Knowledge, Fiction & Imagination

Knowledge, Fiction & Imagination

David Novitz

TEMPLE UNIVERSITY PRESS

Philadelphia

Temple University Press, Philadelphia 19122
Copyright © 1987 by Temple University. All rights reserved
Published 1987
Printed in the United States of America

The paper used in this publication meets the minimum
requirements of American National Standard for Information
Sciences—Permanence of Paper for Printed Library Materials,
ANSI Z39.48-1984

Library of Congress Cataloging-in-Publication Data

Novitz, David.
   Knowledge, fiction, and imagination.
   Bibliography: p.
   Includes index.
   1. Literature—Philosophy.   2. Imagination
(Philosophy)   3. Knowledge, Theory of.   4. Hermeneutics.
5. Romanticism.   6. Fiction.   7. Metaphor.   I. Title.
PN49.N64 1987 801'.3 86-30048
ISBN 0-87722-480-3 (alk. paper)

To Phyllis Shirley Novitz

and

To the memory of Julie Novitz

CONTENTS

PREFACE   xi

ONE   ⁃ The Romantics, Imagination, and Literature   1

⁃ An Excursion into Romantic Theory   2
A Little Imagination   7
⁃ Literature and the New Criticism   11
⁃ Conclusion   19

TWO   A Romantic Theory of Knowledge   21

The Traditional View   22
On Being Philosophical   27
Of Fact and Fancy   29
Hume and the Growth of Knowledge   33
⁃ Conclusion   36

THREE   The Romantic Abyss   37

Idealism, Nietzsche, and Beyond   37
The Rage for Deconstruction   42
In Defense of Deconstruction   45
Presence Regained   48
Realism, Idealism, and the Occlusive Fallacy   55
⁃ A Romantic Realism   63
Conclusion   71

FOUR   The Beholder's Share: Fiction, Imagination, and Emotion   73

The Problem   74
Imagination and Understanding   75

Emotion and Disbelief   79
Conclusion   87

FIVE   The Problem of Interpretation   89

Interpretation, Imagination, and Description   90
A Robust Relativism?   97
Verification   104
The Slide into Incoherence   109
Conclusion   113

SIX   Fiction and the Growth of Knowledge   117

Learning from Fiction   118
Fictional Worlds and Resemblance   121
The Recognition of Resemblances   127
Beliefs from Fiction   130
Skills from Fiction   132
Cognitive Skills and World Views   137
The Exploration of Values   139
Conclusion   142

SEVEN   The Problem of Metaphor   143

The Literal and the Metaphorical   145
Derrida on Metaphor   150
Davidson on Metaphor   153
Meaning, Radical Interpretation, and Metaphor   158
Conclusion   167

EIGHT   Another Look at Metaphorical Meaning   171

An Interpretation Program for Metaphor   172
Construing a Metaphor   175
From Meaning to Emotion   180
Conclusion   183

NINE   Metaphors of Fiction   184

Sentential Metaphors of Fiction   185
Juxtapository Metaphors of Fiction   192
Of Literary Symbols   198
Conclusion   204

TEN   Literature, Imagination, and Identity   206

Geist, *Volksgeist*, and Culture   207
Culture and Colligation   213
Demarcating Cultures   216
The Cry for a Cultural Identity   220
From Cultural to Individual Identity   226
Conclusion   231

NOTES   235

INDEX   257

PREFACE

Even though we learn a good deal from fictional literature, I have long been impressed by the fact that people usually deny this. The more reflective among us reject out of hand the idea that fiction is, or could be, a reliable source of knowledge about the world. And yet it has always seemed to me, and to many others besides, that novels are not just beautiful and imposing verbal constructions. Nor are they idle entertainments. They often have something to "say"; something which, if "said," has the power to affect our thinking, our attitudes, our ways of looking and understanding.

This book is an essay in the philosophy of literature. Its primary aim is to restore to fictional literature its former status as a functional object — allowing that a thing of beauty, bred of the imagination, may indeed instruct, and that it can do so in ways which are richer and more varied than the ways of empirical science.

The question of how we learn from literary works of art, and whether they can properly be regarded as didactic, gives rise to a host of interesting and, I think, important philosophical problems which form the subject matter of this book. In pondering these, I have gradually come to believe that much traditional epistemology is not just at a loss to account for the ways in which we learn from fiction, but is fundamentally wrongheaded. It ignores, and ignores at its peril, the role played by the fanciful imagination in the acquisition and growth of empirical knowledge. In this way, and despite all the warnings of my erstwhile teachers, I have ventured into the territory of the romantics, and to some it will no doubt seem that I too am in danger of expiring of romantic excess.

That I am in no such danger will emerge in the second and third chapters of this book: chapters which discuss and develop aspects of romantic theory without falling prey to the usual romantic fallacies. While fact, on my view, is always bred of fancy, I argue that such an epistemology need not lead to idealism, and still less to the romantic excesses of Friedrich Nietzsche and Jacques Derrida. In this way, by defending what I call a romantic epistemology, and, with it, a romantic realism, I furnish a framework within which it becomes possible to pursue my central thesis and to explain and defend the view that fictional literature is the bearer of insight and knowledge. It is a framework which cannot be developed in all the detail that it deserves in the course of two modest chapters. However, we will find that my discussion does furnish a useful epistemological and metaphysical backdrop against which the central questions of this book take shape and acquire significance.

In the course of writing this book, I seem to have subjected many people, especially at conferences and seminars and philosophical society meetings, to sundry versions of the ideas which now crowd its pages. The discussion and criticisms on these occasions were always appreciated, and I am grateful to those who gave so willingly of their time, and who used conference parties, and sometimes large quantities of alcohol, to pursue these ideas with me. It is not possible to mention all of these people by name, and given what I have just written, it might appear an act of ingratitude to do so.

I am, however, particularly grateful to my colleagues in the Philosophy Department at the University of Canterbury who were always prepared to listen to me, to test my ideas, and who have created a wonderfully congenial environment in which to work. I am particularly indebted to the good sense of Jim Thornton who, although tolerant of my excursions into Derrida and Hegel, never failed to deflate my more nonsensical arguments and to reduce everything to size. Donald Callen was a visitor in this department from July 1981 until July of the following year. I learned much from him and benefited greatly from his close but gentle criticism of the early versions of several chapters of this book.

My postgraduate students were forced to listen to, and read, large tracts of my work. To them I apologize; and my especial thanks to Philip Catton whose perceptive criticisms were always a source of delight. Rosemary Novitz commented helpfully and patiently on early drafts of several chapters. Her willingness to discuss my work with me, and to encourage me in my endeavor, helped more than anything else to bring this book to fruition. Tonia, my daughter, read the Preface and insisted on being mentioned in it. To her, as well as to my son Julian, I must apologize for the endless clatter of a typewriter and for not always being as freely available as I should have been. Lisa Symes helped generously in the preparation of the manuscript.

I am grateful, too, to the editors of various journals who allowed me to test some of my ideas in print and who have given their permission for some of this material to be reproduced here. Part of Chapter Two appeared in the *American Philosophical Quarterly* in 1980; Sections 2 and 3 of Chapter Three appeared in *The Monist* in 1986; Chapters Four and Five contain revised versions of articles which appeared in *The Journal of Aesthetics and Art Criticism* in 1980 and 1982. Different parts of Chapter Six appeared earlier in *Grazer Philosophische Studien*, in 1983, and as "Pictures, Fiction and Resemblance" in *The British Journal of Aesthetics* (22), published by Oxford University Press in 1982. An early version of Chapter Eight first appeared in *Philosophia* in 1985. Responses to some of these articles, both in print and in personal letters, have been most useful.

My most profound debt is acknowledged in the dedication.

Knowledge, Fiction & Imagination

ONE

The Romantics,
Imagination,
and Literature

The novels and plays that we come across from day to day are widely regarded as a kind of entertainment; as a source of amusement to which we attend, not, emphatically, in order to learn anything, but as a stimulating and pleasurable pastime. Whatever the message of a novel or play, we know that we should not take it too seriously: we certainly should not think of it as the literal truth about the world we inhabit. Fiction, after all, is the offspring of a somewhat fevered, and invariably fanciful, imagination. And fancy, we have been told time and time again, tends to mislead rather than inform. If we must have information about our world, it is to empirical science, not the literature of fiction, that we should turn. For it is empirical science which is the source of all useful knowledge: knowledge on which we can depend, and in terms of which we can organize our world.

This attitude to fiction is, of course, a by-product of the scientific revolution in the seventeenth century. The consequent blossoming of Enlightenment fervor in the eighteenth century, and the development of successive versions of positivism in the nineteenth and twentieth centuries, were very largely responsible for the tendency to elevate science as an authority in our lives, and to relegate literature to the status of a mere amusement. It is true that the romantic movement protested vigorously against this view, but its response to the Enlightenment seems now to have been little more than a rearguard action designed to preserve a few favored intuitions. The doctrines of romanticism, although often eloquently and attractively presented, were fundamentally obscure, and did little to undermine the growing hegemony of science.

Science continues to dominate, and continues to furnish the standards of adequacy relative to which we judge others' claims to knowledge. In so doing, it plays a vitally important role, for it successfully eliminates ungrounded pretensions to knowledge, and thereby democratizes knowledge by making it available to all people who avail themselves of the scientific method. In many ways, science seems to have earned its authority, for it tends, by and large, to work. Its claims to knowledge enjoy a predictive utility which is, to all appearances, unmatched by any other putative source of empirical knowledge.

And yet doubts remain. Could it not be that the romantics were correct; that science dehumanizes by quantifying; that it straightjackets our inquiries by looking for knowledge in only one place and by ignoring other fountainheads? This certainly is part of what the early romantics meant to say, and it is a view which continues to linger. In the present century, we have been told by a number of voices that science claims for itself an authority which it does not possess; that it arbitrarily sets the criteria of rationality in ways that suit itself and its practitioners.

By concentrating on the role which fictional literature, and hence the creative or fanciful imagination, plays in the acquisition and growth of knowledge, this book explores some of these claims. It challenges the view that empirical science is the only sure source of knowledge about the world, and argues that it is possible to learn from the fanciful imagination and its products—most especially from fictional literature. In order better to understand the scope and aims of this book, it will be helpful to think of the arguments which follow in at least three different, but related ways. In detailing these in the present chapter, I shall furnish the background against which the central concerns of this book emerge.

An Excursion into Romantic Theory

We can think of the pages which follow as an attempt to resuscitate aspects of the threadbare and frequently maligned epistemological theories of eighteenth- and nineteenth-century romanticism. This is not to say that I shall busy myself with the interminable job of patching up the work of Schelling or Coleridge, of Wordsworth or Nietzsche. Their theories are seriously flawed, and instead of sifting through them routinely, I shall try to preserve only some of their basic insights and will argue that the general direction that they take is in some ways very nearly the right one. Like the romantics who take this view from Kant, I contend that people do not passively record the world about them, but that in coming to know it, they actively construe it in certain ways with the help of the imagination. Furthermore, and contrary to the spirit of Kant, I argue together with some romantics that people can successfully construe their world only with the help of a "poetic," a free-ranging and "unruly" imagination—what I shall call the fanciful imagination; so that it is in the end our ability to fantasize which is essential to the acquisition and growth of empirical knowledge.

The challenge is to state this view coherently. For to insist that our knowledge of nature is the product of our own fanciful imaginings is to allow that what we know, like what we say, does not straightforwardly reflect a settled reality. And it is but a short step from this to many varieties of irrationalism—whether it be a cast-iron solipsism, a lapse into inarticulateness, or, which is much the same, a surrender to a radical and indefensible relativism.

Despite the popular view, the romantic impulse did not wither and die at the end of the nineteenth century. Not only has it survived, but it forms an integral part of our current philosophical landscape. I say this not just because Nietzsche has had an obvious influence on contemporary continental philosophy, but also because the Anglo–American tradition has unwittingly fallen under the romantic spell. Our romantic heritage, one could say, is perpetuated in this century not just by Heidegger, Derrida and Foucault, but also by philosophers as diverse as Gilbert Ryle, Ludwig Wittgenstein, Nelson Goodman, Joseph Margolis, and Richard Rorty. Aspects of romanticism can be seen to survive, even to thrive, in most of the important philosophical disputes of this century—whether it be the idealist/realist controversy; the issues and disputes surrounding nominalism, pragmatism, and relativism; the theory/observation controversy; the fact/value distinction; or the dispute between ethical absolutists and subjectivists. It is true that the crusade against realism takes many forms, but even so, much of its impetus in this century can be seen to derive from one or another romantic epistemology.

All of this suggests that romanticism has had a much wider influence than is usually acknowledged. It attests as well to the fact that philosophers often find certain aspects of the romantic movement attractive and useful. We should not, of course, think that they all find the same aspects attractive, for the movement is a very broad one, including under its aegis a variety of epistemological and metaphysical doctrines. All of these doctrines, however, take root in the Kantian reaction to the passive associationism of David Hume. Kant, of course, had contended that how we experience the phenomenal world depends crucially on our construal of undifferentiated sensation in terms of the pure concepts of the understanding: concepts which are given *a priori*, and over which the individual has no control.

In so arguing, Kant had effectively sown the seeds of romanticism, for there now emerged a number of philosophers—Hegel, Fichte, Schelling, Schopenhauer, and eventually Nietzsche in Germany; Coleridge and Wordsworth in Britain—who took from Kant the idea that our concepts or ideas help fix the nature of reality. Unlike Kant, however, they all discarded the distinction between the phenomenal and noumenal world, arguing that our intuitions (or experiences) are productive, and produce the world as it really is, and not merely as it appears to be.[1] Still more, they seemed to leave little room for any central, unchanging core of concepts, given *a priori*, in terms of which to construe the world. True enough, Schelling does insist that we first construct the world unconsciously, but he also contends that the artist performs the same task consciously; and since the imagination can furnish artists with all manner of ideas or concepts or categories, these will mediate their productive intuitions, and so help create the world of nature.[2] On Schelling's view, the creative imagination enjoys a boundless freedom to create new categories in terms of which to experience, and thereby create, the ultimate nature of the world.

This emphasis on the boundless freedom of the imagination to help create reality is a feature of most romantic thought. There are, it is true, very few arguments for this view, but this should hardly surprise us. Romanticism was a movement in active rebellion against the rationality of the Enlightenment, so that what we find, for the most part, are bald, sometimes dark and profound, statements about the powers and freedoms of the imagination, but scarcely anything which amounts to an argument. This, at any rate, is the case with Coleridge, for he simply insists on the freedom of the "primary" and "secondary" imaginations to mold our experience of nature, and thereby nature itself.[3] A similar emphasis on freedom is found, in a roundabout and more reasonable way, in Hegel. For it is well known that he contends that both the subjective and the universal Mind are ultimately free to construe the world as they will, and in so doing they are said to make the world congruent to themselves.[4] On an altogether different tack, Nietzsche sees our conceptual formation, and hence the categories that we work with, as the product of primeval metaphors, and, echoing the early romantics, he regards the will (or, more precisely, a desire for power and control) as responsible for the elevation of certain of these metaphors into "truths" which shape our sense of reality.[5]

All of these philosophers agree that the concepts which fix reality are in one way or another the products of the individual human mind. All, moreover, emphasize the voluntaristic side of human nature—the freedom of the mind to construe as it wills. These features of romanticism, I shall argue later on, are obviously present in the work of Derrida, and will, to a much lesser extent, be found in what I have to say. But all of us—the romantics, Derrida, and myself—are faced with the same problem: we cannot, on romantic premises, straightforwardly assume a uniformity of concepts and experience from one mind to another. As a result, there seems to be no reason to assume that there is one unified world which all of us experience. This being the case, it is difficult to understand how we could ever communicate with one another, since it would seem that we are all locked into our own private worlds.

One obvious idealist response to such a problem would be to abandon the realist intuitions on which it is premised. Hence an idealist might caution us not to assume that there are discrete human minds, or that the worlds that they "posit" exist independently of each other. This course, however, is not properly open to the romantics, for they wish to preserve, indeed elevate, the notion of the individual self or ego. As a result they insist that there are individual human minds. However, they also insist that there is a very special relationship between an individual ego and what it experiences, for what is experienced is both distinct from the ego and yet a part of it. "The external world," Schelling writes, "lies open before us so that we may find again in it the history of our own spirit." [6] For him the ego is "at the very same time a subjective and objective being." [7]

In the light of what has already been said, it is a relatively easy matter to see why the romantic idealists should think that the objects of experience form a part of the ego. It is more difficult to understand why they should believe that these objects are also distinct from the ego. The most reasonable reconstruction that I can muster starts with Schelling's observation that "inner is only distinguishable in contrast to outer." [8] If we generalize this, it would seem that according to Schelling we can have a conception of X only if we also have a conception of not-X. Moreover, since our conceptions help determine reality, it follows that any object X actually is both X and not-X. Hence anything which is experienced by an individual mind as not being part of itself actually is a part of itself; and that goes for other minds as well, so that all minds and what they experience are actually one universal mind or absolute ego. But if one accepts the initial hypothesis, the universal mind must be what it is not, and so must be nonuniversal, or particular. Hence it would seem that for the romantic idealist there is only one mind, the universal mind, which is also and at the same time one and many particular minds.

Despite this air of paradox and obfuscation, it would seem that the romantics do, after all, tender some sort of "solution" to the problem of whether there can be a single unified world which all of us experience. On their view there certainly can be such a world, provided that all experience, and hence reality, is a function of a universal mind—which, so it seems, it both is and is not. The problem, then, is "solved" by the simple irrationalist device of shrouding it in paradox. But romantic idealists are generally prepared to bite and swallow this bullet, for such paradoxes, so they believe, will be resolved when once we have knowledge of the universal mind or absolute ego—that is, when once mind becomes fully self-aware.[9] Thus Schelling tells us that when once "you have seen the fullness of existence, as it is in itself . . . then you should also know the inner and holy bond between things and the manner in which, through the unity of the essence to which they belong, they become one."[10] The view is robustly optimistic, although the reader, I believe, could be forgiven for not sharing this optimism.

It would seem, then, that the problem posed by romantic idealism is still with us. For it simply is not clear that a romantic epistemology can ever allow us access to a unified world which we can all experience, and about which we can communicate. In this century there have been a number of noteworthy and somewhat curious responses to the problem. Richard Rorty, for instance, effectively denies that it is a problem. He contends that there is no point in thinking that there exists an extra-linguistic world which we can apprehend and to which language corresponds. On his view, experience does not help us to discover the world. On the contrary, it is our choice of vocabulary which helps us to invent it.[11] Here, of course, Rorty is at one with the romantics, although he differs sharply from them by maintaining that if it should turn out that most of us have a similar conception of the world, this can only be because we happen, for sociological reasons, to concur in most of our beliefs. However, as T. S. Kuhn at one time argued, we need not all have the same beliefs—with the unwelcome consequence that there could be as many worlds as there are coherent sets of beliefs.[12]

Derrida, of course, is in broad agreement with Rorty's response to the problem, dubbing any belief to the contrary a confused "logocentrism," an uncritical allegiance to the "metaphysics of presence." [13]

These are the desperate and, so I shall argue, the untenable solutions to the problems posed by romanticism. My aim is to steer a course between the rocks of a naive empiricism on the one hand, and the Sirens of romantic idealism on the other. In so doing I shall argue for certain alternative solutions which, while they preserve the more useful epistemological insights of romanticism (Chapter Two), allow us nonetheless to argue for a robust realism: a romantic realism which allows us knowledge of an independently existing world, rejects idealism, textualism, and pragmatism (Chapter Three), combats conceptual relativism, and argues for the possibility of a correct understanding or interpretation of our world, its objects, and artifacts (Chapter Five). In order to demonstrate all of this, we shall need to be much clearer than the romantics generally are about the arguments in favor of adopting a romantic theory of knowledge. It is to this end that I argue in Chapter Two, together with the best of the romantics, that the fanciful imagination plays a crucial role in the acquisition and growth of empirical knowledge. And this argument, as we shall see later on, turns out to have profound consequences for any theory about the cognitive content of literary works of art.

A Little Imagination

There is another way of looking at the arguments of this book. We can and should see them as a sustained and coherent study of the imagination. In a sense this stands to reason, for I have already stressed that it is among the concerns of this work to resurrect aspects of the romantic theory of knowledge. Consequently, we are bound to attend to questions not just about knowledge, but also about the relationship between knowledge and the imagination. In Chapter Two, therefore, we shall want to know whether what I call the fanciful imagination can properly be considered necessary for empirical knowledge, or whether, as so many have argued, it is an obstacle to it. And this question gives rise at once to a range of related puzzles, for we will want to know what the fanciful imagination is, how it works, and what it does.

To this extent my study of the imagination is a traditional one; it asks many of the old questions. This said, it must at once be conceded that it is in some respects an unusual study, for it concentrates in the later chapters on a range of issues which appear to be only peripherally related to traditional concerns about the imagination. These include problems about metaphor, interpretation, fiction, and our responses to it; problems about the growth of knowledge, emotion, culture, and cultural identity. And although a consideration of all these topics might appear to be at odds with my professed aim of offering a *coherent* study of the imagination, I do nonetheless want to insist that it forms part and parcel of such an account.

My reason for approaching the topic in this way is that I wish to escape the old and tired idiom in which philosophers have traditionally addressed the imagination. The tendency, very often, is to explore the "powers" of the imagination, its *modus operandi*, and the status of its images, without attending to what *people* actually *do*, and actually produce, when they are described as imagining or as being imaginative. The very words "the imagination" suggest that there must be a mental entity, usually a faculty, which does the imagining, which performs certain covert mental acts which are qualitatively different from all other mental acts. This picture is seriously misleading. It is a picture created by the mentalistic vocabulary that we have inherited, and it is the pervasiveness of this vocabulary which makes it so difficult for us to avoid speaking and thinking of the imagination as a hidden faculty engaged in covert operations.

Gilbert Ryle has done much in the present century to dismantle this picture of the imagination. In his seminal work, *The Concept of Mind*, he insists that there is no hidden mental faculty which is responsible for our imaginings. Rather than a faculty, it is the person who imagines, and who does so in many different ways. The concept of imagining, we are told, is a polymorphous one—which is just to say that there are many different activities that count as imagining:

The mendacious witness in the witness-box, the inventor thinking out a new machine, the constructor of a romance, the child playing bears, and Henry Irving are all exercising their imaginations; but so, too, are the judge listening to the lies of the witness, the colleague giving his opinion on the new invention, the novel reader, the nurse who refrains from admonishing the "bears" for their subhuman noises, the dramatic critic and the theatre goers.[14]

Ryle insists, however, that there is no one kernel act which all perform when imagining, and if he is right (as I think he is) then it makes good sense in any study of the imagination to examine (as I will do) a range of human activities, all of which can properly be regarded as involving the exercise of the imagination.

Most of the activities to which I shall attend are related in one way or another to the composition and comprehension of fictional literature. My concern is with what the writer and the reader actually do, and we shall see that although what they do can properly be regarded as imagining, their various activities are nonetheless very different. Authors do not just create fictional worlds and populate them with characters. They also use language in ways which are carefully designed to have specific effects: to breed insights, to encourage emotional responses, to highlight certain values and disabuse us of others. To this end metaphors are coined, symbols are invented and strategically deployed, and a wealth of images and figures is devised with the aim of fostering certain associative and emotional responses. Readers, in their turn, try to comprehend the fiction, and this frequently requires them to interpret certain works. They become "caught up in" the fiction, they "identify" with its characters, they laugh with them and weep for them. Occasionally they come to rethink their world, to "see" things differently, and in such cases they seem to learn from the fiction. Not only this, but with a blush of pride they may turn to a body of literature as the vehicle of their culture, and they may seek and discern within it the marks of their identity.

By inquiring into activities such as these, we will, I hope, promote a better understanding of the imagination. The aim is no longer to explore the hidden workings of a mysterious mental entity, but is rather to explore a loosely connected body of more or less overt activities, all of which can properly be regarded as the exercise of the imagination. Ryle, I have said, is adamant that there is no kernel act of imagining—no one act or set of acts shared by these activities and in virtue of which they can properly be said to be instances of imagining. And although this is basically correct, the analogy that he draws with farming in order to explain his point is misleading. He writes: "Just as ploughing is one farming job and tree-spraying is another farming job, so inventing a new machine is one way of being imaginative and playing bears is another." [15] The trouble with this analogy, though, is that what makes tree-spraying and ploughing farming jobs is their shared purpose. But this is not at all the case with inventing and playing bears, for although they are both instances of imagining, they clearly need not share any purpose. Indeed, what makes them instances of imagining in this case may very well be that they share a core act.

One invents a machine not by following a recipe or a plan, but by tentatively combining certain ideas, or bits and pieces of plastic or iron, or lines and colors on paper. It is true as well that one combines these entities "freely" or "at will," for there are no procedures, plans, or rules to be followed in *inventing* a machine. But much of this, it could be argued, is true as well of the child who plays bears. Certainly the child does not combine lines, colors, or bits of plastic, but it does combine certain actions, growls, and grimaces, and it does so not by following any procedures, but at will. For this reason it seems plausible to suppose that it is the free combination of entities (ideas, actions, plastic parts, and so on) which bear-playing and inventing have in common, and which ensures that both can correctly be described as exercises of the imagination.

It will not do to argue against this by contending that while the imaginings of inventors are curbed or limited by their aims or goals, the imaginings of children who play at bears are not. Even though it is true that the inventor invents within certain constraints, the child who plays at bears can be seen to play within certain constraints as well. Thus the inventor invariably has some conception of the function that is to be served by the envisaged machine, or of the materials out of which it is to be constructed, and this will constrain what is done on the drawing board. But the child is similarly constrained. Bears cannot fly, and nor do they bark like dogs. Proffered growls have to be taken as bear growls and not those of a tiger. It is within limits such as these that the child invents and plays the game.

The activities of inventing and of playing bears plainly do have something in common, for within specific constraints both involve the free combination of certain entities. And it is presumably in virtue of this, rather than in virtue of any shared purpose, that both are properly regarded as instances of imagining. In this respect the concept "imagining" differs from "farming." What makes tree-spraying and ploughing both instances of farming, I have said, is a shared (agricultural) purpose, and not at all a kernel act of farming somehow to be located in tree-spraying, ploughing, feeding the chickens, and painting the barn door. So even if "imagining" is a polymorphous concept, it is quite wrong to construe it, as Ryle does, on the model of "farming."

This is not to say that every exercise of the imagination involves the free or unregulated combination of certain entities. The reader who derivatively imagines a scene described by an author cannot, in so doing, properly combine certain ideas, images, or words at will, for to do so would be to ignore the author's descriptions. One's derivative imaginings, unlike their creative or fanciful counterparts, do not involve the free combination of ideas, images, words, and the rest. And yet derivative imagining is not entirely unlike fanciful or creative imagining. Both usually involve a degree of what I shall call "cognitive disengagement," for it is typically, although not invariably, the case that when one imagines, one ceases to attend to, and is at times barely aware of, one's immediate environment. Both varieties of imagining, moreover, are closely allied to human feeling, although the precise dimensions of this must await examination in Chapters Four and Six.

In a nutshell, then, it seems more nearly correct to regard each act of imagining as bearing what Wittgenstein has called a "family resemblance" to each other act, with no one essential feature common to all. And this, I think, enables us to explain what Ryle regards as the "polymorphous" character of the concept of imagining. For it is now possible to understand why so many different acts, not all of which have any one thing in common, can nonetheless be regarded as acts of the imagination. It seems to follow from this that we can only hope to explore the concept of the imagination with any degree of success by looking at a range of activities which can properly be described as exercises of the imagination. And it is this that I propose to do in the chapters which follow.

Literature and the New Criticism

Although this book contributes to the debate on romantic theory, it does so only in order to provide a framework within which to pursue its central thesis. For this reason, its arguments should be understood first and foremost as a contribution to the philosophy of literature. While it is true that its arguments are primarily concerned with the literature of fiction, their aim is not just to explain the nature of fiction or how we understand and respond to it. They also defend a highly controversial and frequently maligned view of this art form—namely, that it affords, and is important because it affords, genuine cognitive experiences which are of considerable heuristic value.

It is not just that fictional literature influences our beliefs and values, but I shall argue that it also affords knowledge of, and insights into, the world within which we live. It enables us to see things differently, to think anew, to reconceptualize, and in so doing it brings us to notice, and to be sensitive to, aspects of our environment to which we were previously blind. If I am right about this, then the creative or fanciful imaginings of authors, poets, and playwrights will have to be seen as cognitively valuable, and this, of course, is a view which takes root in, and gathers support from, a romantic theory of knowledge. It is also a shamelessly functional and didactic view of literature, one which has been in disrepute ever since the emergence of the New Criticism. And the irony is that, just as I shall attempt to develop and use romantic theory in order to advocate this functionalist view, so the New Critics use romantic theory in order to denounce it.

The New Criticism was a movement in fervent rebellion against all didactic, and hence all mimetic, views of literature. Certainly literature could instruct, but nothing, on this view, could acquire the status of literature simply because it instructed; nor could the quality of instruction ever be a measure of literary merit. It followed that the study and criticism of literature should never be concerned with such incidentals. According to Gerald Graff:

The New Critics set out—and in this they succeeded wholly—to expunge from the mind of the educated middle class what might be called the genteel schoolmarm theory of literature, which had defined literature as a kind of prettified didacticism, and to replace it with a theory of the radical autonomy of the imagination.[16]

And while one can sympathize with this attempt to treat literature as something more than a "prettified" lesson, and to deliver us from "the mishmash of philology, biography, moral admonition, textual exegesis, social history and sheer burbling that largely made up what was thought of as literary criticism,"[17] it is nonetheless true that the New Criticism overplayed its hand. For it set in motion a train of thought and a realm of practice which would eventually undermine the status of literature in the present century, and would ensure that the broad mass of people would cease to take it seriously.

It was, above all, the emphasis that many of the New Critics placed on the autonomy of the imagination and its products which did so much to undermine the mimetic conception of literature. This, of course, was no more than a new phase in the romantic crusade against the Enlightenment, for what we find is at first an ambivalent attitude toward, and later on a growing distrust of, discursive and scientific methods of acquiring knowledge. One of the founding fathers of the New Criticism, I. A. Richards, tells us with a measure of approval that science has altered certain of our patterns of thought and belief, and in so doing has shown religion to be untenable.[18] But he insists nonetheless that it is only poetry, and not science, which can address those questions that concern us most and which give us the moral fortitude to face the world. He says,

For science tells us and can tell us nothing about the nature of things in any *ultimate* sense. It can never answer any questions of the form: *What* is so and so?

it can only tell us *how* such and such behave. And it does not attempt to do more than this.[19]

Our ultimate questions, Richards contends, are not questions at all, and "indicate our desire not for knowledge, . . . but for assurance."[20] They are pseudo-questions which can be "answered" only by the pseudo-statements of poetry, whose proper purpose it is to furnish us with experiences rather than discursive knowledge.[21]

In the wake of Richards, the New Criticism came gradually to the view that literature should not be conceived of as a vehicle for discursive knowledge or rationally based beliefs about the world. Rather, it should be understood as furnishing unitary, wholly autonomous, and intrinsically valuable experiences. "A poem," W. K. Wimsatt, Jr., and Monroe C. Beardsley were later to say, " 'should not mean but be.' " And they added, in unison with most other new critical voices, "it *is*, simply *is*, in the sense that we have no excuse for enquiring what part is intended or meant."[22]

Like most of the New Critics, Richards does allow that literary works, and especially poems, can be "true." However, they are not true because they furnish us with propositional knowledge about the world, but because they present us with an experience which satisfies some emotional need or other.[23] The pseudo-statements of literature, and the experiences they furnish, are always the product of an autonomous imaginative life: an imaginative life, Richards says, which "is its own justification."[24] But Richards's romanticism does not end here. In a later work we are told that the imagination creates all the "myths" in terms of which we construe our world, and that science is every bit as mythical as poetry. However, since science does not answer our "ultimate" questions, it is poetry rather than science which should be seen as the vehicle for "the reconstitution of [our social] order." For poetry is "the myth-making activity which most brings 'the soul of man into activity' (*Biographia Literaria*, II, 12)" and which is " 'the medium by which spirits communicate with one another' (*Biographia Literaria*, I, 168)."[25]

Related attitudes to science, and a similar emphasis on the autonomous, nondiscursive products of the imagination, are to be found everywhere in the New Criticism. The New Criticism, one might say, takes root in the soil of romanticism—so that whether it be T. S. Eliot, Cleanth Brooks, Robert Penn Warren, or John Crowe Ransom, we find in each a similar (if sometimes more intemperate) condemnation of science, a similar view of literature, and a similar romantic view of the imagination. True enough, the details differ, and sometimes the differences are important, but there is nonetheless an underlying core of agreement which characterizes the movement. Most New Critics, for instance, regard the scientific ideal of rationality as seriously destructive of our humanity. John Crowe Ransom is one who argues that the abstractions and classifications of science deny us access to the rich and intricate workings of what he calls "the world's body." Science, on his view, fosters an "interested" and acquisitive view of the world according to which we manipulate it to our own interests. "It is thus that we lose the power of imagination . . . by which we are able to contemplate things as they are in their rich, contingent materiality." [26]

T. S. Eliot, by contrast, regards science as largely responsible for the fragmentation and gradual disintegration of modern society. The scientist's emphasis on specialization leads inexorably to the absence of shared belief, the abandonment of tradition, and the destruction of a sense of community. The result, of course, is the mushrooming of factions, interest groups, and political parties—all of which further undermine the social fabric, and leave us with a pseudo-individualism, a "negative liberal society" in which the sciences foster the illusion of progress. [27] Cleanth Brooks is similarly, but more abruptly, sceptical. In *Modern Poetry and the Tradition* he expresses his doubts about science through the simple device of equating science with lust, poetry with love. On this view, "love is the aesthetic of sex; lust is the science. . . . Lust drives forward urgently and scientifically to the immediate extirpation of the desire." [28]

One can go on in this vein to uncover similar assaults on the scientific ideal of rationality in the work of most of the New Critics. [29] In each case, moreover, the envisaged antidote to the dehumanizing effects of science is roughly similar: it resides in the advocacy and adoption of a kind of romanticism, the essentials of which had previously been articulated in the work of I. A. Richards. For, as we have seen, Richards believes that only poetry, and certainly not science, can solve our ultimate problems. And there is a corresponding tendency among many of the New Critics to "solve" these problems by "depersonalizing" literature—that is, by refusing to regard it as something which serves the interests of its author or audience. More specifically, they deny that the literary work is akin to a scientific instrument through which to manipulate or understand the world. All that literature does and can do, on this view, is furnish the reader with an experience: an autonomous, nonmimetic, nondiscursive experience which is its own justification, and which is bred of the author's imagination.

It is this literary experience which, according to Cleanth Brooks, furnishes us with a nonconceptual mode of cognition that both rivals and undermines the scientific mode. It is an experience which is the product of the author's creative imagination: an imagination which "is not logical" and which "apparently violates science and common sense; it welds together the discordant and the contradictory." This, of course, is the romantic imagination, and Brooks contends that "Coleridge has . . . given us the classic description of its nature and power."[30] Here, then, we have an imagination which can both furnish the reader with genuine experiences and in some sense help create the worlds we live in. These worlds, however, are not constructed "logically," for "in poetry the disparate elements are not combined in logic . . . ; they are combined in poetry rather as experience, and experience has decided to ignore logic."[31] The poetic imagination furnishes us with "a controlled experience which has to be *experienced*, not a logical process, the conclusion of which is reached by logical methods and the validity of which can be checked by logical tests."[32]

According to the New Criticism, there is no contradiction involved in saying that a literary work is wholly autonomous, and yet capable of affording experiences which are, in Cleanth Brooks's words, "founded on the facts of experience."[33] For Brooks recognizes that one's literary experiences may sit uneasily with one's real-life experiences, and that the poem which can accommodate these will be taken more seriously than one which cannot. But this, Brooks insists, need not involve going "outside the poem": it only involves responding to it, as one must, in terms of a given mental set bred of previous experiences. Nor is there a contradiction involved in saying that an autonomous and impersonal work is capable of reconstituting our social order. For we have seen that the New Critics are romantics at heart, and so tend to the view that, like all experience, literary experience is in some sense capable of molding reality. So it is no use attacking the New Criticism, as Gerald Graff does, by asking, "But how could one talk of the work's relation to the 'facts of experience' if with the same breath one prohibited the critic from 'going outside the poem'?"[34] For the answer is clear. Not only do we have to experience the poem in terms of the experiences we have already had, but more important, the New Criticism is tacitly committed to the romantic view that the experience furnished by the literary work helps constitute "the facts of experience." The poem helps recreate the world of "objective" fact, and this view, as we shall see presently, finds a very explicit statement in the work of Northrop Frye.

The New Critics, however, are adamant that a literary experience can be conveyed only through language, and at this point the tensions characteristic of romantic theory begin to emerge in their work. Although "it is never what a poem *says* that matters, but what it *is*,"[35] it is the language of the poem which determines what it is. Thus, for instance, Wimsatt and Beardsley contend that a "poem can only *be* through its *meaning*—since its medium is words."[36] For the most part, the New Critics insist that we need to discern and grasp the meaning which inheres in a literary work in order properly to understand it. But it is difficult to see how a novel or a poem which is said to furnish us with nondiscursive and nonconceptual experiences can do so only through the medium of determinate meanings that are somehow contained in, and expressed by, the work. Either to understand the work is just to have a range of imaginatively induced nondiscursive experiences which help shape reality or our view of it, or it is to grasp the determinate meanings which inhere in the work. The former is reminiscent of romantic idealism; the latter, so it would seem, constitutes a realist view of meanings. It is difficult to see how the two can be reconciled.

According to the New Critics, however, a literary experience is furnished by the language, structure, and discernible meanings of the literary work, and not by the author's or the reader's state of mind. In this we discern the seeds of structuralism, and, as Gerald Graff has argued, "if we follow this line of reasoning far enough, we arrive at the view that it is language that writes the poem, not the poet." But Graff quite rightly insists that the New Critics only dabble with this view, for they certainly do not want to banish the "human subject" from literature. T. S. Eliot, Graff reminds us, wished to banish only the individual personality from the poem, not the "personality of modern man."[37] And I. A. Richards arguably concurs in this view, for while he maintains that the literary work is an autonomous object which allows us to have disinterested or impersonal experiences, this means only that we "respond not through one narrow channel of interest, but simultaneously and coherently through many." Hence to say that our response to literature is impersonal is both to affirm the autonomy of the literary work and is also "merely a curious way of saying that our personality is more *completely* involved" in the work and our experience of it.[38]

It is no part of my argument to suggest that the New Critics were all equally and uniformly committed to the tenets of romanticism. They were not. What I do claim is that the New Criticism is imbued with the spirit of romanticism, and that it imparts this spirit to its post-modernist successors. It is not a little ironic, therefore, that these same post-modernists should accuse the New Critics of the "scientism" that they sought to combat.[39] The coolly analytic technique of "close reading" which was Richards's legacy to the New Criticism, as well as the widely shared belief that it was possible to unpick the meanings, implications, and semantic structures concealed within a literary work, encouraged the view that the New Criticism is party to "a forcible seizure, a 'rape' of the text," and that it "operates, philosophically speaking, largely in the framework of realism."[40] There is, it is true, a tendency in the New Criticism to waver in its romanticism, and to slide between a positive and negative attitude to science on the one hand, and between idealism and realism on the other, so that its body of literary theory abounds with tensions and even contradictions.[41] Nonetheless, as Gerald Graff points out, the assumptions about literature, which are presupposed by the recent attacks on the New Criticism, "were the elementary lessons taught by the New Critics: that literature is not conceptual knowledge, but experience, that it is a dramatic process not static propositions, that it therefore resists the 'heresy of paraphrase.' "[42]

There can be no doubt but that the post-modernists have imbibed the romanticism of Richards, Brooks, Eliot, and Ransom. And it is their allegiance to this aspect of the New Criticism which leads quickly to certain idealist excesses. For as Gerald Graff tells us:

> If we pursue the argument that the experience of literary meaning is not an experience of conceptual statements, we arrive eventually at the conclusion that criticism cannot deal with literature as long as *it*—criticism—makes conceptual statements. Criticism itself must shed its propositionality and become literature. Thus Harold Bloom . . . says that "a theory *of* poetry must belong *to* poetry, must *be* poetry, before it can be of any use in interpreting poems."[43]

On this post-modernist view, there plainly cannot be any propositional truths about literature which are capable of giving the meaning of the literary work. Criticism is not propositional. It consists, at most, of imaginative constructs which, through a manipulative rhetoric, create the impression of telling us the truth about the work. In point of fact, though, it only furnishes us with an experience of the work: an experience, which, like all romantic experiences, shapes our conception of the novel or the poem. But there is, on this view, no one true conception of the work; rather, there are many imaginatively produced conceptions, all with equal claims to validity. In other words, when once one takes seriously the idea that literary works can furnish us only with nondiscursive experiences, we have to abandon the idea that they have determinate meanings, and that it is, or could be, the business of the literary critic to interpret or unpick such meanings. To do so, according to Susan Sontag, is "to impoverish, to deplete the world." It is to detract from the immediacy of experience by setting up "a shadow world of 'meanings.' " [44] It is for all these reasons and more that literary works are sometimes said to be unreadable, and it is the aim of Derrida, Paul de Man, Geoffrey Hartman, and Christopher Norris to show, in one way or another, that this is indeed the case.

These theorists embrace idealist rather than realist solutions to the problems posed by the romanticism of the New Critics. On the one hand, as we have seen, the New Criticism emphasizes an autonomous imagination which, through its literary products, can furnish nonmimetic and nonconceptual experiences that help shape and transform our world. On the other, it insists on a "close reading" of the text, and on the possibility of correctly interpreting the complex meaning of a readily identifiable work—for how else, it asks, can we preserve the notion of a publicly accessible literary work, and with it the possibility of literary criticism? [45]

The problem, I have suggested, is to reconcile, or else adjudicate between, these apparently irreconcilable views. How can a literary work that furnishes only nonconceptual experiences have determinate meanings? And if it does not, how can we hope to individuate the work, or ever know that we are speaking about the same poem, novel, or play? The post-modernist solution is, as we have seen, a desperate one, for it involves denying that there are real, determinate meanings which can properly be discerned within a work. These, at best, are fictions created by the rhetoric of criticism—by the so-called canny critic. [46] For just as the author engages in a kind of imaginative play which produces the literary work, so does the critic; and it is only a canny critic who pretends to have uncovered a clear meaning and a message in the work. To do so, we are told, is to destroy the integrity of the text: it is to "rape" it by putting it to one's own purposes instead of allowing it to produce, through mere play, an indefinitely large set of experiences. On this view, there is no such thing as an appropriate or inappropriate response to the work; indeed, it is not even clear what the work is, for insofar as it does not bear determinate meanings, there is no way in which we can neatly individuate it. The work, such as it is, is simply the occasion and the product of the critic's imaginative play.

These post-structuralist doctrines are not always formulated with the New Criticism in mind. Jacques Derrida, as we shall see, pursues an altogether different strategy—even though it is one which is fully compatible with, and lends strength to, post-structuralist criticism. [47] It is nonetheless true that post-structuralism tends to adopt idealist solutions to the type of problem posed by the New Criticism, for in its own way it emphasizes and elevates the unbridled freedom of the imagination at play, wreaking irrationalist havoc as it goes. My solutions to these problems, I have intimated, are very different. They are realist rather than idealist in character. For even though I subscribe to a romantic epistemology and emphasize the role of the fanciful imagination in the acquisition and growth of knowledge, I also argue that this imagination does not have a boundless freedom and cannot wander wherever it likes (Chapter Two). In the end it is this that saves me from the clutches of idealism, and enables me to argue not only that deconstruction is misconceived (Chapter Three), but more positively that we can interpret literary works without in any sense violating them; that some interpretations can be correct, others incorrect; that a work or its parts may bear determinate, indeterminate, or multiple meanings (Chapter Five); that we can distinguish between appropriate and inappropriate responses to the work (Chapter Four); that there is a difference between fictional and nonfictional discourse (Chapter Six), and that there is also a difference, although of another variety, between literal and metaphorical discourse (Chapters Seven, Eight, and Nine).

In these ways I preserve the view that we can and do learn from fiction; still more, that we can acquire both propositional and nonpropositional knowledge from literary works of art (Chapter Six). And I preserve this view, not by reducing literature to a "prettified didacticism," nor yet by reverting to Northrop Frye's idealist device of allowing the author's creative imagination to appropriate the world and shape it according to its dictates. "Literature," according to Frye, "does not reflect life, but it doesn't escape or withdraw from life either, it swallows it. And the imagination won't stop until it's swallowed everything." [48] I argue, by contrast, that literature can reflect life: that it does, indeed must, indirectly "refer" to it, that it has, and must have, a mimetic function if we are to be able to make any sense of it (Chapter Six). And since I also argue that we can make sense of all unflawed texts (provided, of course, that we construe the word "sense" liberally enough), I am forced to conclude that there are certain crucial cognitive links between literature and the world in which we live (Chapters Two, Six, and Ten). But this is not to say that such links characterize literature, or exhaust what there is to say about it. There is much more that can and must be said, and although I do not say all of it here, it does seem that in this respect the New Criticism points us in something like the right direction.

Conclusion

These are my aims in this book. In sketching them, I have tried to lay bare the issues and concerns which have formed the background to its writing. It is important to stress, though, that while current literary theory raises many issues that are of interest to the philosopher, it is no part of my purpose to enter into the polemics of that debate. For it is a debate which thrives not just on literary flourishes and grand gestures, but also on a good deal of dogmatism and on an eclecticism which at times serves little purpose other than that of bewildering the reader. Here Geoffery Hartman, Paul de Man, and Harold Bloom stand out as beacons of darkness—although it would be wrong to think that all post-structuralist thinkers fit this mold. Some are painstaking in their writing and present arguments which have to be taken seriously.

Arguments, of course, are the stuff of philosophy, and my concern is to see whether there are any sound arguments for or against the doctrines advanced by contemporary literary theorists. Needless to say, not all of these theorists are post-structuralist in outlook. Gerald Graff is one who has fought a lonely and largely ignored battle against post-structuralism and its predecessors, and it is to his voice, and with a sense of indebtedness, that I add my own. But I do so not as a literary theorist. My task is a philosophical one which probes certain very basic issues in order to make the distinctions and furnish the arguments so often overlooked by romantic idealism, deconstruction, and contemporary pragmatism. Were I a part of the polemical tradition of contemporary literary theory, I would no doubt dub myself the first of the post-deconstructionists, and would proceed to found a school or a movement. I have every hope, though, that my arguments will stand without the help of such trappings.

TWO

A Romantic Theory
of Knowledge

People try, both constantly and compulsively, to make sense of
the world about them, and to some extent they are all expected to be able
to do so. Their place in a community, indeed their survival as human
beings, depend on this. Anyone who mistakes chairs for firewood, paintings
for dartboards, or dessert bowls for spittoons will not long be tolerated as a
member of our community. And anyone who takes gasoline as water, cyanide
as talcum powder, or a puff-adder as an earthworm, is not long for this
world. This seems obvious. Equally obvious, but somewhat more trouble-
some, is the fact that knowing how to take or construe the objects of one's
environment does not come naturally. It is something that has to be learned,
often over a long period of time.

What, then, is involved in learning how to construe and so understand
the events and objects of one's environment? In this chapter I shall argue
that it is possible to answer this question only by acknowledging the role
which the fanciful imagination plays in the acquisition and growth of empirical knowledge. It is, I contend, our ability to combine images or entities
at will which lies at the heart of our capacity to make sense of, and to
acquire beliefs and knowledge about, the world we inhabit. In effect, my
aim is to defend a romantic theory of knowledge, one which is completely
at loggerheads with traditional epistemology. It is the view that the fanciful
imagination (or, if you like, our ability to fantasize) is necessary for empirical knowledge. This, if true, must radically affect our beliefs about the

cognitive value of fictional literature, games of make-believe, children's fantasies, and even daydreams.

The Traditional View

Traditionally a distinction is drawn between two different types of imagination: what I shall call the fanciful imagination on the one hand, and the constructive imagination on the other. Part of my aim, I have said, is to emphasize and explain the role played by the fanciful imagination in the acquisition and growth of knowledge. And this is odd, for in traditional epistemology, and certainly in the works of Hume and Kant, the constructive imagination is regarded as crucial to the acquisition of knowledge, whereas the fanciful imagination is regarded as inimical to it.

Not that the concept of imagination has always had a place in western philosophy. Socrates had no room for it. His theory of knowledge as recollection (*anamnesis*) does not require an inventive human mind since, on his view, we come to know only by recalling and examining our past experience of the Forms. This refusal to countenance an originative mind poses a special problem when it comes to explaining artistic creativity, for he is forced to suppose that the artist's creative powers come from without, that they are the product of divine inspiration. In the *Phaedrus* we are told that

if any man come to the gates of poetry without the madness of the Muses, persuaded that skill alone will make him a good poet, then shall he and his works of sanity be brought to nought by the poetry of madness.[1]

Poetry, like all art, is not always rational and may even approach the point of insanity. The vexing thing for Socrates, however, is that the arts are not without insight or value, and it is for this reason that the artist's madness must be laid at the feet of the gods. It is they who are responsible for the artist's madness.

This view of artistic creativity seems to have prevailed right up until the time of the Renaissance. Christians of the Middle Ages, influenced as they were by Plato, preferred to regard works of art as theophanies—that is, as manifestations of a transcendent deity who inspired the work and whose glory was expressed within it. Saint Augustine, however, seems to have been an exception, for although he was a Platonist, he refused to explain works of art as simple imitations—still less as products of divine inspiration. In a letter strongly reminiscent of John Locke and David Hume, he writes:

it is possible for the mind, by taking away . . . some things which the senses have brought within its knowledge, and by adding some things, to produce in the exercise of the imagination that which, as a whole, was never within the observation of any of the senses.[2]

Still, it is only really at the time of the Renaissance, with its increased emphasis on the powers and worth of the individual, that artistic creation comes to be treated less as a product of divine inspiration, and more as the result of the imaginative powers of the individual.

Philosophers waited until the seventeenth century before writing about the imagination, and their comments then were far from flattering. Cartesians were dismissive of the imagination and flatly denied that it could have any role at all to play in the acquisition of genuine knowledge. Descartes writes of "the misleading judgement that proceeds from the blundering constructions of imagination," although he does allow that the imagination may in some ways serve the understanding.[3] Nonetheless, the imagination "inasmuch as it differs from the power of understanding, is in no wise a necessary element in my nature or in my essence."[4] And Nicholas Malebranche is even more explicitly dismissive of the imagination, devoting the whole of the second book of his *Recherche de la Vérité* to establishing that the imagination is the source of all sorts of deceptions and must be severely constrained.[5]

Francis Bacon was not much kinder, for even though he allows the imagination a role in poetry, it has no part to play in the acquisition of knowledge. The imagination, on his view, may "sever that which nature hath joined, and so make unlawful matches and divorces of things."[6] It "hardly produces sciences" but only poetry which is "to be accounted rather as a pleasure or play of wit than a science."[7]

It was left to Thomas Hobbes, though, to explain the workings of the imagination, and he does so naturalistically. "There is no conception in a man's mind," he writes, "which hath not at first, totally, or by parts, been begotten upon the organs of sense."[8] However, after an object is removed from sight, or the eye shut, "wee still retain an image of the thing seen, though more obscure than when we see it." This is what the "Latines call *Imagination*" and what the Greeks call "*Fancy*," and on Hobbes's view, both are to be explained as "decaying sense."[9] Since this involves the "decaying" image of the whole object as it was presented to the senses, Hobbes terms it the *simple imagination*, and he contrasts it with the *compounded imagination* which has the power to conjoin images in one way or another, "as when from the sight of a man at one time, and of a horse at another, we conceive in our mind a Centaure" which is "but a fiction of the mind."[10]

In order to explain the process whereby the compound imagination works, Hobbes invokes an early version of Hume's and David Hartley's associationism. He writes:

When a man thinketh on any thing whatsoever, His next Thought after, is not altogether so casuall as it seems to be. . . . All Fancies are motions within us, reliques of those made in the Sense: And those motions that immediately succeeded one another in the sense, continue also together after Sense:[11]

This "Trayne of Thoughts," we are told, is of two sorts. First, there is the unguided or inconstant imagination in which "the thoughts are said to wander, and seem impertinent to one another, as in a Dream." And yet, even in this "wild ranging of the mind" we can often discern "the dependence of one thought upon another."[12] Hence association is at work even in the unguided imagination. The second sort of association is "regulated" by the dominance of a desire which prompts thoughts appropriate to its satisfaction.

According to Hobbes, those people who readily observe similarities between their ideas, "in case they be such as are but rarely observed by others," are said to have a good wit or fancy. Those who have the power to discern differences between their ideas are said to have a good judgment.[13] But "Fancy without the help of Judgement is not commended as a Vertue," and where it does so function "Fancy is one kind of Madnesse."[14] It was this distinction, and the unkind verdict based upon it, which was (as we shall see) to have so great an influence upon John Locke and many who followed him.

Locke, it is well known, does not explicitly mention the imagination, although he does discuss the power that people have to combine simple ideas into complex ones. He writes:

In this faculty of repeating and joining together its ideas, the mind has great power in varying and multiplying the objects of its thoughts, infinitely beyond what sensation or reflection furnished it with.[15]

Like Hobbes, Locke believes that the mind does this by associating ideas. Such association can take place in a number of ways: either by means of a *natural* correspondence which ideas have with each other, but also, and more particularly, association can occur voluntarily, by chance or by custom.[16] So, for instance,

The *ideas* of *goblins* and *sprites* have really no more to do with darkness than light: yet let but a foolish maid inculcate these often on the mind of a child and raise them there together . . . darkness shall ever after bring with it those frightful ideas.[17]

On Locke's view, whenever the association of ideas is brought about either voluntarily or by chance or custom, we are liable to error. Turning to Hobbes's distinction between judgment and fancy, Locke declares that anyone who can associate ideas, "putting those together with quickness and variety, wherein can be found any resemblance or congruity," has a good wit or fancy. This, however, is to be distinguished from a good judgment, which involves "separating carefully, one from another, ideas wherein can be found the least difference."[18] The fancy is a source of analogies, metaphor, and allusion, and judgment, so we are told, proceeds quite differently from this. Indeed,

if the fancy be allowed the place of judgement at first in sport, it afterwards comes to usurp it . . . . There are so many ways of fallacy, such arts of giving colours, appearances, and resemblances by this court dresser, the fancy, that he who is not wary to admit nothing but truth itself . . . cannot but be caught.[19]

The products of fancy are epistemically suspect, and this is why metaphors, allusions, and figures of speech generally are described as "perfect cheats" when "we would speak of things as they are."[20]

This attack on the fanciful imagination and its products continues well into the eighteenth century. David Hume concedes the power of the (fanciful) imagination to roam at will. He speaks of "the liberty of the imagination to transpose and change its ideas"[21] in "what form it pleases" (*Treatise of Human Nature*, p. 10). However, he soon concedes that "nothing would be more unaccountable than the operations of that faculty were it not guided by some universal principles" (p. 10). And it is the principle of the association of ideas which is posited as the guiding force of the imagination in its constructive function: its function, that is, of affording justified beliefs —what most of us regard as knowledge—about the world. According to Hume, certain qualities of our ideas, namely resemblance, contiguity, cause, and effect, furnish a "gentle force" which causes us to associate distinct ideas. This, he tells us, is the natural function of a healthy imagination, and is responsible for many of our ideas and beliefs about the world around us—from our belief in the continuous existence of physical objects to our ideas of substance and causal necessity.

The principle of association of ideas, therefore, is conceived of by

Hume as "permanent, irresistible and universal," and, according to him, must be distinguished from other principles, which are "changeable, weak and irregular" (p. 225). He goes on to say that the imagination when regulated by the principle of association is "the foundation of all our thoughts and actions, so that upon [its] removal human nature must immediately perish and go to ruin" (p. 225).

Since the fanciful imagination is characterized, in part at least, by the absence of the principle of association, and by the presence of weak and changeable principles, Hume clearly regards fancy as a source of the destruction of human nature (pp. 225–26). It is the origin of "the loose and indolent reveries of a castle builder" (p. 624) and the inventions of poets— each of which is "to be regarded as an idle fiction" (pp. 493–94). However, the principles that guide the fanciful imagination (unlike the principle of association, which guides the constructive imagination) "are neither unavoidable to mankind, nor necessary, or so much as useful in the conduct of life." (p. 225).

Similar claims are made by Kant. In his view, it is the transcendental imagination which plays the essential constructive function of synthesizing the "manifold" of experience by bringing it under certain concepts. As conceived here, the transcendental imagination is a condition of all empirical knowledge, and has the function of bringing diverse and disjoint sensory material under a range of concepts. Some of these concepts, Kant tells us, are "pure" concepts of the understanding, but others are empirical and are derived from our experience in what Kant sometimes calls the reproductive imagination.

The reproductive imagination, however, very closely resembles Hume's constructive imagination, since it is "entirely subject to empirical laws, the laws namely of association." [22] Although the imagination has both a transcendental function and an empirical function, the reproductive imagination operates "within the domain . . . of psychology" (*Critique of Pure Reason*, B152). According to Kant, therefore, our empirical concepts are a product of the principle of the association of ideas, and certainly not of the fanciful imagination.

Like Hume, Kant has harsh things to say about the fanciful imagination. In *Anthropologie* (31, VII, 175) he tells us that "phantasy" is nothing other than the uncontrolled spatial imagination which runs riot in daydreams or nightmares. However, it can be controlled, and when it is we speak of composition. The most obvious example of this is to be found in artistic composition; but even so, whether controlled or uncontrolled, the imagination thus conceived is altogether incapable of performing the normal epistemic functions of the constructive imagination. Fancy, in Kant's words, is "the mere play of the imagination": it is an "unruly" imagination, an imagination ungoverned by rules of synthesis. Such an imagination can combine appearances in whatever way it chooses, and cannot, for that reason, allow us access to the actual or objective appearances of things in the world.[23]

Like the philosophers who preceded them, both Hume and Kant clearly regard the fanciful imagination as wholly inconducive to the acquisition and growth of knowledge. In what remains of this chapter I shall give reasons for maintaining otherwise. In order to do this, it is helpful to begin by attending to the role of the fanciful imagination in the development of what laymen sometimes call "a philosophical attitude." Throughout I shall use the term "fanciful imagination" to mention the ability which people have to fabricate or invent by combining ideas, images, beliefs, words, or physical objects howsoever they choose. It should be stressed, though, that the exercise of this ability need not be covert; it can, and often does, involve the public manipulation of words and physical entities.

On Being Philosophical

Philosophers are often expected by those who are unfamiliar with the intricacies of academic philosophy to be *philosophical* about their fate. They are expected to know how to take the vicissitudes and vacillations of fortune.

To be philosophical in this sense requires flights of fancy not unlike those involved in a game of make-believe. We usually praise as philosophical a response to an event if we believe that it construes the event in a helpful or beneficial way. Thus, for instance, if people regard a personal loss—an injury, death of a loved one, or bankruptcy—not as a disaster, but, say, as conducive to personal growth, or as a gateway to a new life, we may (if we approve of their response) say that they have responded philosophically. However, the response in each of these cases does not include an accurate description of the event; nor is it in any obvious sense a deduction from such a description. Rather, each response involves a specific way of construing a certain state of affairs even though its observable features do not obviously warrant these construals. The response in each case, it would seem, is more or less fanciful. If, for instance, Mr. Carruthers construes death as a gateway to a better life, he has, at the very least, to think his way around what would normally be regarded as the finality of death. And he has to do so imaginatively.

That this involves fanciful acts of the imagination is, I think, abundantly clear. However, should we disapprove of Carruthers's response to his fate, we would scarcely describe it as philosophical or imaginative. On the contrary, we would be much more likely to condemn his imaginings as unimaginative or unphilosophical. And we can do this only because the terms "imaginative" and "philosophical" are often used in a way which is strongly evaluative. Similarly, the words "fancy," "fanciful," or "mere fantasy" are often used to express our disapproval of a person's imaginings. If sufficiently skeptical, we might declare Carruthers's view of death fanciful —meaning only that we think it unlikely, silly, or inappropriate.

We must, of course, take good care to distinguish the evaluative use of the terms "imagination" and "fancy" from their descriptive use. I have used these terms descriptively in order to distinguish various mental acts that people actually perform. Hence in saying that Carruthers's construal of death is fanciful, I neither approve nor disapprove of what he says. Rather, I emphasize the fact that what he says does not describe, and is not inferred from, what we now take to be the facts about death. The strange thing, however, is that although fanciful and manifestly nonfactual, such construals often acquire greater factual status as time passes and come to be regarded as factual descriptions rather than fanciful meanderings. It is not difficult to conceive of Carruthers's philosophical attitude to death gaining greater factual currency with the passage of time. We need only observe that while it is true that the appearance of a corpse does not, in this day and age, suggest that the deceased is about to take up office in a better world, it was not very long ago that the apparent serenity of a corpse was widely taken to suggest that the deceased had abandoned his or her worldly problems and had proceeded to a more tranquil life. It is altogether possible, therefore, that Carruthers's observations about death, although initially regarded as fanciful, should gradually acquire greater factual status, and so come to be regarded as literally descriptive.

What we take to be the facts about death may change, and such changes, it would seem, often result from those flights of fancy which are part and parcel of our many attempts to make sense of this world. Our fantasies, in other words, may come to have a more literal application in the way in which we describe and organize our environment. I am suggesting that what we take to be facts are bred of fancy; and if this sounds outrageous, it seems to me to be no more contentious than the other side of the coin, captured in N. R. Hanson's famous phrase, "Observation is theory-laden."[24]

Such a reassurance, of course, does little to cure one's outrage. How, it will be asked, can I hope to establish that all supposed facts are born of fancy on the basis merely of an account of what is involved in being philosophical? It is to this question that I shall now address myself.

Of Fact and Fancy

To be philosophical is, in part at least, to attempt to make sense of some or other event. Now, one might be inclined to think that we try to make sense of only a few aspects of our lives, and that for the most part everything is plain and obvious. As a result one is inclined to believe that the flights of fancy involved in being philosophical occur only infrequently. But this is not true.

We try almost constantly, using methods of varying sophistication, to read meaning into the vast buzzing confusion which surrounds us. Thus, for instance, an infant has to make sense of, and learn how to take, the amorphous blur of raw experience which confronts it. Unless it can do this it will not survive. For the most part, though, adult confusion and bewilderment occur at a level where, even though we can recognize the objects of our environment, we are nonetheless puzzled by their behavior. A physicist, for instance, may be puzzled by the transformations of matter, a novelist by the purpose of life, or a wife by her husband's behavior. We are all of us "significance seeking organisms" constantly in search of cures for our bewilderment.[25]

It is, as Michael Frayn points out, vitally important to be able to attach significance to the objects of our environment. Not to know that a certain object is capable of easing your hunger or quenching your thirst is eventually to die of starvation or dehydration. Signs and clues of one sort or another are the very stuff of survival, and are epistemic constructions—man-made rather than god-given. Human beings, rather than natural forces or transcendent deities, have the task of sorting and organising the environment. If they do not, they are unable to perform one of the most basic chores necessary for their survival.

And yet this is a chore which, initially at least, is performed in a situation of utter ignorance. We are required, on pain of extinction, to make sense of our surroundings, but we do so neither by bringing objects under empirical concepts and so recognizing them, nor (if we discount the possibility of innate ideas) by appealing to some established body of knowledge and belief. In such a situation there is no room for deduction or induction, for there is nothing to deduce or induce from. The only possible alternative is to respond imaginatively. The fanciful imagination is brought into play.

Of course I cannot pretend to speak with authority about the mental states of the new born infant. My aim, rather, is to explain what must be the case if we are ever to make sense of our environment. My argument, which is transcendental in form, has proceeded by elimination to the conclusion that the fanciful imagination is essential to this task. But I can imagine someone objecting either that I have eliminated too much, or that in my eagerness to reach a favored conclusion I have not taken all possibilities fully into account.

One suggestion might be that I have been too short with induction. An infant, it is said, begins to make sense of its environment inductively, by associating similar sequences of events. Thus, because a specific object or set of properties has led to the cessation of an uncomfortable sensation in the past, the presence of this object on a certain occasion in the future produces the expectation that it will remove the sensation once again. It is in this way, the objection continues, that we come to attach significance to the objects of our environment. At root the process is inductive, and it is therefore contended that I have been too hasty in eliminating induction as the primary means of making sense of our environment.

This same objection may be cast in Humean terms. One might want to maintain that it is the principle of the association of ideas (and not the fanciful imagination) which enables us, in the first instance, to make sense of our surroundings. The claim is that the mind naturally associates similar sequences of ideas, and it is this natural association of ideas which enables a young infant to regard, say, the female breast as a source of nourishment. Hence, when the objection is put in these terms, it is maintained that I have failed to take all possibilities fully into account, for I have not adequately considered the role of the constructive imagination or induction in accounting for the way in which we come to make sense of our environment.

No matter how it is cast, this objection quickly runs into difficulties. The trouble is that we can only associate ideas of discrete objects or events if we are able to individuate the objects or events concerned. Similarly, one can only associate similar sequences of events if one can distinguish these sequences (as well as the events which constitute them), and if one can discern their properties so as to notice similarities of one sort or another between them. Hence induction and association require the prior discernment of the properties and individuation of the objects, events, and sequences on which these modes of inference are based. It is no use, therefore, appealing to induction or association in order to explain the way in which we come to individuate or distinguish the objects of our environment. Both modes of inference require the ability to individuate, and cannot therefore be invoked in an explanation of it.

It seems, then, that if we are to explain how we first order the murk and confusion of raw experience, we need to appeal once more to the fanciful imagination. My claim is that in any conceptual lacuna it is necessary to construe the shapes, shades, sounds, and sensations which confront and bewilder us. We have to place imaginative constructions on the flurry of untamed sensation; we have to speculate or guess as to the character and function of the various happenings around and about. This, in my view, is necessary if we are ever to perform the tasks of individuating the objects of our environment.

But a further objection can be brought against this conclusion, for someone might point out that up until now I have only assumed, but have not shown, that the individuation of objects is the result of a certain task which we all have to perform. If in fact there is no such task, it stands to reason that acts of fancy cannot be required for its performance. The claim is that I have altogether misconstrued what is involved in individuation. It is not as if there is any task to perform at all; rather, the objects of the environment present themselves to the human mind neatly individuated and clearly distinguished from all other objects. This, in effect, is David Hume's position. According to him, since "everything in nature is individual," the impression derived from nature "must necessarily have a determinate quantity and quality," and so too must the idea which is a copy of that impression (*Treatise of Human Nature*, p. 19). It follows, therefore, that our ideas of objects are fixed and determinate in every respect, and hence that objects present themselves to our minds neatly packaged and fully individuated as a result of a causal or mechanical process and not as the result of some task which we perform.

Now, if this is true then there clearly is no need to invoke the fanciful imagination in an account of how we individuate objects. For clearly, if we do not have to perform this task at all, the fanciful imagination cannot play any part in it.

However, the Humean argument in support of this view is inadequate. Our ideas are not determinate in every respect. Even though the flower in my hand has a precise number of petals, to be aware of the flower is not of itself to be aware of the number of its petals. And this indeterminacy affects boundaries as well. While looking at the flower I may be undecided as to where it ends and its stem begins. What is more, a closer and more detailed look at the bloom will not resolve the issue. In this case a boundary has to be imposed, not discovered.

This helps explain why people do not always individuate the objects of their environment in the same way. Indeed, were it the case (as Hume suggests) that objects present themselves to the human mind clearly distinguished from all other objects, we would find it difficult to explain the well-known fact that different people and groups "arrange" their worlds differently. Eskimos, Benjamin Whorf tells us, see many different kinds of snow where I see only two or three. Most of us see seven colors in the spectrum, but others, in certain other societies, see only three. And this suggests that individuation and discernment are not simply passive mechanical processes.

This seems to settle the issue. We can no longer hope to explain how we make sense of our environment by appealing to induction, for in order to reason inductively we have first to perform the more basic task of individuating the objects and events on which inductive inference depends. Nor can we explain individuation as the passive affect on the mind of a mechanical process. Rather, it is the result of a special task that cannot depend on induction and association, but which, if I am right, must involve fanciful guesses or conjectures of one sort or another. Only in this way is it possible to make sense of, and so discern an order in, the bewildering blur of raw experience.

At this stage, someone is bound to object that one cannot conjecture or entertain fanciful guesses unless one does so in terms of certain concepts, ideas, or beliefs. After all, conjectures or guesses are always framed in terms of what we already know or believe. Hence, far from the fanciful imagination being a condition of empirical knowledge, its exercise actually presupposes the acquisition of such knowledge.

Now, I do not wish to suggest that this objection can be disposed of as decisively as the others. However, it seems perfectly conceivable that human beings confronted with and bewildered by the primeval stuff of raw sensation should tentatively construe it, or arrange it, in many different ways, successively modifying each construal in the light of its utility. Such construals are inventive or fabricative in that they involve the arrangement and rearrangement of sensations at will—either through optical or aural fixation, or through figure-ground alterations, or bodily movements.[26] For this reason they qualify for the epithet "fanciful." Still more, they are tentative, for they are readily abandoned when found to be useless or misleading. For this reason they are aptly described as conjectures or guesses; although, of course, they differ from the normal run of the mill conjecture in that they are pre-verbal and pre-conceptual. It might, of course, be true that such conjectures are aided by physiological reflexes, Kantian pure concepts of the understanding, or by innate structures of one kind or another, but this would not alter the fact that they are in some degree fanciful or conjectural.

Insofar as these flights of fancy prove to be useful, they are adopted as being less than fanciful, are eventually relied upon, and so become part of a network of everyday beliefs which we have about our world. Construals or speculations that lead nowhere are quickly dismissed as idle fantasies. The process as I am now describing it is not unlike the process of Popperian conjecture and refutation—one difference being that my emphasis on fanciful conjecture is not confined to the growth of scientific knowledge, but is regarded as a condition of all significant experience or cognition.

Clearly, then, the fanciful imagination is not only required for our first infantile attempts to make sense of the environment. It plays an equally important role in adult attempts to decipher the more bewildering aspects of everyday life. For whenever established knowledge fails us, whenever there is no adequate conceptual apparatus with which to ease our confusion and bridge the gap between ignorance and insight, we fall back upon the fanciful imagination.

We are now at last in a position to understand how what we take to be facts are bred of fancy. We have seen that the fanciful imagination is not only a condition of significant experience, but that we also revert to it in order to make sense of our environment. A fanciful conjecture which fails to dispel a puzzle or confusion may be progressively modified until it does. At this point it ceases to be regarded as fanciful, comes to be relied upon, and is eventually regarded as knowledge.

Hume and the Growth of Knowledge

Needless to say, Hume does not agree with this conception of the role that the fanciful imagination plays in the growth of knowledge. The trouble, as he sees it, is that were we to rely on fancy as a source of knowledge, we would be hopelessly misled. Fancy roams apparently unconstrained and this is why the fanciful imagination is considered radically incapable of affording new knowledge. After all, how can that mental faculty that is thought responsible for delusion and dreams be thought capable of affording knowledge?

Despite these traditional fears, fancy seldom roams unconstrained. Normally, as we have seen, we revert to fancy in order to ease our bewilderment, but it is very seldom indeed that we have no knowledge at all with which to be guided. A scientist's initial conjecture, it is true, may be wild and wide of the mark, but each successive guess, although fanciful, is modified in the light of past failures until it serves its purpose. Conjectures, quite clearly, may be more or less fanciful, and precisely how fanciful one's conjecture is will depend on the extent of one's past relevant experience. Fancy, one could say, is constrained by past experience and, as we shall see, works most often and most efficiently within these constraints. It is also true, though, that when fancy is overly constrained by the burden of established belief, it fails to function at all. For what we take to be the case, and so believe, may stifle our curiosity, inhibit flights of fancy, and so prevent new insights about the commonplace, new inventions, and new discoveries.[27]

We may say that an imaginative response becomes progressively less fanciful as experience limits our choice of responses. When at last we arrive at a response—a hypothesis or conjecture—which serves our (explanatory) purpose, we rely on it and come to regard it not as a guess or a mere product of fancy, but as knowledge. It goes without saying that unless fancy is constrained in this way by past experience, it is hardly likely to furnish us with useful hypotheses in terms of which to negotiate the environment and ease our confusion.

A Humean, however, might still have serious doubts as to whether the fanciful imagination can possibly provide us with knowledge of the actual world. After all, we normally regard hypotheses and conjectures as fanciful only if they fail to explain what we wish to have explained; only, that is, if they fail to furnish us with knowledge. A hypothesis that works is never regarded as mere fantasy. This is why Hume prefers to ascribe the growth of knowledge to the "just," "healthy," or (in my words) constructive (rather than fanciful) imagination.

In one respect our Humean is clearly correct. It is true that successful hypotheses are not mere fantasies. They are, as I have stressed, a product both of fancy and experience. It is true, too, that we tend to regard hypotheses as less than fanciful—indeed, as factual—if they achieve explanatory success. However, it is difficult to see why the contingent success of a conjecture or hypothesis should be taken to establish that it was framed independently of the fanciful imagination. After all, the fact (if it is one) that the world turns out to be as hypothesized is largely a matter of luck and cannot be taken to establish that the hypothesis concerned is fancy free.

This point, however, can easily be granted by Hume. No doubt he would argue that it is not the success of the hypothesis, but rather the fact that it is framed in terms of relevant past experience, which makes it nonfanciful. But even this is not as straightforward as it may seem. Part of the trouble is that it is by no means clear how extensive our past experience should be in order for us to say that a hypothesis or conjecture is not a product of fancy. If we insist that hypotheses are only nonfanciful when they are framed entirely in terms of past relevant experience, then it is arguable that we are no longer talking about hypotheses at all, but about recalled knowledge. If, on the other hand, we allow that our hypotheses or conjectures are not purely products of past experience, then they cannot be entirely divorced from the fanciful imagination.

Nor, of course, is it always obvious whether our past experience is or is not relevant to the solution of a particular problem. We may conjecture one way or the other, but we all know that we are often mistaken on this score.

Clearly, then, the fanciful imagination, insofar as it is required for the formation of hypotheses or conjectures, plays a vital role in problem-solving and hence in the growth of empirical knowledge. This is not to deny that Hume's principle of the association of ideas and induction—that is, the constructive imagination—plays a role in this process. However, I do want to deny that one can explain problem-solving, and hence the growth of empirical knowledge, solely in terms of the constructive imagination.

Briefly, my reason for denying this is that one can learn only what one does not know. By this stage, though, it ought to be abundantly clear that by itself Hume's constructive imagination cannot furnish new knowledge; it merely allows us to recall and apply the old. This is clear from the fact that Hume speaks of the "just" and "healthy" use of the imagination (that is, of the constructive imagination) in situations where anyone other than a skeptic would speak of recalled knowledge. Unless one confines the term "knowledge" to what is logically certain, in which case empirical knowledge becomes unattainable, one must be prepared to describe as *knowledge* those past, recalled experiences in terms of which we fruitfully negotiate the environment. Hume's constructive imagination, therefore, does no more than allow us to recall and apply what we *already know* in new situations; by itself, it cannot furnish new knowledge. The only role that it can play in the acquisition and growth of empirical knowledge is that of guide and mentor to the fanciful imagination.

To say this, of course, is to deny that induction alone can ever add to our body of knowledge. And while such a claim will no doubt raise some eyebrows, it is easily defended. Consider this example: When I walk across a floor I unquestioningly or, to use Hume's term, naturally apply my past experience of floors to the floorboards on which I am about to step. I infer that they too will support me. Now, if one believes that an inductive inference of this sort adds to one's knowledge, one has to maintain that the application of past experience in this situation informs me of something about which I was previously unaware. And this is odd. For whatever anyone tells me, I do want to say that I know, and have known for some time, that the floorboards in front of me will support my weight. I know this in just the way that I know that milk will nourish my cat and that cyanide will poison it. To suppose that I do not know this is either to suppose that I have good reason to doubt it—which I do not have; or it is to suppose that anything which can be doubted cannot be known—in which case we remove all possibility of empirical knowledge.

It is only when there is some doubt as to whether our past experience applies in a new situation that we can actually learn from past experience. In such a case, though, we do not rely on induction for the acquisition of empirical knowledge, for we have to suppose, imagine, or hypothesize that our past experience is relevant to the present situation. Should we find our hypothesis confirmed we will indeed have learned something new, but in such a case the fanciful imagination has once again been brought to play.

Conclusion

I began by saying that adult human beings are normally expected to know how to take the objects of their environment. This emphasis on *taking* is important, for implicit in it is the suggestion (which I have defended in some detail) that the objects of the environment do not simply present themselves in the fullness of their properties to a passive human mind. Rather, we *actively* take them in certain ways. How we take them, I have tried to show, is a function not merely of past experience, but of the fanciful imagination as well. To this extent my argument runs contrary to much traditional epistemology, for I have attempted to remove those vestiges of empiricism (and skepticism) which still affect our attitude towards the fanciful imagination and the epistemological status of its constructs.

THREE

The Romantic Abyss

My argument so far has brought us to the very brink of romantic idealism. If I am right, everything that we take to be fact is bred of fancy, but it seems only a small step from this to the conclusion that there can be no distinction between our fanciful imaginings and the way the world is. And this, of course, is the abyss into which romantic idealists gladly leap. It is a leap, I shall argue, which is at best misjudged, for romantic idealism is simply untenable. However, I shall also argue that the epistemological framework that I have developed is compatible with realism, and, even though I cannot provide a thorough survey of the realism controversy here, I will nonetheless furnish and argue for the bare bones of what I call a romantic realism.

Idealism, Nietzsche, and Beyond

The connection between a romantic epistemology on the one hand and some version of idealism on the other is all too obvious in the work of both the early and the later romantics. In *The System of Transcendental Idealism*, for instance, Friedrich Schelling subscribes to a romantic epistemology according to which the imagination, or more precisely "the productive intuition," is responsible not only for the sense we make of the world, but, in so doing, for the very creation of that world.[1] It is arguable that Coleridge follows Schelling in this regard, for he treats what he calls the primary imagination as "a repetition in the finite mind of the eternal act of creation in the infinite I AM."[2] Unfortunately, though, Coleridge's meaning is not entirely clear. Certainly he is of the opinion that the finite human mind *repeats* the creativity of the universal mind, but since the word "repetition" in this context may mean either that the finite mind *follows* the universal mind in being genuinely creative, or that it merely mirrors the genuine creations of the universal mind, it is difficult to decide to what extent Coleridge deems the primary imagination of the individual to be genuinely creative. Hence, while there are grounds for thinking that Coleridge is as much an idealist as Schelling, this can be disputed.

Romantic idealists, we saw earlier, come in different shapes and sizes. Nietzsche, so it seems to me, is in certain respects as much a romantic and an idealist as Schelling, although, of course, he makes his case differently. He has relatively little to say about imagination, but more to say about truth. What we take to be the truth in this society at this time is, as he says in a well-known passage, no more than a "mobile army of metaphors." [3] And when we look more closely at his defense of this view, we find, first, that Nietzsche means by "metaphor" something very like what I mean by "fanciful imagination"; second, that he totally rejects the view that our truths can ever reveal or reflect a clearly delineated and independently existing reality. Reality does not guide and shape our descriptions; rather our descriptions shape it. Herein resides Nietzsche's idealism.

Although Nietzsche's writings on the topic are neither thorough nor systematic, they are important, for in drawing out the implications of romantic idealism they quickly show how that doctrine leads to cognitive relativism, contemporary pragmatism, and deconstruction. It will be helpful, then, to look more closely at what Nietzsche has to say in order to see why, on his view, a romantic epistemology must lead to these doctrines — doctrines, I should add, which have lately received a good deal of attention and acclaim.

According to Nietzsche, our penchant for "the truth" arises in the first instance because of the individual's attempts "to preserve himself against other individuals" ("On Truth and Falsity," p. 176). To that end, one *invents* a "uniformly valid and binding designation of things," and thereby the contrast between truth and falsity (p. 176). But the individual, Nietzsche contends, is not sincerely concerned with the truth, since "he covets the agreeable, life-preserving consequences of truth; . . . [but is] even inimical towards truths which possibly might prove harmful or destroying" (p. 177).

All cognition, all knowledge, on Nietzsche's view, is the product of metaphor. "A nerve-stimulus," he writes, "first transformed into a percept! First metaphor! The percept again copied into a sound! Second metaphor!" (p. 178). But we deceive ourselves if we believe that these metaphors are capable of telling us how things really are, for "when we talk about trees, . . . we believe we know something about the things themselves, and yet we only possess metaphors of the things, and these metaphors do not in the least correspond to the original essentials" (p. 178). Indeed, it is only because we forget the origins of our language that we can believe it adequate to a nonlinguistic reality. A word, we are told, is no more than "a nerve-stimulus in sounds," but "to infer a cause outside us from the nerve-stimulus is already the result of a wrong and unjustifiable application of the proposition of causality" (p. 177). Indeed, the " 'thing-in-itself' " . . . is also quite incomprehensible to the creator of language" (p. 178).

The idealist in Nietzsche is adamant that nature and its contents are "inaccessible" and "indefinable" (p. 180). The notion of truth, therefore, has nothing whatsoever to do with correspondence to reality. Rather, it is a way of coming to control the world about us so as to meet "important needs with foresight, prudence, regularity" (p. 190); it is a way of securing the "agreeable" and the "life-preserving" (p. 177). Thus all that the individual can do is to construe the world in certain ways, and we do so by construing aspects of our experience in terms which are invariably different from and hence foreign to it. We do so, that is, by coining metaphors. This is what Nietzsche means, I think, when he says that "every idea originates through equating the unequal" (p. 178). We ignore the differences between that which we construe and the terms in which we construe it, and so come to think, metaphorically, of the one *as* the other. But to do all this is just to exercise the fanciful imagination, for Nietzsche goes on to describe the "primitive world of metaphors" as "pouring forth as a fiery liquid out of the primal faculty of human fancy" (p. 184).

Our primal metaphors, if found to be useful, become the established or conventional way of describing and delineating our world. It is for this reason that Nietzsche can write in a widely quoted passage:

What therefore is truth? A mobile army of metaphors, metonymies, anthropomorphisms: in short a sum of human relations which become poetically and rhetorically intensified, metamorphosed, adorned, and after long usage seem to a nation fixed, canonic and binding; truths are illusions of which one has forgotten that they *are* illusions. (p. 180)

It is, therefore, only because we forget that we create our own world, and forget that every person is "an *artistically creating* subject," that we can live firm in the belief that we all have access to the same stable and public world. In fact there is no such world, and were we to remember the origins of our world-view, this would become immediately apparent. And so Nietzsche writes of the ordinary person:

Already it costs him some trouble to admit to himself that the insect and the bird perceive a world different from his own, and that the question, which of the two world-perceptions is more accurate, is quite a senseless one, since to decide this question it would be necessary to apply the standard of *right perception*, i.e., to apply a standard which *does not exist*. (p. 184)

At this point Nietzsche's idealism clearly commits him both to a radical cognitive relativism and an accompanying incommensurability thesis, for he now contends that "between two utterly different spheres, . . . there is no . . . accuracy, no expression, but at the utmost . . . a stammering translation into a quite distinct foreign language" (p. 184).

Nietzsche's idealism does not only pave the way for T. S. Kuhn and Paul Feyerabend, but also, I think, for Richard Rorty and Jacques Derrida. Thus, for instance, we have seen that Nietzsche treats truth not as a relation of correspondence to an extra-linguistic reality, but as a term reserved for those statements or points of view which are "agreeable" and "life-preserving" (p. 177), and which (in Rorty's words) enable us "to cope."[4] To this extent he clearly is a harbinger of Rorty's pragmatism. He also foreshadows Derrida's attack on "logocentrism" — on the view, that is, that our utterances refer to, are guided by, and reflect an extra-linguistic reality. Like Derrida, Nietzsche appears to think that we are confined to a world of signs, for when he speaks of laws of nature it becomes clear that they are not considered by him to be regularities in an external, physical world. A law of nature, he writes,

is not known in itself but only . . . in its relation to other laws of nature, which again are known to us only as sums of relations. *Therefore all these relations refer only one to another* and are absolutely incomprehensible to us in their essence. (p. 186. Emphasis added.)

Still more, according to Nietzsche, everything that we marvel at in the laws of nature

lies really and solely in the mathematical rigour and inviolability of the conceptions of time and space. These however we produce within ourselves and throw them forth with that necessity with which the spider spins. (p. 186)

Here, then, are some of the seeds of deconstruction. Nor are they the only ones to be found in Nietzsche, for his account of rationality is echoed in the work of Derrida. According to Nietzsche, the western ideal of

rationality, and especially its emphasis on literal truth, is bred of forgetful-
ness and of man's "invincible tendency to let himself be deceived" (p. 189).
Our established ways of thinking and speaking, our received truths, are all
the products of free and fanciful metaphors which, because of our desire to
control the world about us, have become frozen as the "true," the "rational,"
way of proceeding. But this

enormous framework and hoarding of ideas, by clinging to which needy man saves
himself through life, is to the freed intellect only a scaffolding and a toy for Its
most daring feats, and when It smashes it to pieces, throws it into confusion, and
then puts it together ironically, pairing the strangest, separating the nearest items,
then It manifests that It has no use for those makeshifts of misery, and that It is
now no longer led by ideas but by intuitions. (p. 190)

Here we have both the recipe and the rationale for deconstruction. We
are required to shake loose our standard ways of organizing, classifying,
thinking about the world. Reason, for instance, is "shown" by Nietzsche to
be an illusion which, if relentlessly pursued, will be the source of its own
destruction and will come grinding to a halt. Literal truths are similarly
illusory, and can be shown to originate in, and to depend on, metaphor.[5] By
dismantling our ordinary set ways of thinking, new possibilities of thought
are opened up to us. We are, in a sense, free to re-erect our structures of
thought in whatever way we wish—creating new insights and visions and
understanding along the way.

There are, however, important differences between Derrida and
Nietzsche, for Nietzsche is never as radical or as thorough as Derrida in
ferreting out the implications of this doctrine. So, for instance, Nietzsche
allows that there are real origins. Cognition, we are told, *really* begins with
metaphor, and there *really* are no literal truths. Derrida, by contrast, has no
room for such notions. There are, for the contemporary deconstructionist,
no origins, no fundamental realities. There are only signs and meanings
bred of the interplay of signs. That is to say, there is what Derrida calls
"writing"—a free play of signs which, as we shall see later on, we freeze
metaphorically when we attempt to devise a literal language.

The upshot of all this is that the romantic epistemology that I have so
far defended and developed tends toward the romantic abyss. It leads to a
number of doctrines, from romantic idealism to pragmatism and deconstruction, all of which are quite hostile to any form of realism.

Two tasks now fall to hand. First, because deconstruction can be seen
to represent what is in some ways the most radical and far-reaching application of romantic theory, it is important to see whether the Nietzschean

and Derridean attack on reason, and its application in deconstructionist practice, can withstand scrutiny. I shall try to show that it cannot. Second, and more positively, I shall try to show that commitment to a romantic epistemology need not commit us to a rejection of realism. When once this is understood, it becomes possible to explain the workings of the fanciful imagination in the creation and comprehension of fiction without commitment to any of the doctrines which have traditionally taken root in the romantic theory of knowledge.

The Rage for Deconstruction

It would be a fearless and somewhat foolhardy expositor who aimed to reveal the essential nature of deconstruction: to give, as it were, an objective specification of that practice. For it is, paradoxically, essential to deconstruction that such a specification is not possible. To suppose that I can convey the intrinsic nature of the practice (or of anything else) through language is to subscribe to what Derrida condemns as "logocentrism": the "myth" according to which language is guided by, and can somehow reflect and latch on to, the true nature of nonlinguistic entities. Logocentrism, we are told, is a product of "the exigent, powerful, systematic and irrepressible desire" for certain nonlinguistic entities which language can "signify." [6] For, as Derrida tells us, such a "transcendental signified" will alone ensure that we can talk about reality, and not merely about talk itself. It is, on his view, this overwhelming urge to "place a reassuring end to the reference from sign to sign" which inclines all of us, in all cultures, to subscribe to the logocentric view that language is subservient to certain nonlinguistic objects, intentions, or ideas. [7]

And yet, if Derrida is to be believed, this same logocentrism is a self-defeating "myth" which has befuddled Western thinking since at least the time of Plato. It gives rise to the idea that there are fixed truths, brute extra-linguistic facts which are present to the speaker and which can be captured in literal discourse. And it falls to philosophy and science to uncover these truths by using the tools of reason, evidence, and argument. In this sense, then, both philosophy and science attempt to "place a reassuring end to the reference from sign to sign." They hope to get away from the realm of speculative conceptions whereby we invent significance in order to reveal the actual facts of the matter and show how things *really* are. So, while philosophy and science are but systems of signs, they pretend, according to Derrida, to transcend those signs. They ignore the formative power of the language which constitutes them, and pretend instead to latch directly on to the way the world is.

According to Derrida, then, both science and philosophy assume the presence in all that they do of a real world, of discernible truths, causes, origins—all of which can be referred to, captured and conveyed in ordinary discourse. It is this that Derrida terms the "metaphysics of presence": a metaphysics which clearly is part and parcel of the logocentric "myth." Derrida, of course, is adamant that this picture of science and philosophy is misleading, that neither furnishes a window to an immutable reality. Rather, each discipline is a variety of what he calls "writing." Each is a system of signs, and every sign gets its sense not from some extra-linguistic entity which it signifies, but from its relationship to other signs within this system.

It is possible, therefore, for philosophy or science or literary criticism to perpetuate its logocentrism (and thereby its metaphysics of presence) only by artificially restricting the sense of certain signs. This it does by making certain terms dominate others. "One of the terms," writes Derrida, "dominates the other (axiologically, logically, etc.), and occupies the commanding position."[8] Examples are many. Philosophy organizes itself around contrasts such as true/false; literal/metaphorical; real/fictional; empirical/transcendental; observable/theoretical; fact/value; serious/nonserious; objective/subjective, and so on. In each case, we are told, the first term assumes a dominance, a priority which is bred of our allegiance to the metaphysics of presence. Given the assumption of this dominance, philosophical analysis is just

the enterprise of returning "strategically," in idealization, to an origin or to a "priority" seen as simple, intact, normal, pure, standard, self-identical, in order *then* to conceive of derivation, complication, deterioration, accident, etc. All metaphysicians have proceeded thus.[9]

To this Derrida adds (in a voice strongly reminiscent of Nietzsche) that "to deconstruct the opposition is above all, at a particular moment, to reverse the hierarchy."[10] Deconstruction, therefore, whether of a text or a discourse, involves showing "how it undermines the philosophy it asserts, or the hierarchical oppositions on which it relies."[11]

Derrida premises this practice on the antilogocentric assumption that "from the moment that there is meaning there is nothing but signs."[12] Each such sign, so the claim goes, gets its meaning not from some nonlinguistic entity which it signifies, but from its interaction with, and hence its difference from, other signs. Usually it is the context within which the sign occurs that helps determine the way in which it is taken to interact with others, but, as Jonathan Culler puts it, "context is boundless": there are no theoretical ways of delimiting it.[13] The temptation, when context fails us, is to appeal to the speaker's intention, but this presupposes that the intention is present to us—another example of our uncritical adherence to the metaphysics of presence. Clearly, then, the ways in which signs interact in any given text may be seen to vary, so that one cannot think of the text, a discourse, or its signs as possessing clear, definitive, and settled meanings. Any attempt to uncover determinate meanings—as one does when one subscribes to the metaphysics of presence—is no more than a distortion which "represses" the actual nature of language.

It is a distortion, moreover, that Derrida hopes to set to rights by showing that for every "settled" meaning, alternative interpretations, construals, readings can be offered which are equally plausible, and which can be arrived at with as much or as little justification. There are, on Derrida's view, no fixed standards, no primary concepts relative to which others are merely derivative or parasitic. And it is the aim of deconstruction to demonstrate this by showing that for any discourse, whether it be philosophy, science, or literature, what is taken to be a fixed and determinate meaning is really fluid and shifting. The literal truth paradigm is an invention: a fancy which suits our purposes, but which succeeds only in disguising, not eliminating, the indeterminacy of meaning. In creating a literal truth paradigm, Derrida seems to be saying, we do no more than speak in Nietzschean metaphors.

This is not to say that we have to abandon the search for, or the regulative ideal of, determinate meaning. Even Derrida concedes that the ideal is positively useful. Nor, as I understand him, is he suggesting that there are no conceptual oppositions—still less that we could ever do without them. What he does seem to say, though, is that such oppositions are of our invention. They are a product of the way in which we choose to fix the play of signs. The important point is that we can often, perhaps always, find reasons for inverting these "hierarchical oppositions," so that they cannot be taken to reflect a settled reality; but this, we are required to understand, is a function of the way in which we employ the signs that constitute our language, and is emphatically not the causal effect of an ever-present brute reality on a passive human mind.

There is, of course, much more than a trace of Nietzschean romanticism in all of this. Like all romantics, Derrida allows that our views of the world are shaped by the categories we bring to it. Like Nietzsche, he is of the opinion that these categories are much more fluid than we normally suppose, but he differs from Nietzsche insofar as he refuses to locate the formation of these categories in the fanciful imagination. To do so would be to pretend to discover a real origin, and would thus be a reversion to the logocentrism which he decries. Although Derrida is more consistent than Nietzsche in this regard, both are adamant that we do not have access to things-in-themselves. To suppose that we do is, in Derrida's jargon, to subscribe to logocentrism and the metaphysics of presence. On his view, brute facts are never present to us. Still more, there is nothing we can say that reveals their essence. Rather, we are locked into our conceptions of the world, where these are shaped not by the world itself but by the categories we bring to it.

Herein resides Derrida's romantic idealism. It differs from Schelling's, for Derrida does not altogether deny that there are things-in-themselves. Rather, he maintains that such entities do not affect us cognitively, that they cannot be experienced, and hence that they cannot be revealed through language. In a nutshell, they are never "present" to us. And it seems but a short step from this to Schelling's idealism; although, so far as I can see, it is a step that Derrida does not actually take.

In Defense of Deconstruction

So much, then, for the main thrust of Derridean deconstruction. The question that we must now ask is, what arguments Derrida has for his attacks on logocentrism and the metaphysics of presence. The short answer is that he appears to have only two, which appear in different forms throughout his many writings. I shall attend to only a few works in which these arguments are deployed, and shall take as my point of departure some of Derrida's statements in *Of Grammatology*.

It is in this work that Derrida launches his well-known attack on Ferdinand de Saussure's so-called phonocentrism: on his tendency, that is, to privilege speech as a form of "direct" communication, over writing, which is thought of as an "indirect" and distorting medium. Of course, there is much in Saussure's writings of which Derrida approves. For one thing, Saussure appears to go a considerable way toward undermining logocentrism, for he insists that signs in a linguistic system are conventional or arbitrary and are never intrinsically or naturally related to a specific meaning.[14] Rather, the meanings that such signs acquire are a function of the differences between them. Meanings, for Saussure, are not "things out there." They are the product of a differential system of signs: a system (*la langue*) which generates meanings through the differences and different relations between its constituent signs. It is this system, Saussure argues, which enables us to perform individual speech acts (*parole*). Now, although Saussure emphasizes (in this way) that all speech presupposes *la langue*, he also insists that writing is derived from and presupposes speech. And Derrida balks at this. He finds himself totally at odds with Saussure's (Plato's, Rousseau's, and, indeed, philosophy's) insistence that writing is parasitic on, and less reliable than, speech.[15]

According to Derrida, the widespread belief that speech brings us much closer to what the speaker means to convey than writing ever can is no more than a prejudice bred of the metaphysics of presence. Those who are infected with this prejudice consider speech a source of insight into the speaker's meaning; while writing, since it invariably floats free of author and context, is believed to give us a questionable, and at times a downright distorted, view of what the author hoped to convey. The speaker's meaning, it is held, is transparent in speech—it is presented or made "present" to us—but is obscured in writing.

But according to Derrida, neither the speaker's meaning nor anything else can be directly present to us as an underived simple. Rather, what we think of as present is always a construct based on our conception of what it is for that thing to be absent. What Derrida is doing, of course, is to deconstruct the "hierarchial opposition" *speech/writing*, but he does so by deconstructing the further, apparently more basic, "hierarchical opposition" *presence/absence* on which it is made to depend. Whereas we ordinarily think that objects can be present to us and that absence has to be explained as the negation of presence, Derrida now argues that we can make sense of the concept of presence only by attributing to it features which belong to the concept of absence.[16]

The thrust of Derrida's argument is perfectly simple: nothing can be known to be present unless we have some conception of what it would be like for that thing to be absent. As Culler puts it, "the notion of presence and of the present is derived: an effect of differences."[17] We can recognize the presence of an object only because of the "traces" in it of its absence—that is, because of our conception of what it would be like for it to be absent. For this reason, Derrida thinks of presence as a meaningful construct, one which depends crucially on certain systematic differences between "signs" for its meaning. If he is to be believed, it follows from this that nothing can be directly present to us. The presence of anything is "deferred" since we have access to it only through a system of signs, so that if the relations between these signs alter, the object could cease to be regarded as present. In a typically convoluted way, Derrida uses the word *différance* to capture the process of coming to think of presence—where this word is to be explained partly in terms of the differences between signs which produce meaning, and partly in terms of the notion of the deferral of both meaning and the immediacy of presence.

Nothing, then, can ever be directly present to us, for it now turns out that all comprehension and all cognition are crucially mediated by signs.[18] It should be stressed, though, that not all of these signs are linguistic, for if I understand Derrida correctly any conception is meaningful and so qualifies as a sign. It is this system of signs in general that Derrida calls *archi-écriture* or "archi-writing," and it is this, we are told, that is a condition of all speech, writing (in the ordinary sense), and cognition. This, we can now see, is why Derrida objects so strenuously to phonocentrism, for if his analysis is correct, speech can no more present us with a speaker's meaning than writing can present us with an author's meaning.

The point is that according to Derrida, nothing is ever directly present to us, including the meaning of what I have just written (or said). Meaning is invariably a construct bred of your (or my) conception of the differences between the signs that I use. And this, Derrida contends, is true of every communicative act. However, it now appears that there can be no originary speech act which does not already presuppose a linguistic structure, a system of signs, or what Saussure has called *la langue*. For on Derrida's view, a shout in a protolanguage can be taken to mean *danger* only if we already have a conception ("sign") of nondangerous things, and if we can already distinguish between this shout and other ones, or between shouts and non-shouts. In other words, the shout can be significant, and hence can constitute a speech act, only if it is constrasted with, and seen to be different from, other signs not present.[19]

Derrida freely acknowledges, though, that it is difficult, indeed impossible, to see how such a linguistic structure (*la langue*) can be developed without initial speech acts (*parole*) which shape and determine the structure. In saying this, he is attempting to deconstruct the "hierarchical opposition" *parole/la langue*, or, if you prefer, *speech act/linguistic structure*. It is not just that he reverses the normal opposition by insisting that speech acts presuppose (rather than create) a linguistic structure, but when once he has done this he insists as well that we cannot simply abandon the established opposition—that we still have to think of speech acts as responsible for linguistic structure. Each way of thinking about language shows the other to be mistaken, so that one is left with an irresolvable paradox or "aporia." Derrida takes this point up in *Positions*:

> There is a circle here, for if one distinguishes rigorously *langue* and *parole* . . . and if one is to do justice to the two principles here enunciated, one does not know where to begin and how something can in general begin, be it *langue* or *parole*. One must therefore recognize, prior to any dissociation of *langue* and *parole* . . . a systematic production of differences, the *production* of a system of differences—a *différance* among whose effects one might later, by abstraction and for specific reasons, distinguish a linguistics of *langue* from a linguistics of *parole*. (p. 28)

All that we have are differences, and by organizing these in certain ways through a process of selection and abstraction—guided always by "specific reasons"—we establish more or less discrete systems of signification. What Derrida appears to be saying is that out of these differences emerge different (Wittgensteinian) language games, which, since they are established for different purposes, are not entirely commensurable. And this explains, even if it does not resolve, the aporia.

We now have some idea of the extent of Derrida's antirealism and of one of the arguments which he uses to dismantle the metaphysics of presence. It is an argument which is integral to the practice of deconstruction, for if it fails, we simply have no reason to deny that our use of language is guided and constrained by the external world (which is present to us in perception). The obvious question, therefore, is whether the argument manages to establish that we cannot have access to a world "out there"? Or, put differently, is it true that cognition is always mediated by a system of signs, by "writing," so that nothing can ever be present to us? If this is true, then the logocentrism on which we all rely turns out to be the myth that Derrida insists it is.

Presence Regained

Derrida's argument, we have seen, starts by looking specifically at language, and is in agreement with Saussure's view that language is, in the final analysis, a system of differences—differences, that is, between arbitrary linguistic units which both Derrida and Saussure describe as signs. We have seen, too, that Derrida's argument against presence emphasizes the fact that one's knowledge of the presence of an object is bred of an awareness of certain contrasts or differences: an awareness, that is, which is based *inter alia* on what it would be like for that object to be absent. And from this Derrida infers that our awareness of presence is based on a system of signs which is not essentially different from the system of signs which constitutes a language. It is for this reason that he speaks of this system of differences as writing in general, as *archi-écriture*.

Derrida, however, can draw this inference only because of an elementary confusion between necessary and sufficient conditions. Systematic differences certainly are *necessary* for anything to count as a system of signs, but they are not sufficient. Something more is required, for when I discern systematic differences of shape and color in the clouds at sunset, I do not discern a system of signs. And yet if such differences were sufficient for signal systems, that is what I should have to discern. There are many systematic differences, both in artifacts and in the world of nature, which do not in any ordinary sense constitute systems of signs. The patterned marks of a curtain or wallpaper are systematically different, but do not constitute signal systems. Cell walls in a plant differ systematically from cell sap; colors in a spectrum differ systematically. None is a system of signs. It is true, of course, that Derrida has not described them as such. However, if he is to be consistent, he should be prepared to do so, for he has already argued that it is only through appeal to systematic differences, and *therefore* a system of signs, that we come to notice the presence of an object.

It seems, then, that Derrida succeeds only in extending the concept of a system of signs, and that in so doing he makes the corresponding expression ("a system of signs") do rather too much work. He is, of course, correct when he insists that we need to notice differences in order to experience an object. And it is true, too, that we cannot do so without having some conception of these differences. But to say this is to say no more than Jean Piaget did when he argued that we can be aware of an object (the "presence" of an object) only if our experience is already differentiated.[20] This, however, does not entail that a system of signs, a language, is required for such awareness; still less that differentiated experience constitutes such a system. Derrida can suppose that it does only by so stretching the meaning of the expression "a system of signs" as to use it inconsistently. For on the one hand, he uses it (in its normal sense) to describe a system which can be used to convey more or less determinate meanings in communicative acts. On the other hand, he uses it to mention "structures of differences" (visible and aural contrasts, for instance) which are not used in acts of communication, and which cannot be so used without a change in communicative conventions.

Perhaps I have been too short with Derrida. For is it not true that one has to have some conception of a tree in order to recognize its presence? And if this is true, must not such a conception be informative, or significant, and so itself a sign? And so it might be argued that one's perception of presence is always mediated by a system of signs which does not differ in any essential respect from a language.

But this argument is problematic. We know from everyday experience that not everything that is significant is a sign in the same sense of this word. The blood on a tubercular person's handkerchief is certainly significant since it *means* tuberculosis, but it is not a sign for tuberculosis (it is in fact a sign *of* tuberculosis) in the same sense that "tuberculosis" is a sign for the disease. H. P. Grice, in his seminal article, treats the first as *natural meaning* (meaning$_n$), the second as non-natural or conventional meaning (meaning$_{nn}$).[21] And I can see no good reason for confusing the two. In much the same way, we can distinguish those of our conceptions that are linguistic and meaningful$_{nn}$ from those which are the causal products of past experiences, and are, at best, meaningful$_n$. The latter may constitute a system of signs (although it would be difficult to see in what sense they could be systematic), but would not constitute a language in any ordinary sense of this word.

So while we do have conceptions, significant conceptions, which are vital to our experience of the world, they need not always be linguistic and, in this sense, a kind of Derridean "writing." My pictorial image, and hence my visual conception, of a cat is clearly nonlinguistic. A young child's conception of a steam engine as a noisy object (evidenced by hands over ears) need not be, and most probably is not, linguistic. Derrida's notion of "writing" treats manifestly different types of conception as essentially the same: as a kind of general language. He offers no worthwhile argument for this, and so far as I can see, there is nothing to be said in its defense.

No doubt anyone who is wedded to the practice of deconstruction will respond to this criticism by attempting to deconstruct or destablize Grice's "oppositional hierarchy" *meaning$_n$/meaning$_{nn}$*. However, it is important to realize at this point that we cannot defend Derrida's argument against presence by appealing to *any* of the findings of deconstruction; this simply because deconstruction can get off the ground only if Derrida's argument against presence works. Hence, to use the findings of deconstruction in order to defend that argument is to beg the question. In other words, it is no use contending (as deconstructionists are wont to do) that my objection to Derrida ignores the fact that there are no semantic stabilities; or that

Derrida could deconstruct certain conceptual oppositions on which my argument depends. These sorts of rejoinders are derived from deconstructive practice, and clearly presuppose the adequacy of that practice. But since this is the very issue in question, no such assumption can properly be made.

But is it true that Derrida's argument against presence is *fundamental* to deconstruction? Why can't the practice survive even if this argument fails? The simple answer, I think, is that as long as Derrida fails to furnish us with a convincing argument against presence, we cannot take his attack on logocentrism seriously. For without such an argument, it remains possible not only that we can experience the external world, but that this world constrains, and should be allowed to constrain, our talk about the world. It remains possible, that is, that some of the "hierarchical oppositions" which Derrida seeks to displace through deconstruction are founded on, and constrained by, a real world which can be "present" to us, and which we can come to know.

In time, Derrida may furnish an alternative and more telling argument against presence, but until he does there is no reason at all to subscribe to the central theories on which deconstruction is based. Even so, we can continue to furnish arguments (in just the way that traditional philosophy often does) which purport to upset certain "hierarchical oppositions" — although such arguments need have nothing whatsoever to do with deconstructive theory and need not entail a denial of logocentrism or the metaphysics of presence. Plato, for instance, although he is the archenemy of all who follow Derrida, can plausibly be seen as having attempted to displace the "hierarchical opposition" *knowledge/memory* by contending that one does not always have first to know in order later to remember, but that there is a sense in which we have first to remember in order later to know. Much more recently, philosophers such as Karl Popper, Gilbert Ryle, and N. R. Hanson have attempted to displace the "opposition" *fact/theory* by showing that facts, far from being prior to theories, are bred of them, so that there can be no such thing as the theory-free observation of facts.[22] Whether or not these attempts at displacement succeed must depend, of course, on strength of argument. What is clear, though, is that the displacement of "hierarchical oppositions" is not peculiar to deconstruction and can continue without the antirealism which it presupposes.

Derrida does have another argument with which to reinforce his attack on presence. This emerges during his discussion of history, and, more particularly, during his discussion of the historicity of our linguistic conceptions. On his view, all discourse is historically shaped: our concepts, our meanings are all influenced by our location in history. As a result, he stresses the unavailability to us of a historical context in terms of which to stabilize the meaning of a given text. The trouble is that our conception of such a context is itself historically determined, so that the context can never properly be regained or made present to us. By the same token, if our concepts and meanings are historically shaped, they cannot "convey" the world as it is, but must always signify some or other conception of the world. Indeed, my conception of your meaning when you speak, or of my meaning when I speak, is historically shaped, a historical construct, so that meaning itself is never present to us in speech or in a written text. It is deferred through conceptions, and hence differences, bred of time. This is why Derrida designates, by the term *différance*, the "movement by which language, or any code, any system of reference in general, becomes 'historically' constituted as a fabric of differences." [23]

According to Derrida, then, it is because our concepts and meanings are historically conditioned that they do not represent, convey, or correspond to a nonlinguistic reality, a "transcendental signified". Rather, every sign signifies some other sign or conception, and so on indefinitely. Between every two signs there is a third that mediates our understanding, so that meanings, like the objects of our environment, are never properly present to us, but are always deferred through history—or, put differently, they are always our own historically shaped constructs.

It is difficult to take this argument seriously. For it seems plain that the historicity of our symbol systems need not lead to textualism—to the view, that is, that we cannot transcend our languages or codes and so achieve a "textually" unmediated awareness of the objects about us. For even if our concept of an elephant has changed with time, this only entails that some of our criteria for applying the word "elephant," and for individuating elephants, have changed. It does not so much as hint at the view that talk about elephants is talk about signs; still less that it is talk about a historically conditioned conception of elephants. Nor does the historicity of the concept affect the fact that there are observable criteria which must be instantiated by a nonlinguistic, nonsemiotic, object if it is to be described as an elephant. To say this might appear to beg the question against Derrida. However, it does not do so, for he can only deny that we can observe nonsemiotic elephants (that is, elephants which are not constructs bred of our codes or systems of signs) if his earlier argument against presence works. But, as we have seen, it does not work. So far as I can see, then, the fact of historicity—the fact, that is, that our concepts are historically located—

does nothing at all to undermine the metaphysics of presence. Derrida, it turns out, has only suggested, but has not shown, that it does.

Certainly our linguistic concepts and beliefs mediate and guide our perception of elephants. But this does not entail that perception is *wholly determined* by our beliefs and linguistic concepts. Were this the case, we could never be genuinely puzzled by our perceptions, nor could we ever acquire new conceptions or beliefs from them. It would not be possible to stumble on, and so discover, objects and events which defy our best efforts at description. But we do make such discoveries, and our fumbling efforts to describe and comprehend them suggest both that our perceptions are not wholly determined by our linguistic concepts, and that in these cases we do not merely talk about talk. We actually talk about a nonlinguistic world, and strive to capture and convey its features in conversation.

It could be suggested that I have interpreted Derrida too narrowly; that despite what he seems to say, he does not think that perception is wholly determined by our *linguistic* concepts. Rather his view is that perception is determined by systematic differences, by signs, codes, or what have you, not all of which are linguistic. In the end his message is that we cannot (as Richard Rorty puts it) experience an elephant "plain, unmasked, naked to our gaze." [24] But if this only means that we cannot experience an object apart from our mental constructs—apart, that is, from the differences and constrasts that we notice, and apart from our various construals and conceptions—then this, while true, is trivially so, for it is just another way of saying that we cannot experience an object apart from our experience of it. It certainly follows from this that we cannot match our observations and descriptions of an elephant with an unexperienced (or noumenal) elephant, but this is an entirely trivial truth and marks no restriction on our powers of observation, description, or verification. We still observe nonlinguistic or nonsemiotic objects in order to ascertain whether we have described them correctly, or whether earlier observations were accurate. Since this is so, there must be a nonlinguistic, nonsemiotic, nonconstructed world: one which is not entirely the product of our current conceptions, signs, and codes, and one, moreover, which exercises some constraint on what we say, on how we organize, differentiate, and codify.

I think this argument both telling and sound. I think, too, that it disposes of a good deal of Derrida. And yet I have no doubt that my argument will be considered by some to be beside the point. For not only have I attempted to vindicate the metaphysics of presence by assuming its adequacy, but it will also be suggested that I have altogether overlooked the fact that Derrida nowhere denies that we use language (or at least take ourselves to use language) in order to communicate about a nonlinguistic reality which we think of as present to ourselves.[25] What he insists on, however, is that there is another (anti-logocentric) way of looking at the matter for which an equally good case can be made. Because strong arguments can be adduced in support of both of these positions, and because each view can be shown to presuppose the other so that neither can readily be abandoned, it is simply arbitrary and an artifice to adopt the one view rather than the other.[26] As Steven Fuller puts it, "If this were mathematics, . . . the deconstructionist would be claiming, in effect, that his discipline's proof procedure undermines the possibility of its ever serving as a decision procedure."[27]

But the trouble remains that Derrida has not as yet given us a sound reason for abandoning the metaphysics of presence. Unless he can develop a defensible argument for the view that the mere fact of differentiated experience establishes that observation is wholly mediated by systems of signs, much of what he says simply falls by the way. Still worse, if I am guilty of complicity with the metaphysics of presence, so too, of course, is Derrida. For he is obliged to use words and phrases referringly to single out practices (grafting, masturbation, speech, construing), objects (signs, texts, discourse, people, science, systems, metaphors), and events (coming to understand, misunderstand, and so on), which he thereby represents (re-*presents*) to the reader. Like all deconstructionists, Derrida is clearly faced with a dilemma. To be consistent, he has to reject the logocentrism and presence which he decries; but to do so is, in the end, to reject the only language available to us. For we apply words in a natural language systematically, and often in accordance with observable, nonlinguistic criteria. To reject this aspect of logocentrism and presence must result in indecipherable nonsense. The only alternative is to adopt the metaphysics of presence in order to argue against it, but this seems manifestly inconsistent.

Derrida is acutely aware of the problem, and proposes to avoid the difficulty in a way suggested by Nietzsche and employed by Heidegger. He proposes to write "under erasure." By placing a cross neatly through the word "sign," for instance, Derrida furnishes us with a mark of the absence of any signified, and so takes himself to have removed the metaphysical baggage which normally accompanies the word "sign."[28] So, too, for the word "literal," the word "metaphor," or any other word or expression which seems to commit him to something that he wishes to deny.

There are, however, very definite problems for the reader in this procedure. For it is never clear what remains to be grasped once a word appears "under erasure." To use the word "sign" *sous rature* is to erase and so eliminate the notion of the signified. But if this does not actually destroy our concept of a sign, it so strains it that we are left wondering what we are to understand by Derrida's use of the word.

Derrida is not unaware of the difficulty and uses his notion of a *trace* in order to circumvent it. In using a word "under erasure," he concedes, one exploits its standard or literal meaning in order to convey a specific sense, but having done so, one immediately disowns this meaning. It is this trace or "echo" of its literal meaning which gives provisional sense to the utterance: a sense which is instantaneously withdrawn and denied. It is important to realize, though, that Derrida sees this move as no more than a strategy. "It is the strategy of using the only available language while not subscribing to its premises." [29] What is more, he allows that this "is in fact contradictory and not acceptable within the logic of identity." [30] But he feels obliged to take this course of action in order to be able to present his view at all. If argument cannot do it, then rhetoric must, and so he writes, "At each step I was *obliged* to proceed by ellipses, . . . letting go of each concept at the very moment that I needed to use it." [31]

Derrida's aim, we can now see, is largely rhetorical. By presenting the illusion of an argument, he is trying to get us to abandon our metaphysical assumptions and to adopt an altogether different view of language. [32] This is no more than what he calls "an adventure of vision, a conversion." [33] Since there are no compelling arguments for his position, we simply have no reason to take what he writes seriously. It would be quite wrong to defend Derrida by suggesting that since his "arguments" do not accept the metaphysics of presence, they need not accept the logical constraints peculiar to that metaphysic. The trouble is that Derrida has to furnish arguments which will convince people who *are* entrenched in the metaphysics of presence that that metaphysics is wrong. This he is unable to do.

Realism, Idealism, and the Occlusive Fallacy

If our sense of reality is always the product of a fanciful imagination, then we can alter fundamentally our view of the world just by imagining in one way rather than another. This, of course, is the message of romantic idealism and forms the basis both of Nietzschean and Derridean deconstruction. [34] According to this view, a romantic epistemology must inevitably lead to idealism, for (it is said) such an epistemology gives us no reason to suppose that there are entities external to our imaginings which constrain or otherwise curb our various construals. On this view, too, there can be no point in speaking about the world as it is in itself; nor is there any point in speaking (as Kant appeared to do) of the mind as it is (or had to be) in itself. There are no pure concepts of the understanding, no brute facts. These are but the products of our imaginings. It is all a construct. There are no objects presented to us in perception; there is no "presence"; for some, even, there is no perception.[35]

The triumph of idealism, however, is far from secure. For the plain fact of the matter, we shall see, is that a romantic epistemology is not irretrievably wedded to an idealist, nor even an antirealist, metaphysic. Those who believe that it is are usually guilty of a number of elementary confusions, and it is to these that I shall now attend.

My account in Chapter Two of the acquisition and growth of empirical knowledge purports to explain how we come to make sense of, perceive, and know the objects and events of our world. The fanciful imagination, I have argued, is crucial to this complex task, and here I find favor with the romantics. But we soon part company, and we do so because those romantics who veer towards idealism commit a widespread, as yet unnamed, fallacy: what I shall call the occlusive fallacy. It is a fallacy common to a romantic and an empiricist epistemology, and in both cases it inclines those who commit it to what is commonly, perhaps mistakenly, regarded as an antirealist metaphysic.[36] The fallacy takes the following form. It is supposed, first of all, that our experience of X, where X is the world and its objects, can be explained in terms of a favored entity or process Y. From this it is inferred that we *really* experience only Y, and that X is no more than an inference from, or a construction out of, Y. Ys are believed to form a "veil," a "barrier," between experiencing subjects and the Xs that were previously considered to be the *bona fide* objects of their experience; and sometimes the Ys even come to be regarded as the ultimate constituents of reality.

The fallacy is obvious. It involves accepting the explanation of what it is to experience the world in order to show that we do not, after all, experience the world—and hence in order to reject the explanation on which this conclusion is based. Put yet more plainly, the rejection of the explanation presupposes its acceptance. If the invocation of Y really is an adequate explanation of our experience of X, then Y or Ying is just what it is to experience X. If, on the other hand, we do not really experience Xs, so that our invocation of Y is not an explanation of what it is to experience X, then there is no need to take the invocation of Y—the "explanation"—seriously, and *a fortiori* no need at all to regard Y as the sole object of our experience.

We cannot avoid the force of this objection by contending that since there is no external world—that is, since there are no Xs—we need to reword the point or purpose of explaining our experience. Someone might wish to argue, for instance, that the aim of an epistemology is not to explain what is involved in experiencing and coming to know the external world, but that it is to explain the *appearance* of this. But any such move, as Hume has long since pointed out, is entirely sophistical. For we naturally assume, and cannot help assuming, that we are all acquainted with a world that exists independently of ourselves and our states of mind. There can be no question of rationally justifying this assumption; it is one which is natural to us, over which we have no rational control, and which cannot be displaced through reason.[37] That we are acquainted with the external world is a proposition which, at least in our uncritical moments, we all take ourselves to know. Indeed, it is a proposition in accordance with which we cannot help acting, and which our every action reveals as something that we unquestioningly believe and clearly regard as knowledge. Any epistemology which denies that we can know this seems wildly implausible, counterintuitive; and the mere fact that an attempt is made to communicate this denial to us as independently existing beings renders it less than coherent and suggests that the view cannot be coherently communicated.

It would seem, then, that to argue on the basis of one's theory of knowledge that we only ever know or experience some favored entity, and not the external world, is to commit the occlusive fallacy. Hence, if it is true that a certain complex brain process is crucially involved in our experience, say, of a marmalade cat, it does not follow from this that we really experience only the brain process and not the marmalade cat, for if the explanation is correct, this brain process is part and parcel of what it is to experience the marmalade cat. Similarly, if, as I have argued, the fanciful imagination is crucially involved in coming to know the world about us, it does not follow from this that we are confined to figments of the imagination. Our fanciful imagination has to be understood as a necessary component in our experience of the world, but this cannot entail that it is something that we experience to the exclusion of the world.

The occlusive fallacy surfaces at many points in the history of philosophy. It is committed by a variety of so-called antirealist doctrines—from phenomenalism on the one hand, to romantic idealism, textualism, and contemporary pragmatism on the other. Empiricists, for example, usually attempt to explain our knowledge of the external world in terms of our experience of it. However, it soon turns out (in the case of Hume, for instance) that we "really" experience only our perceptions (impressions and ideas), and never the external objects of which we take them to be perceptions.[38] Far from explaining how we come to know the world about us, our perceptions form an impenetrable "veil" that actually occludes the external world. Bertrand Russell, of course, moves in the same direction. In one work he maintains that we experience only sense-data, and that we infer the presence of material objects from them.[39] In a later work he changes tack and maintains that we do not infer, but construct, material objects out of sensations; that sensations alone are the true objects of experience.[40]

The same fallacy brings Schelling and Coleridge to romantic idealism, for both, we have seen, treat the imagination as integral to the acquisition of knowledge about the world, and then scurry to the view that we only ever have access to our imaginings.[41] Rorty makes an analogous move. Starting with the uncontroversial observation that our linguistic conceptions enter into and affect the way in which we experience the world, he infers that experience is inherently linguistic, and he writes boldly of the "ubiquity of language." In this way language (rather than the imagination or sense-data or impressions and ideas) becomes the "veil" that somehow cuts us off from whatever is "out there." On Rorty's view it is simply impossible for us to experience the world independently of our language. As a result we can never know that our descriptions and experiences correspond to, or reveal, the way things really are.[42]

By now it should be clear that Derrida is neither alone, nor particularly original, in his attack on the metaphysics of presence. In one way or another, this same attack is to be found wherever we find the occlusive fallacy. Empiricists, phenomenalists, textualists, and idealists all deny that the objects of the external world are ever present to us in experience.

As one might expect, therefore, Derrida is also a party to the occlusive fallacy. For on his view, as you will recall, our experience of (the presence of) an object has to be explained as a construct which is built in part out of our conception of its absence. It is a construct bred of a system of differences: of *archi-écriture*, of "writing" in general. "Writing," then, becomes the "veil" which precludes (or endlessly "defers") presence, so that on Derrida's view we never have access to things themselves, but only to the "general text."

My earlier criticism of this view applies with equal force to Rorty's pragmatism. For we know from the way in which we ordinarily go about observing and describing the environment that our experience is not wholly determined (as Rorty seems to suggest) by our linguistic concepts. It is often the case that such concepts fail to do justice to the complexity of our experience, and in such cases, I have said, we are often forced to cast around and to search for more adequate descriptions of what we have experienced. It may, however, be the case that Rorty does not wish to deny this, and that when he speaks of the ubiquity of language, he is using "language" in a very general sense; at least as general as Derrida's notion of "writing."

Perhaps, then, Rorty wishes only to defend the view that we cannot experience anything apart from either our linguistic or our mental representations of it. He suggests as much, for he writes that "we cannot compare a representation (mental or linguistic) with a non-representation and see whether they 'match' in some stronger sense of 'match' than 'that is what we (or they) say when we (or they) see this.' " [43] However, since our mental representations are essential to the experience of any object, to insist that we cannot experience an object apart from them is, as I argued earlier, to state an entirely trivial truth, for it is just another way of saying that we cannot experience an object apart from our experience of it. While it certainly follows from this that we cannot match our observations of an object with the object in its unobserved state, this is necessarily true and does not limit our powers of observation. To suppose that it does is, of course, to commit the occlusive fallacy, for the mental representations essential to our perception of the world are now deemed to occlude it. There are, however, no good grounds for supposing this to be the case, for we still appeal, with manifest success, to our observations of the world in order to support or challenge descriptions of it.

At this stage it is bound to be objected that the fact that romantic idealists commit a specific fallacy does nothing to show that my romantic epistemology can avoid this fallacy—still less that it can avoid stumbling into the thickets of a romantic idealism. A romantic epistemology, it is said, leaves no room at all for the independent verification of the fanciful construals which lead to knowledge claims. Verification always turns out to be based on fancy—so that whichever way one turns, one is inevitably locked into one's fanciful construals. One cannot have access to the world "out there" and to the actual conditions which make one's construals true or false, and it is this, the objection maintains, that commits my romantic theory of knowledge to some or other form of idealism. That this epistemology commits the occlusive fallacy is sad but unavoidable, for the plain fact of the matter is that it is a commitment forced upon us by any romantic epistemology. The fault, the objection continues, lies with the epistemology, for when once it is accepted, one is forced to abandon realism. Commitment to it requires either that one embrace idealism and so commit the occlusive fallacy, or else that one seek refuge in much more blatant inconsistencies.

This objection soon flounders. The assumption is that realism requires the "independent verification" of our knowledge claims, but that a romantic epistemology precludes this since it insists that verification is, at root, dependent on certain fanciful imaginings. But this is odd. The epistemology that I have defended maintains that the fanciful imagination is fundamentally involved in the acquisition and growth of empirical knowledge. As a result, it would seem that what the objection actually requires is that we should be able to know "how things are" independently of (what I have argued) is the only means of coming to know this. And to require this is either to require the impossible, or it is to reject out of hand, and for no good reason, the account that I have given of the acquisition and growth of empirical knowledge.

Still worse, it seems that this objection, if it applies at all, must apply to every epistemology. For whatever the theory of knowledge, there can be no question of one's ever being able to verify a statement independently of one's means of coming to know whether it is true or false. Hence, if this objection is to be taken seriously, it would seem that all epistemologies are committed to a version of idealism. It is no criticism of my romantic epistemology, therefore, that it is not "realist" in the required sense, for it is now apparent that according to the objection at hand no epistemology can avoid this fate. Indeed, if we are to follow the logic of the objection, the very notion of a realist epistemology becomes incoherent, for such an epistemology would be required to provide a means of coming to know the unknowable. It seems plain, then, that what is needed is not a different epistemology, for all can be subjected to analogous objections. Rather, what seems to be needed is a better understanding of the concept of realism. Clarification of this concept will not only enable us to understand what the accusation of antirealism amounts to when it is directed at a romantic epistemology, but it will also help clarify and sharpen my contention that a romantic epistemology is not wedded to idealism, that it can be realist.

Michael Dummett conceives of the realist/antirealist dispute as a metaphysical disagreement regarding the objectivity or independence of the truth conditions for a given statement, whether it be a statement about the physical world, numbers, or fictions. The realist believes "that statements of the disputed class possess an objective truth-value, independently of our means of knowing it: they are true or false in virtue of a reality existing independently of us." [44] The antirealist, by contrast, believes that the truth-values of, and hence the truth conditions for, disputed statements are never objective in the sense of being "evidence transcendent," but are "verificationist," and so depend on the "sort of thing that we count as evidence" for the statements. [45] Truth-values and truth conditions, according to the antirealist, never exist independently of our states of mind and our means of knowing.

This, of course, is not the same conception of realism as the one at work in the above objection. For there the claim was that my romantic epistemology was irretrievably antirealist since it precluded the *independent verification* of our knowledge claims. Dummett's conception of realism, by contrast, has nothing to do with verification. On his view, realism with regard to a particular statement involves commitment to the (metaphysical) belief that its truth-value obtains independently of our knowledge of it. The realist distinguishes truth conditions from the empirical conditions (assertability conditions) under which we declare a statement true. To fail to distinguish the two (as in the above objection) would be to adopt what Dummett regards as an antirealist stance. This, however, is not to say that, on Dummett's version of realism, truth-values and truth conditions are unknowable. It is only to say that they exist independently of our knowledge of them and that it is in principle possible that our experience will always fail to reveal them.

But Dummett's account of realism, although helpful, is suspect. On his view, as we have seen, the realist is one who maintains that "statements of the disputed class possess an objective truth-value." This, however, entails that a reductionist who *denies* the truth of the statement "There are material objects," and who contends that it is objectively the case that there are only sense-data, is, for all that, a realist with regard to the disputed statement since it is believed to be objectively false. And this, to say the very least, is odd, for we want to say that a phenomenalist of this ilk is strongly antirealist with respect to the statement in question. There is another, perhaps a more telling, reason for doubting the viability of Dummett's account of realism. On his view, if we construe idealism as a reductionist thesis according to which the ultimate constituents of reality are our ideas or imaginings, then this, contrary to popular opinion, is a realist thesis. For, as Dummett tells us, the idealist's disagreement with other philosophers, is a disagreement over *what there really is*. But it is not difficult to see that idealism can also be shown to be antirealist in Dummett's sense of this word. For according to the idealist, the truth-value of a statement such as "Ideas are the ultimate constituents of reality" must, if it is true, be dependent on the human mind. So it would seem that by following Dummett's construal of realism and antirealism, we reach the conclusion that idealism, when construed as a reductionist thesis, is both realist and antirealist. Something appears to have gone wrong.

Part of the problem is that Dummett appears to be working with at least two, and most probably three, different senses of "realism." In the first sense—Dummett's chosen sense—to be a realist with regard to a disputed statement is to maintain that the statement is objectively *true* or *false*. In the second sense—the sense in which realism is concerned with what there *really is*—it is to maintain that a given existential statement is true *rather than* false. Hence, in this second sense, a phenomenalist may be a realist with regard to existential statements about sense-data, but antirealist with regard to existential statements about material objects.

There is, however, a third sense of "realism" lurking in the background to Dummett's thought. It emerges in his explanation of antirealism which, it will be recalled, is regarded as the view that the truth-values of, or the truth conditions for, disputed statements are never objective, but depend "on the sort of thing we count as evidence" for the statement. There is a slide here from the purely metaphysical sense of "realism" advocated by Dummett to one which is epistemological in import (even though it does wear metaphysical undergarments). For antirealism at this point becomes closely allied to what we would normally think of as cognitive relativism: to the view that statements cannot be known to be objectively true, and that what we count both as true and as knowledge depends on the sets of ideas, paradigms, world views, pet theories, and so on, which we bring to our observation of the world. This version of antirealism, however, is not properly contrasted with realism in either of the first two senses and is, in fact, compatible with both. It is properly contrasted only with epistemological realism: the view, that is, that we can transcend our sociohistorical conditioning in order to know whether or not a statement really is true.

It is now an easy matter to resolve the problems which beset Dummett's account of the concept of realism. Idealism, we can now see, can be realist in the first sense of this word, since the idealist maintains that it is objectively true that ideas are the ultimate constituents of reality. However, it is plain that in the second sense of the word, idealism may either be realist or antirealist. It will be antirealist with respect to the statement

"There are material objects," and realist with regard to the statement "Ideas are the ultimate constituents of reality." In the third sense, however, idealism is normally antirealist, for it standardly rejects epistemological realism. So while it is true that on Dummett's account of realism, idealism appears to be both realist and antirealist, the apparent paradox is easily resolved when once one realizes that Dummett uses the word "realist" in more than one sense.

A realist in any of these three senses will maintain that there is always some "fact of the matter," some way in which things *are*, independently of one's state of mind, which makes the disputed statement true or false. However, we have seen that in the first two senses, realism is a purely metaphysical doctrine, but that in the third sense it is an epistemological thesis. It seems plain, I think, that the objection to my romantic epistemology has been based on something like the third sense of "realism." For, as we have seen, it contends that my romantic epistemology is antirealist because it does not allow us to verify our knowledge claims independently of our fanciful imaginings. Here "realism" seems to be contrasted with something like cognitive relativism, although it remains true, of course, that realists of this variety are also metaphysical realists, but wish in addition to maintain that it is always possible to become acquainted with the objective truth conditions for, or the actual truth-value of, a given statement.

It is customary nowadays to oppose relativism, not to realism, but (in the wake of Hans-Georg Gadamer) to objectivism.[46] This has at least two advantages. First, it prevents unnecessary confusions between epistemological and metaphysical realism; second, it enables us to see that a cognitive relativist may be a metaphysical realist in either of our two senses given above. It has the disadvantage, however, of hiding the close relationship between, and, at times, the common origins of, idealism and cognitive relativism. For both, as we have seen, may take root in a romantic epistemology—although this, of course, is not to say that such an epistemology need give rise to either.

A Romantic Realism

We are now, at last, in a position to explain and defend my earlier contention that a romantic epistemology can be realist. It can be realist not just in the sense that it allows that there are independent or objective truth conditions for empirical statements, or in the sense that certain entities exist independently of us, but also in the sense that it does not commit its proponents to cognitive relativism. It enables us to explain how we come to know the world "out there," and how we can properly use our experience of that world as a touchstone in terms of which to gauge the truth or otherwise of our various pronouncements. Until now, I have argued negatively for this position by criticizing the view that our imaginings somehow occlude the real, publicly accessible, world. It is time now to follow a more positive line of argument.

In Chapter Two I argued that whenever we run out of knowledge and established belief with which to solve our puzzles, we are forced, if we are curious enough, to conjure up or imagine certain solutions to these puzzles, and so ease our confusion and bewilderment. It is when our imaginings are found to work, I argued, that we tentatively adopt them, come to believe them, and eventually treat them as knowledge. To this I can now add that each such adopted construal or imagining can serve as a concept, a category, a way of ordering or regulating our experience; so that on my view all concepts, all categories, and hence all significant experience, find their origin in the imagination. This, in summary, is my explanation not just of how we come in the first instance to know our world, but also of how we come to perceive it.

It is only when our imaginative construals ease our confusion, when they "tame" our experience and enable us to negotiate the world better, that we come to regard them as adequate to the world in which we live. As long as our imaginings continue to serve us in this way, we can have no good reason to doubt them. As a result, we naturally assume that these construals, and the experiences bred of them, adequately reflect the way things are. There is no question of our having to justify this assumption; it is, as Hume pointed out, something entirely natural to us and over which we have no rational control. "Nature," he writes, "has not left this to [our] choice, and has doubtless esteemed it an affair of too great an importance, to be trusted to our uncertain reasonings and speculations."[47]

But even if Nature has not left this to our choice, it is still the case that our experiences and perceptions are very much a product of the sort of organism that we are. The tautness of the ear drum, the relation of the anvil to the hammer to the sickle in the middle ear, the structure of the retina, the shape of the eye lens—these all affect the nature of our perceptions. Still more, the sorts of things to which we are biologically and emotionally vulnerable help determine how we construe the world about us: things that knock, bump, and injure are singled out and are to be avoided; precipices are one thing, hills, dales, and plains another; deserts are not oases; foes are not friends. Water is to be distinguished from sulfuric acid, which, in its turn, is to be distinguished from mother's milk. And, for the most part, we make and sustain these distinctions because they are useful. They do not only help us to negotiate the world, but they also ensure our survival among people, as well as the survival of those who depend on us. Consequently it seems that what we regard as an accurate or a true description is tied to our most fundamental wants and hence our most fundamental values.

All of this suggests, of course, that there is also a social dimension to the acquisition and growth of human knowledge. The child's fanciful construals are modified and refined in the light of the parent's response. There can be no doubt but that the human (social) response to a misconstrual plays a large, sometimes a crucial, role in bringing the individual to reconsider, to imagine anew, to think again. Fanciful construals, one could say, come to be accepted not just when they enable us to negotiate the brute facts—the rocks, the precipices, the snares which surround us; but also when they enable us to negotiate a social state of affairs—the world of people with whom we interact and on whom we depend.

This is not to say that our experiences are wholly determined by our cultural or social milieu. Some (for instance, religious experiences) might be, and all, it is true, are either undermined or reinforced by the society in which we live. But it is at best misleading to suggest that, because we experience the world within the bounds of certain social traditions, our experience must be *determined* by our culture or sociohistorical background. For one thing, many construals, although socially acceptable, never receive explicit social approval, so that individuals often make sense of their environment on their own. It is, for the most part, only when a person or a group of people disapprove of a particular construal that a social response—in this case a negative social response—is explicitly formulated. But we should not infer from this that tacit social approval and explicit disapproval shape the individual's experience and therefore determine what eventually counts as knowledge. For it is a fact well known that individuals are not always guided in this way. Like Galileo, they repudiate social disapproval and proclaim as knowledge doctrines that their peers refuse to countenance. If this were impossible, we could never intentionally undermine or deliberately challenge the world views or Kuhnian paradigms within which we were reared.

It is sometimes suggested, not least by Rorty, that our language, our concepts, our beliefs—all of which are culturally or socially acquired—mediate and shape our experience of the world, so that it is in *this* way that our knowledge is irretrievably shaped by our sociohistorical background. But this, too, is false. Certainly our linguistic conceptions influence our perception and our construal of the world about us, but I have already shown that our experiences may confound our descriptions, beliefs, and concepts, and, in this way, our sociohistorical conditioning. Consequently, it does seem to be possible to have experiences which are not wholly determined by one's location in society and history. In these cases (cases of nonvisionary, nonhallucinatory experience), there remains an input, a sensory input, which clearly is, and has to be, independent of our social and cultural environment.

It is true, of course, that the overwhelming majority of our experiences *are* conceptually mediated, and hence are strongly influenced by our cultural milieu. For all that, though, I have suggested that some experiences are, and must remain, untouched by concepts and cultures. In order to see this more plainly, we need to distinguish different varieties of experience. More particularly, we need to distinguish the most basic, fundamental, genetic experiences discussed in the previous chapter, from the vastly more sophisticated and informed experiences that we have of cultural objects and processes. There is, as we have seen, the very basic level of experience in which infants who are utterly devoid of knowledge, and hence quite without language or any conceptual apparatus, come to distinguish the objects of the environment on which their survival depends. At this level, experience is neither conditioned by nor a product of social conditioning, for in order to become socialized in the appropriate sense, one has *first* to experience the relevant social forces. And it is evident that this experience cannot be explained by appeal to socialization or social conditioning, for, *ex hypothesi*, the infant is still unaware of any social environment and has still to come to know it.

This, of course, is not to suggest that infants somehow have direct access to the world "as it is in itself" (whatever that may mean); for, as we have already seen, they cannot make any sense of the world apart from a set of fanciful construals which are tentatively projected on to it. What is clear, though, is that at this, the most basic, level of experience, there is and can be no room for sociocultural or conceptual influences. There can, by contrast, be no doubt at all that social and historical influences enter into, and affect, our experience of the world at a level which is more sophisticated than the very basic, genetic, level so far discussed. How we watch and experience a game of football; how we view an artwork, a chemical process, an economic transaction, or a war plane, and what is seen in each, is overwhelmingly a product of our cultural background. But this, I shall argue later on, need not entail that there is no correct way of viewing each, and that we cannot guard against undue cultural, social, or historical influence. All of this, however, constitutes a large and important question, one which cannot be dismissed lightly, and to which I shall return time and again throughout the course of my argument—most obviously when dealing with the problem of interpretation in Chapter Five.

For the present, all that we need to notice is that it is the success of our imaginative construals—whether or not they are in some measure a product of our social environment or past experience—which brings us, eventually, to treat them as knowledge. That we are socialized, and that our socialization places constraints on certain of our fanciful construals, reinforces our natural tendency to assume that there is a public world which, under ideal conditions, can be perceived by everyone. Only in our most sophistical moments do we doubt the independent existence and stability of the external world, and, given our natural inclinations and needs, these skeptical doubts soon lapse. Indeed, were we to follow them, our very survival would be at stake. Such construals—for they are just imaginative construals—constrain us to silence and inaction; both of which must have disastrous consequences for our well-being and eventual survival. Hence it would seem that we have abundant reason for assuming, and no good reason for doubting, the continued, independent existence of an external world which all are capable of perceiving.

So even though we do not know the world, or any aspect of it, apart from our imaginative construals, romantic realism contends that there is nonetheless an external world which is the measure of all our descriptions and pronouncements. It reaches this conclusion via the simple device of applying its own teachings. For the imaginative construal according to which there is an independently existing external world is the one which best allows us to negotiate the world and make sense of our experience of it. Any other imaginative construal about the world and its mode of existence simply flounders. This construal allows us to make sense of the fact that the world has to be discovered, that it is not simply the product of our will, that our imaginative construals do not straightforwardly shape it, that it is intractable and is not molded by our states of mind. And yet, the indispensable role played by the fanciful imagination in coming to know the facts of our own existence suggests that the facts are not simply found or directly apprehended; nor, as we have just seen, are they whimsically invented. They are, it would seem, both found and invented. That, at least, is the import of a romantic realism.

It is because our imaginings are fallible and open to revision that idealists and pragmatists are lured to the view that our imaginative constructs invariably occlude whatever is "out there"—so that we never have access to the actual truth conditions for a given statement, but only to its assertability conditions. To argue in this way is, of course, to reject the view that we can ever have access to some "fact of the matter," some objective state of affairs, in virtue of which a given statement is, and can be known to be, true or false. Sometimes, as with Dewey, truth comes to be regarded as "warranted assertability"; but since what is assertable on the basis of current evidence is fallible and open to revision, the truth or falsity of a statement is no longer thought of as something settled or fixed, but as a floating affair which depends rather more on which imaginative construals we currently accept than on how the world actually is.

There is no need, however, to adopt this antirealist expedient. A romantic realist can concede that one's imaginative construals, and hence one's claims as to the truth or falsity of empirical statements, are always fallible and open to revision, while at the same time insisting that the external world *is* observable. Following Hilary Putnam, such a realist will argue that by observing under ideally correct conditions, we can discover the furniture of the world about us, and in this way come to know not merely that a particular statement is assertable, but that it is true.[48] For instance my announcement that there is a bull in the room next door may be true or false, and will be known to be true if, on observing under the correct conditions, we discover a bull in the room next door.

For the most part, the appropriate conditions for observation are well established and settled, although the romantic realist allows that what these conditions are is not always unproblematic. For if we have learned anything at all from the philosophy of science, it must be that what we deem to be the appropriate or ideal conditions for the observation of a specific phenomenon may alter with the growth of knowledge pertinent either to that phenomenon or to ourselves. In other words, our initial assumption (which is often no more than an imaginative construal) about appropriate conditions for observing something or other may need to be revised in the course of time (with the help of further imaginative construals). This is not at all the same as saying that we constantly interpret and reinterpret such conditions. For the most part, as I have already said, our construals regarding the appropriate conditions for observation achieve stability, become settled, and enter the corpus of established knowledge. Those that work and continue to work, we cannot but regard as correct and as capable of revealing the actual nature of the world. An ideally correct condition for observation is one which has always worked and which, on the basis of past evidence, we assume will always continue to work.

According to the romantic realist, therefore, when we discover those conditions in virtue of which a statement can be said to be true or false, and when we do so on the basis of detailed and thorough observation, we thereby discover (some of) the truth conditions for that statement. We discover an objective state of affairs in virtue of which the statement is either true or false. In so doing, we observe by using the best known methods of observation which are required for the purpose. This must, of course, include imaginatively derived categories, concepts, and beliefs: ones which have been shown to work and which have always proved useful in the past. Certainly such observations can be mistaken. We can and do misperceive, and as a result all knowledge claims which are based on observation are fallible and open to revision. Nonetheless, if our observations are meticulous, the evidence plain and overwhelming, we can properly assert not just that we have found a statement to be true but that we are acquainted with the objective state of affairs which makes it true. That we could be wrong matters not at all, for as long as we have no good reason to doubt our claim, we are justified in asserting it.

To say, as the romantic realist does, that there are objective states of affairs, is, of course, to say that these states of affairs exist independently of our experience of them. The romantic realist insists that the structure or intrinsic nature of these states of affairs does not depend on us: on our linguistic concepts or on our imaginative construals. Unlike what Dummett and Putnam have called metaphysical realism, romantic realism steadfastly maintains that we can observe objective states of affairs, and that we do so with the indispensable help of our imaginative construals.

Both metaphysical and romantic realists subscribe to the correspondence theory of truth, but, as one would expect, they construe this theory very differently. The metaphysical realist maintains that a statement is true only if it corresponds to how things are "in themselves" — that is, only if it corresponds to some objective state of affairs *independently* of our means of knowing it. And at least one problem with this view is that it effectively posits a noumenal world that becomes the touchstone of truth. As a result it is never possible for us to ascertain whether a given statement is true. In this sense at least, the theory is entirely unworkable. We do describe statements as true or false, and we do so with a considerable amount of success — in the sense that these descriptions usually turn out to have predictive utility and obvious survival value. The metaphysical realist, it seems to me, is unable to explain how we are able to apply the word "true" in an informative and useful way.

The romantic realist, by contrast, subscribes to a version of the correspondence theory which does permit an adequate explanation of the concept of truth. On this view, an empirical statement is true, and can properly be said to be true, only if it corresponds to an *observable* state of affairs which it purports to be about. If a particular apple is said to be bruised, then the statement will be true if the apple in question is found to exist and is found to be bruised. True enough, what we observe to be the case is in a certain sense a product of our imaginative construals, but this, as we have seen, is not at all to say that we invent or somehow conjure up objective states of affairs. It is only to say that the fanciful imagination is crucially involved in our observation of them. To infer from this (as metaphysical realists appear to do) that we do not really have access to a world "out there" is, as I have already argued, to commit the occlusive fallacy. According to the romantic realist, there is no distinction to be drawn between a world "out there" and the world which it is possible to experience under ideally correct conditions. Hence, according to this view, there is no distinction between a phenomenal and noumenal world (Kant) or between truth conditions and assertability conditions (Dummett). The world which we all observe under ideally correct conditions is the one and only world.

Indeed, it should be clear from what I have already said that romantic realism is able to preserve all of the intuitions that Kant's noumenal world was designed to preserve. And it does so by insisting *first* that the way the world is, is not "up to us" and does not depend on our conceptual apparatus, imaginings, or desires; *second*, that the way in which we sometimes experience the world (under abnormal, inappropriate, or idiosyncratic conditions) need not reveal the way the world is; and *third*, that there are many unobserved (but very few, if any, essentially unobservable) aspects of the world. In this way, there remains something—a world, if you like—which is constant and unaffected by our cognitive states; but it is something, the romantic realist argues, to which we can always have access through experience or observation.

Certainly we do not always perceive the world in the same way. But the romantic realist contends that it is as a matter of fact the case that evidence, recalcitrant experiences of one sort or another, conflicting beliefs, and the weight of argument, eventually effect a convergence in the way in which we see the world. As a result, agreement is or will be reached, not just about the correct conditions for observation, but also about the truth conditions for certain statements. Truth, on this view, is closely linked to survival value, and hence, as I have already stressed, to our most fundamental wants.[49] For we come to rely on, and to treat as true, those construals which best enable us to make sense of, and to negotiate, the world. Moreover, since human beings are fundamentally similar, since they are endowed with the same basic physical and mental apparatus, and since they are vulnerable in more or less the same sorts of ways, the romantic realist contends that they share the same fundamental wants, and will therefore tend to agree about the conditions under which certain imaginative construals are either to be accepted or to be rejected. Hence the romantic realist assumes as a fundamental tenet that people share most of their basic beliefs about the world.[50] Still more, since we are all *naturally* inclined to the view that those imaginative construals which 'work' also reflect the way things actually are, there can be no point either in doubting this, or in attempting to justify it.

This, then, is the realism that I have defended. The alliance of realism and romanticism I have called a romantic realism, and, according to it, to say that the statement "There is gold under the floorboards" is true, is just to say that if one were to look (in appropriate conditions and using established, well-tried methods) one would find gold. A counterfactual conditional analysis of this sort is essential to any realist epistemology which aims at coherence. It is plain from all that I have argued that a romantic realism purports to allow us access to the furniture of the real world. According to it, one can discover the truth-value of a particular statement, and one can do so independently of what one might have wanted, believed, or imagined to be the case. This, I have stressed, is not to say that beliefs and imaginings play no part in perception. They plainly do; although those that do are not usually purely faddish or passing beliefs, nor are they purely gratuitous or fond imaginings. Rather, those beliefs and imaginative construals on which we depend in perception are invariably well tried, have been found to work, have lost their tentative status, and now form part of the bedrock in terms of which we experience and understand our world. That this bedrock may shift, sometimes gradually, sometimes suddenly and radically, is beyond dispute. What does seem clear, though, is that such a bedrock is required for experience and understanding, and that it is at root a product of the fanciful imagination.

Conclusion

A romantic epistemology—one, that is, which grounds our knowledge of the world in the fanciful imagination—brings us to the very brink of idealism. It brings us, in more picturesque terms, to the rim of the romantic abyss. My task in this chapter has been to show that there is no need at all for any of us to tumble into the abyss, even when we subscribe to a romantic theory of knowledge.

Romanticism takes many different forms, and Nietzsche, I suggested at the outset, was in some respects as much a romantic and an idealist as Schelling before him. It was he, I argued, who set the stage for Derrida and Rorty—both of whom owe much to the romantic movement. For Nietzsche, we have seen, regards our sense of reality as grounded in the fanciful imagination: more specifically, in nonlinguistic metaphors bred of fancy. When once we forget the origins of what we take to be the real world, we treat all descriptions of it as the literal truth, as "fixed, canonic and binding." It is the job of the philosopher, Nietzsche contends, to dismantle this structure of ideas which so confines and stifles our thinking. It is in this way that Nietzsche furnishes the romantic impulse which guides so much of Derrida's thinking.

But Derrida, we found, bases his attempt to deconstruct our ways of thinking and organizing the world on two specious arguments which purport to show that we have access only to a system of signs, to "writing," and never to a world "out there" that is present to us in perception. In this way, Derrida offers his own version of idealism—one, I have argued, which cannot withstand scrutiny. But having shown this, it was important to show—more positively, as it were—that a romantic epistemology need not lead to any version of antirealism. To suppose that it does is usually to commit the occlusive fallacy. Romantic realism, I have argued, is not prone to any such fallacy, and in the end allows us access to a public, observable world: one which is present to us in experience, and which we can capture in language. Precisely how our language latches on to this world is an important question which I have not considered here. It is one to which I shall return when dealing with the problem of metaphor in Chapter Seven.

FOUR

The Beholder's Share: Fiction, Imagination, and Emotion

At times, as we have seen, people engage in the act of imagining; at other times, they respond to and try to understand the imaginings of others. My concern so far has been with the act of imagining, its role in the acquisition and growth of knowledge, and the metaphysical consequences of asserting such a role. In this way I have developed a theoretical framework within which to attend to some of the philosophical problems posed by fictional literature. It is time now to look more closely at these problems, and I shall begin with an explanation of what is involved in responding to, and coming to understand, the imaginings of others—most especially as they are embodied in the literature of fiction.

Our imaginings serve a variety of purposes, and the job of understanding and responding to them is correspondingly various. When a scientist imaginatively formulates a hypothesis in an effort to understand the world in which we live, we treat it as being about the world, and we try to see whether it accurately reflects the way the world is. We try to see whether it is worthy of belief, whether it will eventually afford propositional knowledge. But not so in the case of literary fiction. When a favorite author imaginatively delineates a fictional scene, we do not, if we understand what fiction is all about, attempt to see whether it accurately reflects the way the world is.

This brings some to the view that there is nothing at all to be learned from fictional literature: that although it delights us, it can only mislead by exciting the passions and confusing the understanding. The prejudice runs deeper than this, for the recent trend among Anglo–American philosophers is to speak of the growth of knowledge only in the context of scientific inquiry. The tendency is to concentrate on the growth of propositional knowledge, as if to suggest that it is the only knowledge that really matters. In effect, this means that all other varieties of knowledge are ignored, and fictional literature is simply discounted as a source of insight and knowledge.

Part of my aim in this book is to reverse this trend, to redress the wrong, by showing that we can and do acquire knowledge from fiction. However, we can do so only if we first understand the fiction, and we cannot hope to achieve this unless we respond appropriately to it. It is with the question of response, and more especially with our emotional responses, to fiction that this chapter is concerned.

The Problem

It is often remarked that anyone who mistakes a fictional work for a factual report or a history has not properly understood it. A person who responds to *Hamlet* by attempting to save Polonius's life, or to *Middlemarch* by attempting to locate and read Casaubon's research, has only partially, and at best improperly, understood these works.[1]

Equally commonplace is the view that an appropriate emotional response to a fictional work is often integral to a proper understanding of it. But this is puzzling, for such a response seems to involve treating fiction as fact. We all tend to believe that we can rationally be moved only by what we take to be actual calamities or real quandaries. It is silly, we think, to mourn fictional deaths or celebrate imaginary victories. Hence, it would seem that in order to be rationally moved by the fate of Othello, one must believe that Othello is a real person. Put differently, one must believe that Shakespeare's play is a history or a factual report—and, as we have just seen, anyone who believes this has not properly understood the play. Consequently it appears that any reader who is rationally moved by a fictional work does not properly understand it. Conversely, if the reader does adequately understand the fiction, an emotional response to it must be irrational.[2]

We clearly have a problem. However, I shall argue that it is a problem bred of confusion, and shall try to show that far from an emotional response to fiction precluding a proper understanding of it, one can understand fiction properly only if one is in a position to be moved by the fortunes and misfortunes of its characters. A condition of being appropriately moved by, and so understanding, fiction, I shall argue, is that one should respond imaginatively to it.[3] Rather than treat *Middlemarch* or *Hamlet* as histories, the reader must take it as if there are certain people, must make-believe, fantasize, or imagine that they live in certain places and do certain things.

What precisely this amounts to is by no means clear. Nor is there much clarity about what is to count as *properly* understanding fiction. Both questions can be adequately answered only as this chapter progresses. Despite this, it is obvious, even at this early stage, that talk about properly understanding a literary work is by no means incomprehensible. We know that it is possible to grasp the meaning of an utterance without recognizing, for instance, that it was intended as a joke. We might mistakenly think it a warning or a threat, and in such a case we fail, in a perfectly ordinary sense, to understand it properly. In a similar way, one may grasp the meaning of most, even all, of the sentences in a fictional work, and still not understand the work properly—perhaps because one has not recognized it as fiction or because one is unable to grasp its theme. Obviously there is much that remains to be said about this, and it is a point to which I shall return presently.

For the time being let us consider a likely objection to the claim that we need to become imaginatively involved in fiction if we are to understand it properly. In this way we will be able to explain the claim and initiate a defense of it which will eventually result in a viable account both of how we can rationally be moved by the fortunes or misfortunes of fictional characters and of how we come to understand fictional literature.

Imagination and Understanding

While it is true that one will not properly understand a novel like *Pickwick Papers* unless one treats Samuel Pickwick as a fictional person, it is nonetheless arguable that this does not require that a reader should imagine Pickwick. The author, it may be said, has already imagined him and his activities. All that the reader has to do in order to understand the work is to understand these imaginings—where this involves recognizing them as imaginings of a certain sort. And (the argument continues) just as I do not have to imagine that there is a wolf present in order to recognize or understand that my child imagines this, so I do not have to fantasize in order to understand the imaginings of an author.

The advocates of this view need not deny that readers may, and often do, respond imaginatively to novels and plays. The claim, though, is that even if this does occur, such responses are not necessary for a thoroughgoing comprehension of fictional literature. Rather, it is maintained that one responds appropriately to, and begins to understand, *Pickwick Papers* by noting in the first instance that the statements which it contains are not true of our world. The comprehending reader may be said to preface the novel with the words, "It is imagined that . . ." where the sentences which follow tell us what has been imagined. All of this is understood, first, by *knowing* what to expect of fictional literature; and second, by *knowing* the meanings of its constitutive sentences.[4] Hence it is concluded that understanding *Pickwick Papers* requires knowledge of a certain sort, but does not require the reader's imaginative participation in the life of the novel.

But this leaves something important out of account. Consider the case of a child playing wolves. The view, as we have seen, is that I understand not merely *that* a game is in progress, but the game itself, by entertaining statements such as: "The child imagines that the shadow is a wolf." "She imagines that it is eating the boy." "She imagines that it is smacking its lips." Here, it is maintained, I understand the game by understanding what is imagined, and I understand this without imagining it myself.

Certainly I will be able to understand aspects of the game in this way, but it soon becomes apparent that I will not be able to grasp it fully. The trouble is that by responding in the suggested way, I prevent myself from entering into the spirit of the game. By prefacing my descriptions of the child's cries of alarm, her ravings, raptures, and distress with the words "She imagines that . . .," I effectively deny that these events are real, that her reports apply to the actual world, and by so discounting her utterances and refusing to take them seriously, I "distance" myself from the game and become unable to experience its nuances of feeling and heights or depths of passion. I become a mere bystander who is prevented from feeling the fears, excitement, and tensions that the game generates. As a result, I am increasingly unlikely to know what to look for in the game; I will not have the appropriate expectations and beliefs, and after a while I will, in all probability, be bored by the increasingly meaningless gestures, grimaces, and growls, and will consider the whole unworthy of attention.

It seems, then, that one is unable to grasp the full impact of the game, and so properly understand it, by responding in this way. Of course, my use of the words "full impact" to explain the notion of properly understanding a game is not intended to suggest that a "complete" grasp of all aspects of the make-believe (whatever that could amount to!) is required in order to ensure that one has properly understood it. Whether one understands the game properly depends on whether one has adopted an adequate *way* of understanding it—where the latter is to be explained as a mode of understanding which permits or enables one to grasp (but cannot ensure that one will grasp) all of what are normally regarded as the salient or important features of the game. Hence, one can be said to understand a game properly without grasping all of its salient features and so without having a proper or full understanding of it.

It is in this sense that one cannot properly understand a child's game of wolves by prefacing one's descriptions of it with the words "She imagines that . . . ." To do so is to adopt a skeptical attitude toward it: an attitude which prevents one from becoming involved in the game, and so from experiencing the emotional tensions which are part and parcel of it. And, as I have said, emotional involvement of this sort creates certain expectations, and so directs the player's attention to some of the game's more important features. The curl of a lip or the shape of a hand may be vital to the game, but are only noticed, and only achieve significance, because of expectations bred of emotional involvement. Not to be able to notice these features is to fail to understand the make-believe properly.

These considerations apply equally to the problem of understanding fiction. Understanding *Pickwick Papers* is not merely a matter of understanding that Dickens has imagined certain things. Of course, if one is to understand the novel at all, one has to understand that Dickens imagined that there was a man called Pickwick, that he was fat and jovial, and so on. But this, although in some sense necessary for properly understanding the novel, is by no means sufficient. The trouble is that in this context the phrase "It is imagined that" is used to assert that the propositions which follow are not true of the actual world, that they describe events and states of affairs which do not actually obtain. By attending to this fact, one effectively discounts the narrative by regarding it as inapplicable to one's actual situation: one refuses either to believe or disbelieve it since it does not purport to describe the actual world.

It is a fact of our experience, and a commonplace of psychology, that one cannot become emotionally involved in the plight of characters in a narrative if one discounts the narrative in this way. By constantly reminding oneself that the narrative is neither true nor false of the actual world, that it is a mere product of fancy or a total fabrication, one effectively "distances" oneself from the action of the novel. One does not allow oneself to be "drawn into" its imaginary world or to be "caught up in" its various intrigues or romances.[5] As a result, one can neither share the emotional turmoil of its fictional characters nor experience the tensions generated by its plot. To respond to fiction in a way which does not permit such involvement is to respond to it in a way which cannot promote a full understanding of the work. For, as we have seen, it deprives the reader of emotional experiences integral to understanding fiction; emotional experiences that would otherwise furnish whole sets of expectations in terms of which it is possible to notice other, sometimes vital, aspects of the work.

The same, I think, would be true of anyone who responds to *Pickwick Papers* by actively disbelieving it; incredulity is an obvious psychological barrier to emotional involvement. This, however, is not to say that one has to believe the novel in order to understand it. Statements of fiction, I have stressed, are not intended as assertions about the actual world, but are assertions about an imaginary world. For this reason they are neither false nor true of our world, and it is as misguided to believe them as it is to disbelieve them. The person who refuses to leave the room with J. Alfred Prufrock or who journeys to Elsinore in search of Yorick's skull is as silly as the person who doubts whether Anna Karenina really came to grief under the wheels of a locomotive. If one is to understand fiction properly, one has to do so not by believing or disbelieving it, nor, indeed, by discounting it. One has to entertain its statements in a different and rather special way by making-believe—that is, by imagining or taking it as if there is a man called Pickwick who does certain things and visits certain places. Such make-believe, far from involving belief or disbelief, involves responding to Dickens's descriptions of Pickwick, not, as we shall see, by considering what Pickwick would be like if he actually existed, but by considering what Pickwick is like in a possible, but non-actual—that is, in an imaginary —world. This alone enables the reader to know what Pickwick is actually like in the imaginary world delineated by Dickens. And such knowledge, we shall find, is often the occasion of our emotional responses to fiction.

To respond to *Pickwick Papers*, or, indeed, to any work of fiction by considering what the hero would be like if he existed in our world is to respond inappropriately to it. Such a response fails to take account of the fact that the imaginary world of the hero is delineated by a set of statements, not all of which will, in all likelihood, be compatible with statements about the actual world. Hence to consider what Pickwick would be like if he existed in our world is not strictly relevant to one's comprehension of *Pickwick Papers*. To understand this novel we have to know what Pickwick *is* like in *his own* world, not what he would be like in ours. In other words, to treat the statements of fiction as counterfactual conditionals is not to treat the fiction as an imaginative construction at all. It is to suppose that the statements of fiction, although hypothetical, are nonetheless assertions about the actual world. And this is not the case. What is more, to treat such statements as counterfactuals in anticipation of coming to understand the work is to assume that the world of the novel is in all respects the same as the actual world—and this, of course, is hardly likely.

It seems, then, that in order to understand fiction, a reader must neither believe nor disbelieve the statements of a work, but, by making-believe, must regard them as true or false of an imaginary world. A reader does this in much the way that a geometrician does when she (or he) supposes that the short line sketched on her blotter is four meters long. She knows that the line is not really this length, but, like the reader who knows that Pickwick is not really a person, she disregards (certain of) the facts of her immediate situation. Hers is an imaginative act; an act of fancy, if you like.

Such imaginative acts, however, are by no means free to take whatever form we wish. They are importantly constrained—either, as it were, by authorial decree, or by pencil marks on our geometrician's blotter. One is not at liberty, when reading *Pickwick Papers*, to respond to it by creating one's own imaginary world. Anyone who does so will not have understood the novel. In other words, the reader's imaginings are not what Gilbert Ryle calls "creative" or "originative" imaginings, but are "loaned" or "derivative." [6] They are directed and constrained by Dickens's descriptions. Consequently, we may say that in order to understand a fictional work (rather than understand *that* it is fiction), readers have, as it were, to imagine along with the author: they have to make-believe by thinking their way into the author's imaginary world. And once immersed in this world, the reader treats fictional characters as persons, allowing them their rights, fearing for them, laughing at them, pitying them.

Emotion and Disbelief

So far I have tried to show that one can properly understand fiction only if one responds to it in a way which enables one to be moved by it, to feel its tensions and to identify emotionally with its central characters. Failing this, I argued, one is deprived of beliefs and expectations in terms of which to notice and appraise vital aspects of the work. The only way in which one can respond emotionally to fiction and understand it properly, I have suggested, is by responding imaginatively. Anything other than imaginative involvement will amount either to discounting the fiction, or to disbelieving and so misunderstanding it, or else to believing and hence being deceived by it. And while deception may promote an appropriate emotional response, it cannot, of course, promote a proper understanding of the work.

Needless to say, it does not obviously follow from the fact that discounting, disbelieving and believing, are inadequate responses to fiction that an imaginative response must be adequate. Nor is it immediately clear that this is the only other possibility. In order to provide arguments which show that it is, I shall now consider two attempts to solve the problem of how we come to be moved by fiction, neither of which seriously considers imaginative involvement as a possible solution to the problem.[7]

According to Eva Schaper, puzzles as to how we are moved by the plight of fictional characters arise out of the fact that an emotional response to an object presupposes certain beliefs about it ("Fiction and the Suspension of Disbelief," p. 31). And yet, if an object is known not to exist, or is known to be no more than a creature of fiction — a cardboard figure without blood, nerve, or sinew — it is difficult to regard one's beliefs about it, and hence one's emotional responses to it, as warranted and so as rational. Despite this, Michael Weston and Eva Schaper, unlike certain other philosophers, are of one mind in insisting that there are good reasons for being saddened by the fate of Anna Karenina, by the death of Mercutio, or even by the plight of Black Beauty.[8] What these reasons are, however, and how we come to be moved by fictional characters, is the subject of some disagreement.

Weston's approach is disarmingly simple. He reminds us that "we can be moved, not merely by what has occurred or what is probable, but also by ideas" ("How Can We Be Moved," p. 85). In this he is undoubtedly correct, for it is plain that one can be upset not only by the maiming of one's child, but also by the thought of this — even where there is little likelihood of its happening. What one responds to here, Weston tells us, is the thought of a certain possibility which, on account of one's values or priorities, one finds upsetting.

Of course, the ideas that upset us in the real world need not upset us when they occur in fiction. The thought of someone actually falling into a fire is usually upsetting, but when Captain Scarlett falls into a fire in my daughter's favorite television serial, she remains unmoved because she knows that Captain Scarlett is indestructible. This is why Weston insists that it is the idea of Mercutio's death taken against the background of *what this means in the play* which saddens us. He writes: "To be moved by Mercutio's death is to respond in the light of one's interpretation of that episode in the context of the play, and hence is part of one's response to the sense we see in the play as a whole" (p. 86). This, then, is Weston's solution to the problem of how we can be moved by the fate of Anna Karenina. It is a solution which clearly does not demand the reader's imaginative involvement in the heroine's situation. If Weston is to be believed, it would seem that my account of understanding fiction, and more particularly, of what is involved in being moved by fiction, must be incorrect.

As far as it goes, Weston's account is both sound and useful. The trouble is that it does not go far enough, for in order to take his solution seriously we need to know what exactly he means when he says that in order to be moved by Mercutio's death one must "respond in the light of one's interpretation of that episode in the context of the play" (p. 86). It is not enough to explain this, as Weston does, by appealing to "the sense we see in the play as a whole" (p. 86). We need to know much more about how we come to grasp the sense of the play. Weston has little to say about this, and for the most part avoids questions regarding the way in which we have to entertain, consider, or respond to statements of fiction if we are properly to understand them. To believe or disbelieve them, I have argued, is insufficient, and Weston obviously agrees with this (p. 83). However, he simply remains silent about appropriate ways of responding to statements of fiction.

Not that there are or could be that many candidates. One can distinguish only a few cognitive responses to fiction which can, with any trace of plausibility, be considered a help in explaining how we come to be moved by fictive events. These are believing, disbelieving, knowing, and, of course, making-believe or imagining. Believing and disbelieving have already been tried and discarded. My claim, of course, is that we respond appropriately to the statements of fiction only if we respond imaginatively—that is, that we have to respond by imagining the situations or lives of its fictional characters in terms closely specified by the author. The only other possibility appears to be that the readers of a fictional work *know*, and must know, that they are reading fiction, and that this somehow enables them to respond emotionally to the fiction.

This lies at the heart of Eva Schaper's account. According to her, knowing that a work is fictional and, of course, knowing what fiction is enables us to know and hence to believe that its statements are not intended as reports about actual events. If we know that the play is fictional, then we know that Hamlet is not a real person and that he does not really kill a man hiding behind an arras. Based on this knowledge are certain second-order beliefs about the events which occur in fiction, and, according to Schaper, these are the beliefs which sadden or elate us (p. 39).

Schaper's proposed solution does not so much as mention the reader's imaginative involvement in fiction. Instead, it appeals to our knowledge of fiction and to second-order beliefs bred of that knowledge. It is a solution, though, which should not be taken too seriously. According to Schaper, it is because of our second-order belief that Anna Karenina has been abused by both her husband and lover, and has no one to turn to for help, that we can be moved by her fate. But this will not do at all, for according to Schaper such second-order beliefs presuppose the first-order belief that they are not true of the actual world. This, she tells us, is the disbelief we must have in order to respond appropriately to Tolstoy's novel (p. 35). Hence, if Schaper is correct, our second-order belief presupposes first-order disbelief, but this, of course, is totally implausible, for we have seen that if we are to disbelieve the statements of fiction, we must believe that they are asserted of the actual world. However, if we know what fiction is, then we will also know and consequently believe that its statements are not intended to be true or false of the actual world. They are assertions about an imaginary world, but not about the actual one. Hence anyone who satisfies Schaper's condition of knowing what fiction is will be unable to disbelieve its statements.

Perhaps I am being unkind to Schaper. It may be that the first-order disbelief required in order to understand fiction amounts to the belief that the statements of fiction are not applicable to the actual world, or, conversely, to the disbelief that they are applicable. And this, of course, is altogether different from disbelieving such statements themselves. But even if this is the point of Schaper's insistence on disbelief, it is still by no means clear that she is able to offer an adequate account of how we come to be moved by fiction.

Certainly we need to know that a work is fictional if we are to respond appropriately to it, and this undoubtedly requires that we should not believe that its statements are either true or false of the world that we inhabit. In this respect at least, Schaper's reconstructed argument is correct, for in order to recognize that a literary work is fictional, one has to acknowledge the fact that the statements contained within the work are neither true nor false of the actual world. However—and here lies the rub—we have already seen that readers who attend to the factual vacuity of statements of fiction, who constantly remind themselves that such statements are mere fabrications, are thereby prevented from responding emotionally to these statements. As a result, whatever second-order beliefs one holds about Anna Karenina, it would seem that since on Schaper's account one is required to attend to their factual vacuity, it becomes psychologically impossible to be moved by them.

Schaper is unaware of the problem. Certainly we know that statements of fiction are mere fabrications, and we know too that they are not asserted of the actual world. Nonetheless, if we are to be moved by creatures of fiction, we must find ways of ceasing to attend to what we know: explicit knowledge must be rendered tacit. Earlier I suggested that anyone who prefaces statements of fiction with the words "It is imagined that . . ." retains the explicit knowledge that the statements which follow are mere fabrications and are inapplicable to our actual situation. Such a person persistently attends to this fact and so cannot take the fiction seriously and cannot be "drawn into" or "caught up in" the world of fiction.

The problem, then, is to explain how the explicit knowledge which is required in order to understand that a work is fictional can be rendered tacit so that we can properly understand the fiction. The solution, I would venture, can be found only in an appeal to the imagination. It is, as we have seen, a commonplace of psychology and epistemology that an imaginative response to an event allows us to "escape from," or to suspend our awareness of, the stark facts of our immediate situation. Daydreamers, like all other people who embark on imaginative adventures, cognitively disengage from their immediate situation. And the same applies to the readers of Tolstoy's *Anna Karenina* who allow themselves to respond imaginatively to the work. They cease to pay attention to the fact that Tolstoy's descriptions are neither true nor false of the world in which they live. Instead they take his descriptions to be true or false of an imaginary world: the world which they, as readers, imagine in the light of his written words. Put differently, we could say that our explicit knowledge of the fact that *Anna Karenina* is fictional, and hence what Schaper regards as our first-order disbelief, becomes the occasion of our imaginative entry into the work. And it is only by responding in this way that we can suspend our knowledge of the fact that statements of fiction are not worthy of belief. By suspending our knowledge we do not forget or become ignorant of the fact that the statements of the novel are neither true nor false of the actual world; but we do not attend to this fact when responding imaginatively to the work. Explicit knowledge has become tacit.

But what is involved in responding imaginatively to fiction? In part, we have seen, such a response involves thinking of or considering the world described by the author. To this I can now add that if we do so without a mind to whether or not these descriptions are true or false of the actual world, then we *are* responding imaginatively. Such imagining, we have seen, is derivative rather than creative, loaned rather than originative.

This is how, in Schaper's jargon, one acquires second-order beliefs that are capable of moving us. Do not think that because these beliefs are derived from our imaginative involvement in fiction that the emotional responses based on them must be similarly imaginative or make-believe.[9] Certainly we can make-believe that we have a particular emotion when responding to fiction, but there are no good reasons to suppose that this must be so, and there are strong empirical and conceptual reasons for supposing otherwise. A first point to notice is that we can only make-believe that we are scared (in any ordinary sense of this expression) if we believe that we are not really scared.[10] The trouble is that many theater-goers and readers believe that they are actually upset, excited, amused, afraid, and even sexually aroused by the exploits of fictional characters. It seems altogether inappropriate in such cases to maintain that our theater-goers merely make-believe that they are in these emotional states. And it will not do to maintain, as Walton does, that the make-believe is automatic or nonreflective.[11] As we have seen, make-believe emotional states are always conscious or reflective inasmuch as they involve the belief that one is not really in the make-believe state. Our theater-goers, however, do not share this belief. They believe that they are really afraid or sad, and it is therefore at odds both with our concept of make-believe, and with the available evidence, to maintain that they automatically or nonreflectively make-believe that they are in these emotional states.

Nor will it do to suggest, as Walton does, that theater-goers or readers merely experience physiological sensations of fear (what he calls *quasi-fear*) and thereupon make-believe that they are afraid.[12] Consider this case: someone reads of Maggie Tulliver's death and feels sad. Tears roll down her cheeks and are furtively wiped away. There is a lump in her throat, and her voice, on speaking, is choked, husky, and unsteady. Occasionally she wipes her nose, which has turned an ominous red. In such cases we have a host of public manifestations and "inner" or private sensations that are standardly associated with sadness. There is both first-person and third-person evidence of a logically adequate kind for maintaining that the reader is genuinely sad, but none at all for the assertion that she makes-believe that she is sad.

Why does Walton regard this evidence as insufficient for ascribing genuine sadness to the reader? Mainly, I think, because he is of the opinion that if one is genuinely saddened by an event in fiction, one must believe that the event has actually occurred. Consequently, one must in some sense have been deceived by, and so have misunderstood, the fiction.[13] He altogether overlooks the fact that an imaginative response to fiction can generate beliefs about fictional events which are capable of moving us—even though we know that the events portrayed in the work have not actually occurred. Our imaginative response to the work enables us to put such knowledge in abeyance, and ultimately permits us to respond emotionally to the plight of fictional heroes and heroines without being deceived by the fiction. Had Walton attended to this aspect of our imaginative involvement in fiction, he might have seen that there is not only an "epistemological window between the real world and fictional ones," but an emotional and attitudinal window as well.[14]

But there is more to be said. Walton is adamant that although Charles experiences sensations of fear (so-called quasi-fear) when watching a horror movie, he is not really frightened since he does not experience the "slightest inclination to flee or call the police."[15] Surely, the argument goes, if he were genuinely frightened he would engage in the appropriate behavior. My account, however, explains the fact that Charles can respond appropriately to the fiction, be genuinely scared by it, and still not engage in all the behavior that one might expect in the equivalent real-life situation. On my view, the job of reading a novel or viewing a film does not require incessant imaginative involvement in the work. Total imaginative absorption of this sort could very well lead to a close identification with the feelings and emotions of the hero, but it will undermine one's capacity to appreciate these works as literature or cinema. Rather, as one reads a novel or views a film, one moves in and out of imaginative absorption. One feels what it would be like to be in the hero's shoes, but, unlike the hero, one does not remain in his shoes. One abandons the imaginative mode from time to time in order to reflect on the work and one's response to it. One assesses the structure of the work, the overall development of the plot, its themes, and then, having done so, one begins once more to respond imaginatively to the fiction.

The sophisticated and informed reader moves in and out of imaginative absorption with relative ease. A child finds this more difficult, becomes "caught up in" the fiction, and has to be reminded from time to time that it is just fiction. It is precisely because Charles can break the spell, because he can withdraw from utter absorption in the work in order to reflect both on it and his response to it, that he feels no urge to flee—even though he finds his imaginatively induced beliefs about the slime genuinely frightening. It is this ability to move in and out of the imaginative mode which helps explain the pleasure we sometimes feel in being moved by a tragedy, or in being angered by the wickedness of the villain. For when we disengage from the work and reflect on our emotional response to it, we can, depending on our values and interests at the time, experience a range of meta-emotions. We may, for instance, take pleasure in the fact that we are so sensitive to the fate of Anna Karenina, or we may become irritated and annoyed by our maudlin response to her quandaries.

Leaving this on one side, it should be stressed that whether one is actually moved by the beliefs which one acquires as a result of one's imaginative involvement in fiction must, in the last resort, depend on what sort of person one is. It will depend on one's general outlook, one's values, the significance one attaches to these beliefs in the context of the fiction, and, not least, on how emotional one is. The important point, though, is that beliefs bred of imaginative involvement in fiction *can* result in an appropriate emotional response, whereas those that are not imaginatively derived cannot. For unless we respond imaginatively to fiction, we cannot escape our knowledge of the fact that the work neither describes nor purports to describe the actual world. And it is this, we have seen, which impedes an appropriate emotional response to the work. Anyone who does respond appropriately to the fiction, by, say, experiencing grief or moral outrage is said to have *identified* with certain creatures of fiction, and we say of such people that they are "caught up in" the fiction, that they find it "absorbing," and that they have been "drawn into" it.

It is because Schaper overlooks the imaginative dimension of our response to fiction that her account of how we can be moved by the fate of Anna Karenina must fail. It is only when one responds imaginatively by "thinking one's way into" the situation of our heroine—that is, when one considers what it is like in her world to be deprived of her husband's protection, and when one considers this *without* a mind to whether it actually happened—that one can acquire beliefs about Anna which allow us to feel the urgency, dread, and hopelessness of her situation.

What the many comprehending readers of a novel actually imagine, we have seen, is very largely determined by the author's descriptions. I say "very largely" because, in some small measure, readers may contribute imaginatively to the authorial creation without thereby ceasing to understand the work. To the extent that they follow authorial descriptions, readers are said to understand aspects of the work, and the beliefs bred of such understanding are regarded as well grounded and rational. What is more, given an adequate understanding of their significance within the fiction, a reader can reasonably be moved by them. Clearly, then, our feelings for Anna Karenina are not rendered irrational by the fact that she is a creature of fiction. They can be irrational, but only if they are based on false, unwarranted, hence irrational, beliefs about our heroine. Thus, for instance, anyone who, on reading *Anna Karenina*, comes to believe that Anna is in love with Levin, and who therefore feels sorry for her when Levin marries Kitty, has at least one unfounded and hence irrational belief about the heroine of Tolstoy's novel, as well as an irrational emotion based on that belief. The mere fact, therefore, that the object of one's emotion is fictional does not render the emotion irrational; it is only when the emotion is based on an irrational belief that it can be regarded as less than reasonable.

Conclusion

One can properly understand fiction, I have argued, only if one is in a position to be appropriately moved by the fate of its characters. An emotional response such as this brings into sharp relief features of a work that, while vital to a proper understanding of it, would otherwise pass unnoticed. Any response to a fictional work, therefore, that prevents emotional involvement must also preclude a full understanding of the work. My aim in this chapter has been to show that it is a condition of being appropriately moved by, and so understanding, fiction, that one should respond imaginatively to it. And I have shown that this is the case, first, by considering the inadequacy of alternative responses, and second, by showing how an imaginative response avoids these inadequacies.

To believe fiction, we have seen, is to be deceived by it, and while deception may promote an appropriate emotional response, it can never promote a proper understanding of the work. To disbelieve or to discount the work, on the other hand, prevents us from acquiring those beliefs necessary for an appropriate emotional response to it. Rather than respond to fiction by believing, disbelieving, or discounting it, I have argued that one must respond imaginatively by making-believe. Such imagining, we have seen, is for the most part derivative, and involves thinking of or considering the fictional world described by the author without a mind to the factual vacuity of his or her descriptions. It is this, I have concluded, which allows us to acquire beliefs about creatures of fiction which are capable of moving us.

We found, though, that Weston's and Schaper's accounts of how we come to be moved by fiction do not so much as mention, let alone require, a reader's imaginative involvement. Schaper's proposed solution turned out on closer inspection to require a knowledge of fiction which, far from promoting, would actually inhibit the beliefs necessary for an appropriate emotional response to it. While such knowledge is required in order to recognize that a work is fictional, I argued that it must in some sense be placed in abeyance, or become tacit rather than explicit, if we are to be moved by the fiction. And this, we found, could only be achieved by responding imaginatively to the work.

Weston's solution, while both lucid and useful, was found to be incomplete. He argues that in order to be moved by a fictive event one must respond to it in terms of the sense that one sees in the play. And while this is certainly true, he fails to specify what is involved in grasping the sense of a play. He says very little about appropriate ways of entertaining statements of fiction. Belief and disbelief are simply discarded, but a more positive account is never offered, and the possibility of an imaginative response to the statements of fiction remains unconsidered.

But is it not circular, you will ask, to maintain in unison with Weston that in order to be moved by an event in a play, one must in some sense understand the play? After all, I have argued that one can properly understand a play only if one is able to be emotionally affected by it.

This would undoubtedly be circular were it true that the process of coming to understand fiction is a linear or sequential process, working in one direction only. But understanding fiction is not like understanding a game of dominoes. It is not as if each sentence in the fiction, once understood, becomes a condition of understanding the next: as if the meaning of each is "placed" one alongside the other until the work is understood. Coming to understand fiction is more like exploring an irregularly constructed three-dimensional web. Different parts of the fiction are interconnected at a variety of points and in various ways. Earlier incidents or descriptive passages in a novel sometimes achieve greater significance in the light of what is read later on. And when once these passages are more fully understood the poignancy of some other fictive incident may become apparent; and this, in its turn, may promote the comprehension of yet another passage. There is no circularity in this, only an acknowledgment of the complexity of what is involved in coming to understand fiction.

FIVE

The Problem of Interpretation

There are occasions, not many, it is true, when the story-line and theme of a novel are entirely obvious to its readers. On these occasions, readers find nothing that is obscure within the work, nothing that needs unraveling. Until now my discussion of our response to, and comprehension of, fiction has been confined to precisely these cases: cases in which the reader always grasps the content of the work, but is then required to do something more in order to understand the work as fiction.

But what of those works where the reader is unable to understand what is happening to the characters, where their lives are obscured by the nature of the text, and where the language used comes between the fiction and the reader's comprehension of it?

Normally we insist that such readers need to interpret these works or their parts if they are ever properly to understand them. The trouble is that it is not at all clear what the interpretation of literary works involves. Nor is it clear that readers can discern settled and correct answers to their questions by engaging in this activity. Deconstruction, as we have already learned, denies the possibility of determinate meaning, and some cognitive relativists concur in this view by arguing that there can be no way of deciding between competing interpretations: no way, that is, of deciding which, if any, is true and which false. Although the latter doctrine takes a number of forms, it usually draws strength from the claim that since the beliefs and concepts central to an interpretation are either wholly or largely determined by the situation of the critic, there can be no neutral way of verifying competing interpretations.[1]

We already have perfectly adequate grounds on which to dismiss the claims of deconstruction, for, as we have seen, unless it can furnish sound arguments against "logocentrism" and the metaphysics of presence, we simply have no reason to take its views about the indeterminacy of the text seriously.[2]

Relativism, however, poses an altogether different and vastly more difficult problem—although, as we learned earlier, it may also take root in those antirealist doctrines bred of a romantic epistemology. Needless to say, cognitive relativism has been widely discussed and seriously challenged.[3] Of late, however, a new, supposedly more robust, relativism has emerged which claims not only to avoid these challenges, but also to vindicate a kind of skepticism about interpretation.[4] My aim in this chapter is to defend a realist, or, as it is usually called, an objectivist account of the interpretation of fictional literature against the claims of the so-called "robust" relativist. In so doing, I shall show that the arguments adduced in support of a "robust" relativism altogether misconstrue the epistemic structure of interpretation. I shall begin, therefore, with an explanation of this structure—an explanation which effectively undermines all varieties of relativism about interpretation, and which ensures the possibility of correctly understanding not just fictional literature, but any cultural product whatsoever.

Interpretation, Imagination, and Description

Readers of fiction are often required to solve certain puzzles, answer certain questions, dispel confusions, or eliminate doubts about the meanings of individual words, phrases, or sentences in a text, about the theme of a work or its plot, about the actions, motives, or machinations of fictional characters, or about the political or religious significance of the work to a certain group of people. Attempts to do so are commonly regarded by critics and readers alike as interpretations, and it is my claim that the creative, originative, or fanciful imagination plays a crucial role in the interpretation of fictional literature.

On my view, whenever existing knowledge and belief fail to bridge the gap between ignorance and insight, we are forced, if we are curious enough, to conjecture, fantasize, or hypothesize as to the answer to our various questions.[5] One might, for instance, be puzzled by aspects of certain fictional works, and so might suppose or imagine, say, that Willoughby intends to seduce Marianne Dashwood; or that the word "apeneck" conveys Sweeney's bestiality. Yet again, one might imagine that *The Turn of the Screw* is a story of sexual repression; or that Falstaff hopes, through his antics, to rise to prominence in Hal's entourage. These are all guesses: imaginative construals designed to answer certain questions and so solve certain problems. Each is tentatively projected on to the work, and to the extent that it removes our confusion, it is adopted as a provisional answer to our question. We gradually come to rely on it, to believe it, and if it enables us to negotiate the work better—that is, to understand other sequences within it, or to have appropriate expectations about future events in the narrative—we will eventually treat it as knowledge.

Of course, such answers are not derived, either deductively or inductively, from our existing knowledge or beliefs, for *ex hypothesi* we have neither sufficient knowledge nor the requisite beliefs to solve these problems.[6] Rather, the answers that we offer are the products of our creative or fanciful imaginings. Having said this, we must take care not to confuse these imaginings with those that merely elaborate and develop the fictional world sketched by an author. A reader may quite gratuitously imagine that Anna Karenina has pearly teeth, jet-black hair, and a very straight nose— even though Tolstoy does not describe her in this way, and even though no puzzle is solved or question answered by imagining her in this way. Here the reader contributes to the fiction by fantasizing within the "limits" set by Tolstoy's descriptions. Should the reader transgress these "limits" by imagining Karenina to be (or to do) other than Tolstoy's descriptions allow, we will maintain that the novel has not been properly understood. Nonetheless, these imaginings are not designed to explain the work, to ease our curiosity, or to answer our questions. If they are interpretations at all, they are interpretations in a very different sense of this word.

Indeed, it would seem that we often operate with two quite distinct senses of "interpretation": one in which interpretations involve fanciful conjectures intended to answer certain questions or solve certain puzzles, and another in which interpretations involve the fanciful, largely subjective, and entirely gratuitous elaboration of the work. The trouble is that in speaking of interpretation we sometimes confuse these two senses. The performances of concert pianists, for instance, are frequently regarded as interpretations—where this may mean two quite different things. In some cases pianists perform, and so interpret, certain works without attempting to solve any specific puzzles or answer any questions about the work. Theirs is an elaborative contribution to the work: they merely weave their fanciful variations within the "limits" of the score, and so come to perform the work in ways which they regard as straightforward and uncontrived. There are, however, situations in which pianists may quite properly be puzzled about how best to play a piece, and in these cases their performances (interpretations) involve problem-solving of one sort or another. Confusion between these two kinds of interpretation is encouraged by the fact that they often (quite contingently) affect each other. Interpretative problem-solving may be strongly influenced by one's (interpretative) elaboration of a work, while one's elaborations, in their turn, may be influenced by one's answers to earlier questions or puzzles. But all of this is a reason for emphasizing, not blurring, the distinction between these two types of interpretation.

Thomas Leddy has recently argued that this distinction cannot be sustained.[7] If elaborative interpretation really is gratuitous, he contends, it is not interpretation at all, but merely "wool-gathering." His claim is that I have failed to recognize this, so that "on Novitz's view one could imagine the color of hair of every character and still be doing a kind of interpretation."[8] On the other hand, if elaborative interpretation is not gratuitous, then it must attempt "to *realize* the character" in a performance or a reading while trying to offer the best performance or reading possible. As a result, either elaborative interpretation is not interpretation at all, or it is a kind of elucidatory interpretation—albeit one which is neither true nor false.

What this objection overlooks, however, is that it is possible to "realize" a character in a reading or a performance without trying to achieve the best reading or performance possible. There are occasions when readers or actors simply imagine a character in one way rather than another—as tall rather than short, as fair rather than dark. They do so despite the fact that there is no question, problem, puzzle, or task which exercises them. Their imagining is entirely gratuitous, but nonetheless results in a character being more fully "realized." Like the actor, the reader responds elaboratively, and this response is assessed not in terms of its truth or correctness, but in terms of its inventiveness, imaginative power, or virtuosity. If I am right, this is properly regarded as a case of elaborative interpretation. It involves an imaginative response which, even though it helps "realize" the character, is entirely gratuitous insofar as it is not part of a specific attempt to achieve a certain goal, or answer a question, or solve a puzzle.

My interest, of course, is with interpretations which attempt to answer certain questions or solve certain puzzles about a work, for it is only in these cases—where elucidations and explanations are offered—that questions about empirical adequacy, truth, and falsity properly arise. A reader's subjective elaborations of *Anna Karenina* are not candidates for empirical appraisal, for they plainly are not offered as substantive claims about the work, but are the private fantasies of one reader. The moment, however, that they influence an explanation of the work, or are challenged by someone else's explanation, they may themselves be treated as attempts to explain, and will be subjected to empirical assessment of one sort or another.

Interpretation in this sense always involves the fanciful formulation of conjectures or hypotheses which are designed to answer certain questions and so solve certain problems. If an initial conjecture fails to answer the question, is wild and wide of the mark, we are forced to think again, to imagine anew—but on this occasion our imagining will be directed or controlled by our knowledge of at least one failure. It is therefore true that wild and uninhibited leaps of fancy, far from promoting an adequate understanding of the fiction, will in all likelihood mislead us as to its import and content. Nonetheless, as we have just seen, the fanciful imagination may be progressively constrained and directed by knowledge and beliefs bred of past experience, and as a result may eventually afford new insights and understanding.

There are, needless to say, many different experiences which may serve to constrain a reader's fanciful response to fiction. Perhaps the most trivial of these constraints is the perceived word on the printed page, which, when taken together with our knowledge of the English language, inevitably limits the scope of the reader's imaginings. Thus, for instance, the rules of reading English require that on perceiving the letters "d," "o," and "g" clustered together, one should read "dog," and that one should normally understand this word in its standard or dictionary sense. Still more, anyone who is acquainted with the genre of the novel knows that one should respond to the novel in virtue of the words and sentences of which it is composed. And such knowledge inevitably directs and constrains the reader's fanciful imaginings so that not any imaginative response to the work will be an appropriate or useful response.

Not only does such knowledge inhibit our flights of fancy, but, more important for my purposes, it also helps determine what we find puzzling or problematic in a fictional work. A person who knows the meaning of the sentence "A dog is barking" will be less puzzled by a work containing this sentence than a person who is ignorant of this fundamental. Indeed, the reader who knows the meaning of the sentence can correctly be said to understand it without in any sense having to decode, decipher, or interpret it. In the sense of interpretation with which I am concerned, it is simply inappropriate to speak of readers interpreting the meaning of a sentence if its meaning is already known to them. The need for interpretation only arises when one does not, or is unable to, understand—although the quest for understanding, I hasten to add, is not always linked to a quest for meaning.[9]

There is, of course, a vast body of belief which pertains to fictional literature. Some of these beliefs are widely regarded as true and often pass as knowledge. They may include beliefs about, or knowledge of, the function of a comma, a paragraph, or a chapter; about the dictionary meanings of certain words, of the letters of the alphabet, or of certain aspects of the genre that we call the novel. When once in possession of such beliefs, certain features of the fictional work no longer stand in need of explanation; they are features which we regard as "given" in the work, and which are "transparent" in the sense that they can be understood without recourse to interpretation.

Clearly, not everyone is in possession of the same beliefs and items of knowledge. Consequently, what puzzles one person about a work may be obvious to another. Thus, for instance, if you know that Willoughby is deceiving Marianne (in *Sense and Sensibility*), you will regard this as a "transparent" feature of the work, and your statement, "Willoughby is deceiving Marianne" will count as a description of one aspect of this work. But if what you know is unknown to me, I may very well be mystified by Willoughby's behavior. As a result, I merely conjecture or fantasize when I utter the words, "Willoughby is deceiving Marianne." Even though we both utter the same words, it is plain, I think, that we perform different speech acts: you *describe* and I *interpret* an aspect of the work. The difference between the two acts is not merely, as Robert J. Matthews has cogently argued, that interpretation is "epistemically weaker" than description.[10] It is also that interpretation involves fanciful imaginings which are designed to take us beyond what we already know or believe. Descriptions, by contrast, merely involve the linguistic application of our recalled knowledge and beliefs.

By arguing in this way, I am able, I think, to avoid many of the problems which beset the search for a distinction between interpretation and description. If, as Monroe Beardsley suggests, the distinction is to be based on the content of an utterance, we are left with the difficulty not just of determining which contents are descriptive and which interpretative, but also of explaining why one and the same sentence can be used both to describe and to interpret.[11]

Nor will it do to distinguish description from interpretation on the basis of the relative stability of their respective objects. According to Joseph Margolis, stable objects are *described*; unstable ones "whose properties pose something of a puzzle" are *interpreted*.[12] But the trouble with this, of course, is that our perception of stabilities is itself unstable. How we see the world depends importantly on the beliefs that we bring to perception—so much so that objects are only taken to have certain properties for as long as our beliefs (and theories) about them endure. Since empirical beliefs change, there can be no way of knowing which properties of any object are stable, which unstable. Unless "stability" (and hence "description") is explained in terms of enduring beliefs and knowledge, Margolis runs the risk of reducing all empirical descriptions to interpretations. Indeed, C. L. Stevenson seems to take Margolis's position to its logical conclusion, and despairs of ever distinguishing description from interpretation. Description, he argues, is always selective, and always involves construing certain marks or shapes in certain ways; and this, he maintains, amounts to a low-level interpretation of the work.[13]

It is plain, however, that describing cannot be reduced to interpreting. The epistemic structure of the one is manifestly different from that of the other. Interpretation, we have seen, involves the controlled exercise of the creative or fanciful imagination in an attempt to dispel the uncertainty and confusion bred of ignorance. It involves flights of fancy which are mediated and constrained by our past or present experience. Description, on the other hand, does not require the exercise of the fanciful imagination. It is not intended to banish the speaker's puzzles or uncertainties. On the contrary, a serious or sincere description presupposes the absence of uncertainty, puzzlement, or confusion, and hence neither involves the formation nor the refinement of hypotheses.[14] Rather, as we have seen, it involves the linguistic application of our recalled knowledge and beliefs.

One might be tempted to contest this way of drawing the distinction, either on the grounds that we can interpret without in any sense being puzzled or curious, or on the grounds that we can sincerely describe an entity even when we do not know what it is that we are describing. But this onslaught soon founders. In the case of describing, it is plain that when we sincerely describe an entity without knowing anything about it, it is merely that we wrongly take ourselves to know something about the object, and so misdescribe it. Sincere descriptions can, of course, be incorrect, but even when we describe incorrectly we must (if we are sincere) believe that we are acquainted with, or know certain things about, the object of the description.

If we are aware that we do not know anything about it, then we cannot seriously attempt to describe it. We may tentatively construe it in one way or another, but this, I have been at pains to show, is quite different from describing.

The claim that we can interpret a work without being curious or puzzled about it is also misplaced. Sometimes the confusion resides in a failure to distinguish elaborative interpretations from those which attempt to elucidate and explain. Since my concern in this chapter is to know whether interpretations can bear a truth-value, and since this question gains currency only when asked of elucidatory interpretations, my claim pertains only to elucidatory, not elaborative, interpretations. And it is plain that an interpretation which seeks to explain can do so only if the interpreter is puzzled, confused, or curious about the object of interpretation. After all, why should one seek to explain or elucidate if one already knows, or believes that one knows, the answer to one's question or puzzle?

Despite the triteness of this observation, it is sometimes suggested that we do read, understand, and therefore interpret, novels in the elucidatory sense without being the least bit puzzled by their contents. But this is misleading. Of course one can read and understand a linguistic construction without being puzzled by it. Nothing that I have said is intended to deny this and I have already affirmed the possibility. My point is that in any such case we do not come to understand the construction by interpreting it; rather, we understand it in virtue of what we already know or believe. The mere fact, therefore, that I have understood (or misunderstood) does not entail that I have interpreted. We suppose that it does only because when one's grasp of a work is challenged, one often defends it by using locutions such as "On my reading," or "On this interpretation," where this suggests that in reading the work I must have interpreted it. But such an inference is unwarranted. My understanding may simply be the product of what I already know or believe; although now that it (and hence some of my beliefs) are being called into question, I will no doubt be inclined to regard it more tentatively, and may in the end be forced to offer my reading as an elucidatory interpretation of the work. Thus, it is only when we overlook the distinction between understanding and interpreting that we think it possible to interpret (in the elucidatory sense) without being in any way puzzled about the object of interpretation.

I have now come some of the way toward providing an adequate account of the epistemic structure of interpretation. There is, of course, much more that can be said. Nonetheless, my claim is that when once minimally acquainted with this structure, we have at our disposal an instrument with which to demolish relativistic arguments against the objectivity of interpretation.

A Robust Relativism?

On my view, a coherent relativism can only ever entail that critics who subscribe to different systems of belief and value will frequently offer different interpretations of the same work. This is as obvious as it is true, and for a philosopher it is both uninteresting and unproblematic. The interesting claim is that there can be no way of resolving these differences, of discovering that one interpretation is correct and another false. However, it has been widely argued that on close inspection this claim turns out to be radically incoherent.[15]

Joseph Margolis disagrees.[16] True enough, he insists that a robust relativism must allow disputing critics access to a common conceptual scheme. And he stresses as well that it is no part of his thesis to maintain that all judgments should be construed relativistically, for this, he correctly observes, would have the embarrassing reflexive consequence of relativizing truth ("Robust Relativism," p. 38). In this way, Margolis avoids the incoherence of a radical relativism.

Nonetheless, he is adamant that it is inappropriate to describe interpretations as true or false (p. 44). Rather, they should be understood as taking values such as probable, improbable, or equiprobable (p. 37). The reason for this is that since fictional works are "culturally freighted phenomena" (p. 44), a number of competing principles may be jointly relevant to the validation of any interpretation of such a work (p. 38). The "competing principles" which Margolis has in mind are presumably derived from those culturally determined "myths," from Freudianism to Catholicism and Zen Buddhism, which (he has argued elsewhere) color our perceptions not only of sizeable portions of reality, but of works of literature as well.[17] Interpretation, on his view, involves the imaginative application of such principles: an imaginative exercise which is sometimes thought of as being akin to that of the practicing artist since it is supposed to add to, or even complete, the work.[18] Thus Margolis tells us that "interpreting" suggests "a touch of virtuosity, an element of performance."[19] Moreover, since in assessing interpretations "we are more interested in certain powers of imagination, the logical rigor associated with truth and falsity simply does not apply."[20]

These observations together constitute the cornerstone of Margolis's relativism. But it is not an entirely secure cornerstone. Part of the trouble is that from the very outset Margolis tends to confuse elaborative with elucidatory interpretations. While it is true that cultural considerations may color both our elaborations and elucidations of a fictional work, it is only in the former case that interpreting suggests "a touch of virtuosity" to which truth and falsity do not properly apply. In the latter case—where interpretations are intended to explain—questions of truth and falsity are still very much alive. It is, of course, true that cultural backgrounds influence both the content and the goals of interpretation, but this has no bearing on whether or not an individual interpretation with a specific explanatory goal can be true or false. Even within one and the same culture, literary interpretations can have an indefinitely large number of aims; as many aims, in fact, as there are possible puzzles or questions about a work. And it is obvious, I think, that discussions about the adequacy of any elucidatory interpretation must be informed by a knowledge of the question which the interpretation seeks to answer. I shall argue that, once given this knowledge, there is no reason why one cannot assess the truth or falsity of the interpretation.

If one's aim is to know the meaning of a word or a sentence, or the motives of the villain or the station master, then a given interpretation either will or will not afford correct answers to these questions. It is relative to *these* queries and puzzles that we have to assess the accuracy of the resulting interpretations. An interpretation which contends (relative to the appropriate question) that it was Willoughby's aim to marry Elinor can be shown to be false, while one that maintains that it was his aim to marry a wealthy woman can be shown to be true. No doubt there are highly fanciful, elaborative interpretations according to which Willoughby's early childhood experiences and subconscious drives inclined him to marry Elinor, and no doubt, too, such an interpretation can "give us a new way of looking at" *Sense and Sensibility*. What it cannot do, I shall argue, is furnish a correct answer to the question "Whom did Willoughby wish to marry?" Rather, it furnishes us with an answer which is manifestly false. The correct answer, of course, is that Willoughby wished to marry a woman of Miss Grey's wealth and social standing. Certainly he regretted his treatment of Marianne and he continued to think fondly both of her and her sister, but even so, he wished to marry only a woman of Sophia Grey's fortune and standing.

It is Margolis's reluctance to acknowledge that such an interpretation could possibly be true which has made his remarks the target of sustained criticism. According to Monroe Beardsley, while "the story of 'Jack and the Beanstalk' . . . can no doubt be taken as Freudian symbolism, as a Marxist fable, or as Christian allegory," this is far from being a genuine interpretation of the work, and is no more than a "superimposition" on it.[21] Or, as E. D. Hirsch tells us, it involves determining the "significance" of the work, its relevance, that is, to our current concerns and favored theories, but it does not give us the meaning of the work.[22] The point, presumably of Hirsch's remark is that since one can determine the relevance of a literary work to a particular concern (that is, its "significance") only if one has already grasped its meaning, interpretation can never be a matter of discerning the relevance of a work to a particular historical or cultural concern.

Both authors believe that the earlier Freudian interpretation of Willoughby's motives fails to give an accurate account of the content of *Sense and Sensibility*. Their criticisms, however, although they do not altogether miss the mark, fail to observe a number of crucial distinctions. We should notice for a start that readers are frequently puzzled by the relevance of a work to, say, their religious beliefs, or perhaps to a particular event; and they may seek to dispel this puzzle imaginatively—that is, through interpretation. Thus, for instance, one may feel that *Macbeth* ought to be able to "say something" about the assassination of Anwar Sadat, but one may be puzzled as to what exactly it does "say" about this event. As a result, and contrary to Hirsch's claim, one may attempt, interpretatively, to determine the relevance of the play to this event. Despite Beardsley's suggestion, this clearly is not a "superimposition" on the work. It is a genuine (elucidatory) interpretation of an aspect of the work; it is not, of course, an interpretation of the meaning concealed "within" the work.

Second, we should note that there will be occasions when one is not at all puzzled by the relevance of a work to a particular theory or religion, but where one chooses nonetheless to elaborate the work in terms of that theory or religion. Thus, for instance, one may think of Emma Woodhouse and her relationship to her father and Mr. Knightley entirely in terms of Freudian theory. And this, of course, is an instance of elaborative, not elucidatory, interpretation. While it may, perhaps, constitute what Beardsley calls a superimposition, it is not of itself an attempt to explain the meaning of the work, and so does not of itself constitute a distortion of that meaning.

Such distortions only occur when one's goal in interpretation is to explain the meaning of a work or its parts. According to Beardsley, it is when this goal is subverted by the "myths" that mediate the interpretation that we have a "superimposition" which distorts the true meaning of the work. Suppose, for example, that a critic wishes to grasp the meaning of *Hamlet*, where this is construed (according to popular critical practice) as the meaning which Shakespeare and his contemporaries would have attached to the play. Beardsley's contention is that any attempt to achieve this goal in terms, say, of Marxian economic theory, must constitute a distortion of the meaning—a "superimposition" on the meaning—which "lies hidden in the work." It must do so because Marxian theory, not being of the appropriate time and place, cannot reveal anything about the Elizabethan understanding of *Hamlet*. At best it imposes an anachronistic conception on the meaning which is properly a part of the work.

Margolis, however, will have none of this. On his view, anyone who claims that a critical tract does not give the meaning of a work, but is merely a superimposition on it, must be able to tell where the meaning of a work ends and where superimpositions begin. But to do this, he informs us, requires a comprehensive theory of the identity and individuation of literary works and their properties. The trouble, according to Margolis, is that it is difficult to come by such a theory. Literary works of art, he tells us, enjoy a cultural existence. They are "culturally emergent entities," and since "culturally freighted phenomena are notoriously open to intensional quarrels, that is to identification under alternative descriptions" ("Robust Relativism," p. 44), there can be "no sharp demarcation line between what is internal and what is external" to them (p. 42). Consequently, Margolis would have it that there is no obvious way of telling which meanings lie concealed within, and which are external to, a literary work. On his view, therefore, until we have a "theory in terms of which superimpositions and 'genuine' interpretations can be demarcated," interpretations in terms of cultural "myths" (that is, so-called superimpositions) may well enable us to attribute a perfectly plausible meaning to a literary work (p. 42).

As a result, since it is always possible for different critics to use equally plausible and yet competing principles (or cultural "myths") when interpreting a fictional work, Margolis believes that it must also be possible for them to arrive at equiprobable and yet incompatible interpretations of the meaning of a work. Given the cultural dimension of a literary work, and given, as a consequence, the fact that different critics individuate works and distinguish their properties differently, Margolis maintains that there can be no question of deciding which, if any, of these interpretations is true. It is this claim which lies at the heart of his "robust" relativism.

The case for a "robust" relativism, therefore, depends crucially on the assumption that since fictional works enjoy a cultural habitat, they cannot be neatly individuated. For when once we are able to individuate a work, we will also be able to discern what is internal to it, and will, as a result, be able to speak, and speak properly, of meanings concealed within it and meanings superimposed on it.

But is it true that we cannot furnish an adequate theory in terms of which to identify and individuate literary works? I think not. Strange though it may seem, Margolis has himself furnished us with an excellent theory which, when taken together with some of my remarks about the epistemic structure of interpretation, is adequate to the task. Literary works of art, he argues, are physically embodied and culturally emergent entities.[23] "A work of art," he tells us, "can be identified as such only relative to a favourable culture with respect to the traditions of which it actually exists" ("Works of Art," p. 193). And earlier he tells us that "the recognition that a given work of art actually exists *and has the properties it has* depends on the cultural traditions in terms of which a particular physical object may justifiably be said to embody a particular work of art" (p. 191. Emphasis added).

If Margolis is to be believed, therefore, it ought to be possible to individuate a literary work, and so determine its properties, provided that one knows which cultural traditions are operative at a given time. On his view, such knowledge, inasmuch as it gives us access to the (culturally emergent) properties of a literary work, must also allow us to decide which properties are internal and which are external to it. And this, in its turn, will allow us to determine the meaning of a work or its parts, and to distinguish it from meanings which, in Beardsley's words, are merely superimposed on the work.

But Margolis denies that his observations can be applied in any straightforward way to literary works of art. He does not, of course, deny that one can have the relevant cultural knowledge in terms of which to identify a work and its properties, for to deny this, he fears, is to embrace a radical and incoherent relativism. Nor is his denial founded on the fact that it is difficult to acquire the pertinent knowledge. Such difficulties are undeniable, but they are also undeniably contingent; and the contingent difficulties involved in coming to acquire the relevant cultural knowledge cannot establish a relativism. Rather, his is a conceptual objection, founded on what he takes to be the "logic" of interpretation. Literary works of art, he says, "often cannot themselves be ascribed a coherent design . . . without imputing by interpretation properties that yield a plausible" account of the work as a whole (p. 193). In other words, the ascription of certain kinds of properties to a fictional work depends "on the identification of the work *under a certain description* (or interpretation)" (pp. 193-94). It follows from this that we cannot claim to know, independently of a specific interpretation, that properties of a certain (unspecified) sort inhere in the work. "The nature of the work," Margolis tells us, "is not first fixed and then interpreted"; rather the work is "identified *for* relevant description and appraisal *when* 'it' is interpreted" (p. 194). It is this which makes it impossible for us to verify an interpretation by appealing to the properties of a literary work.

So while Margolis believes himself to have offered a theory of the identity of literary works and their properties, he plainly does not believe that his theory in any way supports the view that it is possible to determine the truth or falsity of a literary interpretation. It is time now to show that Margolis is wrong.

The claim is that because the ascription of some properties to a literary work of art depends on the identification of that work under a certain description or interpretation, one can only have interpretative access to these properties. The reason for this, you will remember, is that works of art are "culturally freighted phenomena" and do not enjoy a stable set of properties. The properties that they are taken to have will always depend on the culturally determined values, beliefs, theories—and hence interpretations and descriptions—that we bring to the work. And, of course, since all of these may vary, the properties of the work must also be taken to vary.

But this conclusion is patently misleading. The plain fact of the matter is that there *are* cultural stabilities: enduring beliefs, theories, values, in terms of which we perceive all manner of objects—whether they be ashtrays, sea shells, or works of art. Against the background of these stabilities, natural objects are seen to have, and cultural objects do have, a stable range of properties.

It would seem, then, that in order to perceive the properties of an artwork, one needs to acquaint oneself with the relevant cultural stabilities. And one can do so in a variety of ways: by consulting dictionaries, encyclopaedias, history books, anthropological investigations, sociological studies, and so on. Of course, not every critic will have easy or immediate access to such sources, and may, as a result, be puzzled by certain aspects of the work. It is in such situations, I have argued, that elucidatory interpretations are called for: interpretations which may subsequently be verified by acquainting oneself with the cultural background against which the work and its properties emerge.

So it simply is not true that the process of discerning and describing the properties of a literary work of art amounts merely to interpreting the work. In my view, Margolis is much too impressed by the fact that culturally based theories and beliefs mediate our descriptions and interpretations of works of art. It is this, I suspect, which leads him to overlook certain important distinctions between describing and interpreting, and to speak at times as if the two are the same. What he fails to appreciate is that cultural "myths" do not only enter into our descriptions of artworks, but thoroughly mediate our descriptions of all artifacts and natural objects—so that whether Margolis knows it or not, he is, in the end, committed to regarding all descriptions as covert interpretations.

It follows, therefore, that unless the distinction between describing and interpreting is to collapse altogether, Margolis must concede its application to literary works of art. And, as we have seen, there are good reasons for doing so. Elucidatory interpretations of a literary work, I argued at the outset of this chapter, are only ever called for when our available knowledge and beliefs are unable to banish whatever puzzles or confusions we have regarding the work. In such cases we are required to engage in imaginative or fanciful speculation in order to alleviate our curiosity and cure our ignorance. Descriptions of a literary work, by contrast, never involve speculation, but merely involve the verbal application of what we already take ourselves to know. Acknowledged ignorance, in other words, while a condition of (elucidatory) interpretation, precludes description. Consequently, while it is true that interpretations imaginatively impute certain properties to works, descriptions never do. They merely mention the properties which we recognize in the light of what we already know or believe.

Contrary to Margolis's suggestion, therefore, the fact that we identify a literary work under a certain description does not entail that we thereby interpret the work and so merely "impute" properties to it. If it is true, to use Margolis's example, that Stanislavsky was *describing* Chekov's plays when he identified them as tragedies, then Chekov's famous rejoinder can only amount to the claim that Stanislavsky has misdescribed his plays.[24] Identifying descriptions can, of course, be false or misleading, but this is not to say that they are interpretations. Conversely, to interpret a work is never thereby to identify it under, or by means of, a certain *description*. It is true, of course, that if an interpretation is to comprehensible, the interpreter must identify whatever is being, or is to be, interpreted. This is frequently done with the help of noncontroversial descriptive phrases such as "the object on the wall" or "the novel you are reading," where what follows is a set of interpretative statements. To say this, of course, is not to say that descriptions are interpretative; still less that a work is "identified *for* relevant description . . . *when* 'it' is interpreted" ("Works of Art," p. 194). It is only to concede what must already be obvious, namely that descriptive and interpretative phrases can inhabit the same critical tract.

There is, then, no reason at all to suppose that the identification of a work under a certain description ever involves the interpretative imputation of properties to it. Nor, of course, is there reason to think (as Margolis undoubtedly does) that critical interpretations somehow complete the literary work, and so create certain of its properties. Indeed, if Margolis's theory of the individuation and identity of works of art has any virtue at all, it is the virtue of explaining how we can discern the properties of a fictional work independently of interpretation. On his view, such properties are jointly a function of the physical object in which the work is embodied (the printed pages), and of the culture in which the work emerges. If this is correct, and I think that it is, knowledge of the physical object and its cultural setting will allow us to discern, to know, and hence to describe, the properties of the work. And this is important, for it furnishes us with an independent means of verifying any given interpretation; it provides us with a way of coming to know whether interpretatively imputed properties actually inhere in a particular work. It is, of course, true that the ability to discern these properties on any given occasion may itself be the result of prior interpretative acts which have produced knowledge of (or established beliefs about) the work and its properties. However, I argued earlier that the act of applying such knowledge or beliefs is never itself interpretative. To claim that it is, is merely to confuse description with interpretation, and is to misconstrue the epistemic structure of both.

If I am right, the case for a robust relativism fails. Since we can know the properties of a work independently of any specific attempt to interpret it, we have at our disposal a means of verifying different interpretations of the work. Not only can interpretations be true or false, but they can be known to be true or false.[25] Needless to say, there will be cases in which we are undecided as to the truth or falsity of an interpretation, but such uncertainties will always be the result of a contingent, and usually remediable, lack of knowledge. As such they entail neither a radical nor a robust relativism.

Verification

It is one thing to interpret a work, and altogether another to verify an interpretation of it. Any attempt at verification, I have already argued, must be guided by our knowledge of the questions that the interpretation purports to answer, the puzzles that it purports to solve. Within the practice of literary criticism, some questions are asked more frequently and are arguably more important than others. Thus, for instance, since the *Hamlet* that we read today can only be regarded as identical with the *Hamlet* of yesterday if it has retained its meaning through time, critics frequently attempt to recover the original meaning or meanings of that play and its parts. This, after all, is the mark of identity of a literary work, and in order to say, as we so often do, that a work has withstood the "test of time," or that it is "universal in its appeal," we have to assume constancy of meaning. Hence, even though there are many aims which a critic may legitimately have in interpreting *Hamlet*, the aim of uncovering its original meaning or meanings is not only recurrent, but of primary importance.[26] In what follows, therefore, I shall assume that the primary goal of interpreting a literary work is just to recover those meanings which could reasonably have been imputed to it by its author and contemporary audience.

In my view, Margolis's theory of literary works as physically embodied and culturally emergent entities comes a long way toward explaining the process of verifying such interpretations. And I have already shown, if only in skeletal form, how this is possible. It is time now to fill in some of the detail, and to explain more fully one of the major preoccupations of literary criticism.

Literary works of art are physically embodied. In most cases they inhabit white pages suitably inscribed with black ink. Once given the appropriate linguistic and literary conventions, these pages may properly be regarded as a text. Normally we assume that the text furnishes us with a good deal of the evidence necessary for discerning the theme of a work and the meaning of its parts. This is why we begin the task of coming to understand a novel by attending in the first instance to its vocabulary and syntactical constructions.

It should come as no surprise, then, to find that we frequently begin the task of verifying an interpretation of the meaning of a work by attending to words and sentences on the printed page. Since interpretation is called for only when we are curious or puzzled, and since curiosity and puzzlement are always a function of what we happen either to know or not to know, one person's interpretation may quite easily be verified by another who happens to know, or who happens to be in a position to discover, the answer to the question which occasioned the interpretation. Since the text of a literary work gives us more evidence than anything else for discerning its meaning, the text becomes the first, and a necessary, port of call for anyone who wishes to verify an interpretation which purports to give the meaning of that work.

This, of course, is not to deny that a literary text standardly conveys whatever its author intends it to convey. If H. P. Grice is to be believed, success in linguistic communication involves the hearer's or reader's recognition of whatever the speaker or author intended to convey by using a particular linguistic device.[27] However, it should be stressed that recognition of the author's very complex intention is facilitated by the development of linguistic conventions which the author uses in the (not infallible) belief that they will convey to a reader whatever the author means or intends to convey. Reciprocally, the reader will suppose (again not infallibly) that the use of specific conventional devices on a particular occasion conveys whatever the author intended to convey.

Although I cannot defend Grice here, there is much to support both his view and the related view of E. D. Hirsch that linguistic meaning is an affair of human consciousness.[28] However, it is a vastly different matter to suppose, as Hirsch unquestionably does, that the interpretation of literature, inasmuch as it involves a search for "determinate meaning," is always in the last resort a matter of uncovering authorial intention.[29] The trouble with such a view, as Monroe Beardsley has pointed out, is that authors, like speakers, make mistakes.[30] Occasionally authors will invoke the wrong convention. They may be guilty of malapropisms or of unintentionally ambiguous constructions, and as a result they may fail to say what they mean. The resultant passages have a meaning which is different from the authors' meaning; and any appeal to authorial intention, while it may tell us what an author meant to convey, will tell us very little, if anything, about the meaning of the passage in question.

Even though Hirsch correctly emphasizes an important genetic relation between linguistic meaning and human mental states, his skepticism about the text as a source of meaning and as a criterion for verifying interpretations is largely misplaced. Hirsch simply overlooks the well-known fact that in any natural language there are many established devices which are used in a range of standardized ways in order to convey authorial intention. Such devices enjoy what Grice calls a "timeless," as opposed to an "utterer's occasion," meaning; and they are used by an author precisely because it is believed that they will serve to convey whatever it is that is meant or intended.[31] Certainly the origins of these devices must be explained in terms of human intention, but they have long since escaped the complete influence of the individuals who use them. They have acquired an independence which allows them to be the bearers of meanings that may be left entirely untouched by the particular intentions of an author on a specific occasion.[32] It is no longer the intention which gives the device meaning; rather, it is frequently the standard meaning of the device which allows us to attribute a particular intention to the author.

If I am right, any text which is written in a natural language must contain a vast number of conventional linguistic devices. Consequently, acquaintance with the relevant conventions (which are themselves partly definitive of a culture[33]) will enable us to discern the meaning of some of the words, phrases, and sentences in the text. Meaning, quite clearly, is itself a culturally emergent property; so, too, of course, are the theme and plot of the work, as well as its ambiguities and vaguenesses. Having said this, it is tempting (but totally mistaken) to conclude that any interpretation of a literary work which its text is "able to bear"—that is, which reflects the conventional meanings of its various words and phrases—is to that extent true or correct. The trouble with this is that a word can only bear its standard meaning if it is used in accordance with established usage, or, to put the matter differently, if it is used in the appropriate context.[34] Since it need not always be obvious from the text alone whether a word is being used conventionally, we may not be able to tell whether the word bears its standard meaning on this occasion. And if we cannot tell from the text alone, it would seem that the text cannot be regarded as a touchstone for correctness in interpretation.

Despite this, it would be unnecessarily precipitate to dismiss the text either as a source of meaning or as a ground for asserting the validity of an interpretation. While it is true that a consideration of the text alone is never sufficient for ascertaining the meaning of a work or the adequacy of its interpretations, we have already seen that a consideration of the text plays a necessary part in this process. However, since it only plays *a part*, something else must be required if we are ever to know that an interpretation is true or false.

Well, what is it that is required? In a recent article, Jack Meiland tells us that we must consider the text in "relation to impersonal (social) linguistic conventions."[35] A similar view is held by Svante Nordin, who maintains that texts must be considered in their social context. Nordin is of the opinion that interpretations can be known to be true if we attend both to the text *and* to the linguistic conventions of the community in which the text occurs.[36] Both views seem to me to be basically sound, but neither is developed in sufficient detail. The main problem is that there is no explanation of how social and linguistic conventions help determine whether a given interpretation "fits" the text. Nor is there any clear account of the nature of these conventions. Clearly, not any conventions will do, but little has been done to delineate the requisite ones.

A moment's reflection, however, will suffice to show that when once we know that a work is a tragedy and not a parody, an allegory and not a comedy, we are immediately able to tell how certain of its words and sentences are being used: literally or figuratively, metaphorically, ironically, and so on. Moreover, just as the utterance "You are about to die" has one meaning when we take it as having the illocutionary force of a threat, and another when we take it as a prediction, so "Goldilocks" has one theme or meaning when we take it as a child's adventure story, and another when we take it as a psychological or political statement. And, of course, if we know to which genre, category, or class the story belongs, then we can appeal to this knowledge, as well as to our knowledge of the conventional devices used in the text, in order to validate certain interpretations of the tale and eliminate others.

But how are we to tell to which genre or set of genres a work belongs? Is this not itself the object of interpretation? The short answer is that it may, but need not, be. Not all art lovers come to a work swaddled in ignorance. The trained observer is usually acquainted with many genres and with the tell-tale signs of genre membership. Not only can most observers tell a painting from a novel, but they can usually distinguish kinds of paintings and kinds of novels. This (cultural) knowledge, Kendall Walton argues, often mediates our perception of the work: we see it as belonging to, or as being in, a particular category, and this affects both what we look for in the work and, most important, what we see in it.[37] So while it certainly is true, as Margolis has argued, that "no distinction of genres, periods, art forms, styles and the like can be supposed to be discovered *simpliciter*"—that is, without the benefit of some knowledge of the relevant culture—it need not follow from this that "some suitably selected alternative system of categories" can always displace the genre to which the work is seen to belong.[38] By Margolis's own admission, a rational critic's knowledge of the culture in which the work appears must prevent the arbitrary displacement of our critical categories.[39]

Needless to say, there will be occasions when we cannot readily classify a work, occasions when we are puzzled about the appropriateness of confining the work to one genre rather than another. Any resolution of this problem invariably requires close attention to a range of conventional clues which (when taken together with some knowledge of the appropriate period of a culture) will enable us to tell to what genre or set of genres, if any, the work belongs. Critics may consider the title of a work, the manner in which a story is told, its written style and formal composition. They may consider its choice of vocabulary, date of publication, and even its length. Anyone conversant with literary art forms will invariably look to certain of these (and other) conventional clues when attempting to determine genre membership. Of course, not everyone knows that these are salient features of literary genres. But this is something that can be learned, and provided that we have acquired the requisite knowledge, there is no reason why we cannot come to know to which category of art, if any, a work belongs.

Context, of course, need not be explicated solely in terms of genres, art forms, styles and their conventional signs. Should we wish to verify the interpretation of a work which does not obviously belong to any established genre or style, we would almost certainly turn our attention from generic to genetic considerations. In such a case, we try to discern the various properties of the work—in this instance, how certain words are being used—by attending perhaps to the biography or autobiographical jottings of an author, or, possibly, to the linguistic conventions of the period in which the author wrote. We may attend, too, to the history of the period, to other of its literary products, or to the works of writers known to have influenced the author.

It is clear from this that attempts to verify an interpretation may become increasingly, indeed alarmingly, esoteric. A critical discussion which starts with apprently innocuous questions about the proper way of reading a contemporary work—whether to stress it in this way or that—may quickly lead to a specialized inquiry into the proper way of reading hexameter verse of the fourth century. It would seem, then, that our attempts to verify interpretations may acquire the form of a social or historical inquiry, and provided that we allow, as Margolis does, that social and historical knowledge are possible, it must also be possible to furnish grounds which help establish that a given interpretation of a fictional work is either true or false.

The Slide into Incoherence

Perhaps, though, I am too rash in assuming that social and historical knowledge are possible. It is sometimes argued that we are all products of our own historical situations, and we see and understand in terms of conceptual schemes and "myths" bred of those situations. This is precisely the specter that Thomas Leddy raises when he writes:

> What then of Novitz's objectivism? Is it sound? He claims, as we have seen, that dictionaries, encyclopedias, histories, sociological investigations, anthropology, and other "social stabilities" can tell us the objective meaning of texts, e.g. how the linguistic contemporary of Shakespeare would have interpreted *Hamlet*. Does he intend to use Catholic history, Marxist sociology, or Structuralist anthropology? Will he use Samuel Johnson's dictionary or Diderot's encyclopedia, each of which expresses many of its author's beliefs and prejudices? Or will he use our own dictionaries and encyclopedias? It is likely that these works are also influenced by the interpretive myths which Margolis has described.[40]

The suggestion is that it might not, after all, be possible for us to come to know those conventions or cultural stabilities which, on my view, will enable us to discern the meaning that Shakespeare and his contemporaries could reasonably have attributed to *Hamlet*. This, of course, is not Margolis's position, for he rightly sees it as heralding a slide from his "robust" relativism to a less tenable, so-called weaker relativism. According to this view, the interpretation of a literary work depends crucially on the beliefs, associations, concepts, and values of the critic. Since these, in their turn, are historically and culturally determined, critics who belong to different cultures or periods of a culture, and so subscribe to different systems of concepts and beliefs, will "see" things differently, and will invariably offer different interpretations of the same literary work. Lionel Trilling is just one among many critics who subscribe to this view. According to him, a poem "is a thing which submits itself to one perception in one age and another kind of perception in another age." This, we are told, "makes it a thing that we can never wholly understand."[41]

This is what I shall call a radical relativism. Notice, though, that radical relativists such as Trilling and Leddy do not merely subscribe to the moderate and (incontestable) thesis that the conventions and material conditions prevalent in our society are likely to influence our interpretations of fictional literature. Rather, they maintain that such conventions and conditions inevitably affect our construals.[42] We are ensnared in Kuhnian paradigms, stifled in ideological closets, and able to see, and think about, works only in terms defined by our culture. The view that we can suspend the influence of an age or escape the bounds of our culture is, according to our skeptic, as far-fetched as Wellsean time travel or telepathic communication.

But why should our attempts at interpretation *inevitably* be affected by the conventions and contingencies of our particular culture? An answer to this question begins to emerge when once we realize that radical relativists are often of the opinion that one can master another conceptual scheme only if one has access to those experiences on which the beliefs and concepts are founded.[43] Presumably, then, the argument is that since we can never return to the past, we can never know that our approach to a particular work embodies the appropriate beliefs and concepts. Indeed, even if we could return to the past, it still is not clear that we could know this, since we would have no way of telling whether we had experienced the appropriate stimuli and so mastered the relevant concepts.[44] If we accept these premises, then it will indeed seem to follow that our interpretations must inevitably be influenced by the values, associations, beliefs, and concepts which are bred of our culture, or period of our culture, since we are inevitably confined to them. Nonetheless, it is all too obvious that insuperable problems arise when we take the radical relativist's premises seriously.[45]

For a start, if it is true that a contemporary critic inevitably operates with a conceptual scheme that is crucially different from that used, say, by Elizabethans, then it is impossible for our critic to know, not only whether a contemporary interpretation is better than its Elizabethan counterpart, but whether it differs from it.[46] If this is true, relativism about interpretation loses a good deal of its force. For whereas the doctrine is standardly taken by its adherents to show that it is possible to have different and competing interpretations, none of which can ever be said to be true, it now transpires that there is no way of knowing that such interpretations are different from, and in competition with, each other.

An equally nasty consequence of radical relativism arises when we realize that we no longer have suitable criteria for identifying Shakespeare's *Hamlet* from one performance to another. Normally we would appeal to the meaning of Shakespeare's words in a designated text as a vital criterion in the re-identification of his plays. Some semantic shifts will of course be tolerated from period to period, but if the meanings of all the words in the text are deemed to have changed gradually and imperceptibly since Shakespeare's time, then it is no longer the play that Shakespeare wrote. Unfortunately, if the relativist is to be believed, there can be no way of telling whether I attach the same meaning to Shakespeare's words as he does. Consequently, when the Bard refers to *Hamlet* he might be speaking of a totally different play from the play to which I refer by using the same title. Reference itself becomes relativized, so that disputing critics in different cultures or periods can never know that they are speaking about, or arguing about, the same literary work.[47] The possibility of rational disputation about the interpretation of literary works is totally undermined.

These considerations serve, I hope, to cast considerable doubt on the viability of any radical relativism. Not all relativists, I hasten to add, are embarrassed by the consequences of their doctrine. Some of these consequences are not only welcomed but are elevated into new doctrines, which in their turn become part of the relativist's armory.[48] But there is one consequence of the doctrine which radical relativists cannot endure: on its premises, human communication itself becomes impossible. The trouble is that there is no reason at all why the considerations that are taken to establish a radical relativism between different communities should not also be made to apply between different individuals. As an individual human being, I am bound to have certain experiences, and, according to a stimulus theory of meaning, certain beliefs and concepts, which you do not share, and in terms of which I will inevitably interpret your utterances. I will tend, therefore, to project my point of view rather than yours on to your various pronouncements. Consequently all communication fails.

It is no use trying to avoid this conclusion by arguing, as a Quinean might, that provided we belong to the same "speech community" we will have more or less the same stimuli and hence the same web of beliefs and concepts.[49] Any such defense plainly puts the cart before the horse, for it is sameness of stimuli which determines speech communities, and not the other way around.[50] It now seems, though, that since individuals have an endless capacity for experiences or stimuli unique to themselves, there can be no way of knowing that any two people share the same beliefs or concepts, or attach the same meanings to the same words.

This conclusion is literally indefensible. Skeptics who believe it are condemned to silence, can never state their case, and consequently cannot reasonably hope to persuade us of its truth. What is more, our social practices, our literary, scholarly, and journalistic conventions, the innumerable cases in which listeners are known to respond appropriately (or inappropriately) to what we say, cumulatively provide overwhelming evidence for the view that we can and do communicate. Communicative practice provides no grounds for supposing, and considerable evidence for denying, that we are ensnared within particular world-views, ideologies, or conceptual systems. Certainly the views of one's age or culture may influence one's perception or understanding of a given literary work, but we commonly recognize and guard against undue influence.

The claim that we can never know another culture or age is plainly fraught with difficulties. To establish this, however, is not to explain how we actually acquire such knowledge and so manage to recover the original meaning of a work such as *Hamlet*. Much, of course, has been done by

Donald Davidson and Hans-Georg Gadamer to show how we can acquire such knowledge, and I shall take this question up in more detail when considering the problem of the comprehension and interpretation of metaphor.[51] Suffice it to say at this stage that we cannot begin to grasp the conventions of another culture or age unless we assume that its inhabitants share most of our beliefs about the world. For, as Davidson insists, unless we do so, we can have no reason at all to regard the inhabitants of other times and cultures as fully rational and fully human.

In other words, we begin to make sense of Shakespeare's age, not by suspending our twentieth-century beliefs (as if that were possible), but by assuming that Shakespeare and his contemporaries share most of our beliefs about the world. This assumption may, I suppose, turn out to be false, and if so, we will come in time to revise our assessment of Shakespeare's rationality and even his humanity. It is much more likely, though, that we will come to realize that there are certain of his beliefs—very few when all are considered—that we do not share. However, we can only recognize this because we already share with him and his contemporaries a framework of beliefs, and it is in terms of these that we gradually come to understand the conventions of the Elizabethan world. Happily, of course, we do not have to start this process from scratch. There are scholarly works which already form part of our critical, historical, and anthropological canon and which are taken to explain those beliefs and cultural stabilities that are peculiar to the Elizabethan world. These works are included in the canon because their explanations are successful; they provide what Davidson has called "the best holistic fit," and they do so by making the most coherent sense of all those features of the culture that we deem to be worthy of attention.

Hence when Leddy asks of me whether I intend to use Catholic history or Marxist sociology, Johnson's dictionary or Diderot's encyclopaedia, in coming to know the cultural stabilities of the Elizabethan age, I have at my disposal a perfectly straightforward reply. I will use those works that give the most coherent, and in this sense, the most successful, explanation of the age and its culture.

Conclusion

Any elucidatory interpretation of a literary work may be said to be true if the properties which it imputes to the work can be independently discovered within it. The process of discovery, we have seen, depends crucially on the acquisition of the relevant cultural knowledge: knowledge of conventions, practices, traditions of one sort or another. It is only in the light of such knowledge that it is possible to discover and observe those features of the work which help determine its character and identity, and which furnish a touchstone for correctness in interpretation.

If this is correct, Margolis's relativism with regard to the interpretation of fictional literature fails. It is a relativism, we have seen, which depends crucially on the belief that works of art are "culturally freighted" objects, the properties of which are not always well defined or available for inspection. Indeed, if Margolis is to be believed, these properties emerge only in contexts where culturally based beliefs and theories (so-called myths) are interpretatively applied to the works. On Margolis's view, therefore, works of art are incomplete, and the task of completing them falls to those who attend to, and wish to understand, the works. The resultant interpretations are said to involve "a touch of virtuosity, an element of performance," for in interpreting a literary work of art the reader is required to imagine properties which can plausibly be imputed to the work, and which, in being imputed, actually become a part of it.[52] However, as we have seen, Margolis is of the opinion that these interpretations are importantly, indeed vitally, influenced by the cultural baggage that each individual brings to the work, and since not everyone carries the same baggage, the view is that at least some of the properties of an artwork are inherently unstable.

It is, I am convinced, the specter of instability which brings Margolis to the view that interpretations can never properly be said to be true. What is more, since the "myths" involved in interpretation are thought to determine the nature of some of the properties of an artwork, Margolis has argued that no description of the properties of an artwork can ever serve to validate an interpretation of it. Indeed, we have seen that in the final analysis Margolis cannot countenance any clear distinction between describing and interpreting the culturally significant properties of a literary work of art.

In part, my aim in this chapter has been to show that Margolis, while interesting and persuasive, is wrong. His relativism, I have argued, fails not only to distinguish elaborative from elucidatory interpretation, but fails as well to draw appropriate epistemic distinctions between description and interpretation. It is no doubt true that culturally determined "myths" may influence the way in which we interpret artworks. What Margolis overlooks, though, is the fact that to interpret a work may *either* be to elaborate *or* to elucidate it, and that in the latter case questions of truth and falsity do properly arise. If the aim of an interpretation is to elucidate, to answer a question, to solve a problem or a puzzle, then it is in principle possible, I have argued, to verify the interpretation, even where this is an interpretation of the culturally significant properties of the work.

On my view, all objects, and not just "culturally freighted" ones, are perceived in terms of cultural "myths" of one sort or another—although this, it should be emphasized, does not commit me to any relativism whatsoever. Margolis's mistake is to suppose that these "myths" are chronically unstable, for they plainly are not. They are often enduring and form part of those stabilities which help characterize a society and its culture. It is our knowledge of these stabilities which allows us to discern and describe the properties of the (natural and cultural) objects which surround us.

By adopting Margolis's theory of works of art as physically embodied and culturally emergent entities, I have, I think, shown that an elucidatory interpretation of a work of art may be verified simply by acquiring the appropriate knowledge of the cultural traditions against which the work and its properties emerge. To know, or to be acquainted with, the appropriate aspects of a culture is to be able to describe the properties of the work, and these descriptions will serve to verify an elucidatory interpretation of it. Skepticism about the possibility of acquiring the relevant cultural knowledge (such as that suggested by Thomas Leddy) results in utter incoherence, and, as we have seen, is literally indefensible.

Of course, what we look for when verifying an interpretation will very largely be determined by the interpretation itself. This, however, does not entail that what we find is wholly determined by the interpretation. It is a commonplace of everyday experience that we do not always find what we look for, or look for what we find. The properties of a literary work are no exception, and, we have seen, can be known independently of any given interpretation.

Thus, for example, if I am acquainted with the meanings of certain words and the rules of accepted behavior in eighteenth-century England, I will know, on reading *Sense and Sensibility*, that the Dashwood family has lived in Sussex for many years, that Mrs. Dashwood has recently been widowed, that Elinor is older than Marianne, and that Willoughby treats Marianne shabbily. Like so many other readers who are acquainted with the relevant cultural knowledge, I do not hesitate to assent to these propositions and to assert their truth. They describe what, for me, are "given" or "transparent" features of the work: features which will serve as a touchstone for the correctness of any interpretation offered by a person who is puzzled by the work, or by certain of its parts. Any interpretation of *Sense and Sensibility* that accurately reflects any one of these features is to that extent true, this despite the fact that it need not be an exhaustive interpretation of the work.

It is simply false, then, that "there is no clear-cut agreement about what is in" a literary work of art.[53] Certainly critics may disagree about this, but there is no reason why such disputes cannot be resolved through the acquisition of the relevant cultural knowledge. We can and do discover that particular beliefs and concepts are inappropriate to the interpretation of a specific play. The critic who maintains that Lear is properly thought of as the victim of his own illiberal and nondemocratic form of government can easily be shown, by appeal to historical evidence, that he or she is interpreting the play in terms which are wholly foreign to an Elizabethan conception of a sound political order. There are historical facts, often reliably recorded, to which critics can and do appeal in order to resolve critical disputes. Nor is it simply that the critic calls these facts "into play *if he wishes*."[54] Rational disputation is essential to critical elucidation, and it is this that forces the critic to consider the available research and to bow to the weight of evidence.

I do not, of course, wish to suggest that every interpretative disagreement will in time be happily resolved—although I have argued that those which resist rational resolution do so for purely contingent reasons. Nor do I wish to suggest that fictional works are never highly complex, vague, or ambiguous, or that a true interpretation can never find them so—although, in so doing, it need not exhaust these complexities and ambiguities. Of course fictional works and their parts can bear many (more or less determinate) meanings. To acknowledge this is to acknowledge their interest and their charm, but is not to accept either a radical or a "robust" relativism.

SIX

Fiction and the Growth of Knowledge

Perhaps the most obvious legacy of the Enlightenment is the widely held belief that empirical science alone can furnish us with useful knowledge about the world. Any claim to knowledge which is not based on, or amenable to, scientific enquiry is generally regarded as bogus, as a kind of quackery to be shunned by all who are not simple-minded or superstitious. David Hume, as a figure of the Enlightenment, persuaded his heirs that the deductive arguments of traditional metaphysics, while perhaps logically certain, were empirically vacuous. On his view, if our claims about the world were to be properly founded and justifiable, they would have to be derived not from deductive system-building, but from sense experience. On this view, as we have already seen, the fanciful imagination turns out to be no more than a source of error which, if relied on, will lead to the total destruction of human nature.[1]

We are already acquainted with the romantic reaction to all of this, and we have seen how easily it tumbles into an untenable idealism. Perhaps because they are reassured by the failure of romantic metaphysics, Anglo–American philosophers of this century continue, for the most part, to speak of the growth of knowledge only in the context of scientific enquiry. As a result, those working in the wake of Popper and W. V. Quine have tended to concentrate on the growth of propositional (or sentential) knowledge, as if to suggest that it is the only knowledge that matters, or, still worse, that it is the only knowledge that grows.[2] This tendency has not only hampered the epistemological enterprise, but has encouraged many to ignore the products of the fanciful imagination, and especially works of art, as a potential source of knowledge. As I have already intimated, my aim in this book is to reverse the trend, and I shall do so in the present chapter by attending to one art form in particular, namely, fictional literature.

Learning from Fiction

Novels are typically regarded as works of fiction, but it is well known that not all statements in a novel need be fictional. Some may be assertions about the actual world—assertions that, if true, afford knowledge of that world. Others, however, express the author's creative or fanciful imaginings. They express fabrications, inventions, fantasies, and are properly regarded as fictional statements. If they cohere, they will describe and delineate what I shall call a "world" of the author's imagining—a fictional or an imaginary world.[3] Attentive readers who understand the text of a fictional work will derivatively imagine this world, and may very well be moved by what they imagine.[4]

It is of considerable interest that readers who respond to fiction in this way frequently claim to have learned something from the fiction. The claim is not merely that they have acquired knowledge about the fictional work and its imaginary world, but that they have learned something about the actual world in which we live. Not only does fiction impart knowledge of the real world, we are told, but it helps us to understand and to come to terms with what would otherwise be baffling. It imparts insights, skills, and values of one sort or another, and in so doing helps us to see the world differently.

That we learn about our world from fiction seems clear enough. The problem is to know how this is possible, for if fictional statements are not true of the world we inhabit, it is difficult to understand how we can learn about the world from such statements. And while there have been many attempts to answer this question, even a cursory glance at the literature reveals a tendency for explanation to cease at the very point at which one might have expected it to begin.[5] Although I cannot examine this literature here, it would seem that one reason for this failure is that many theorists uncritically suppose that there can be only one way in which we learn from fiction. This assumption compels them to explain a range of diverse phenomena by appeal to a single principle, and what better way of doing so than with the help of unexplained metaphors and obscure expressions?

It goes without saying, though, that there are many different things that one can learn, and that they are not all learned in the same way. One does not learn tennis in the way that one learns history; nor does one learn science in the way that one learns to be moral. Similarly, since there is a number of different sorts of things that one may learn about the world from fiction, it seems unreasonable to suppose that they must all be learned in a single way.

What is it that we learn from fiction? First, I think it plain enough that people sometimes acquire propositional beliefs about their world from the novels and stories that they encounter. Such beliefs—propositional beliefs about the furniture of the world and what has happened in it—I shall call factual beliefs, and it is clear that some of these beliefs may be true and others false. Hence we may say that in learning from fiction we sometimes acquire true or false factual beliefs. Of course, the mere acquisition of a true factual belief does not amount to the acquisition of propositional knowledge. It is only when we are justified in believing that p that we can appropriately be said to know that p. And although I shall have more to say about the process of justification later on, it is my claim that in learning from fiction we can acquire propositional knowledge about our world.

Of course, as I have already hinted, factual beliefs and propositional knowledge are by no means the major component of what we learn from fiction. As we know from the many censorship boards all over the world, it is possible to acquire certain values or attitudes from fictional works. These may, of course, affect and be affected by one's beliefs, and will at times be integrally related to them.

In addition, it should be stressed that a good deal of what we learn from fiction is practical rather than propositional or attitudinal. We often acquire not just factual beliefs and values, but also a range of skills from the novels that we read. These skills fall into at least two classes. First, there are skills of strategy. A favorite hero may furnish us with purely practical strategies for handling a tricky situation: strategies which we may adopt when we find ourselves in a similar situation. Alternatively, a fictional work may impart intellectual strategies by enabling us to take more aspects of a problem into account, and in this way to think more comprehensively and efficiently about it. In the latter case fiction extends our thinking by drawing to our attention previously unconsidered aspects of a problem.

The second class of skills, however, does not merely extend our thinking, but radically alters it. Fiction may impart what, for want of a better term, I shall call conceptual or cognitive skills: skills which offer radically new ways of thinking about or perceiving aspects of our environment.

Novels and plays, we shall see, may enable us to place new and helpful constructions on an otherwise baffling array of events. They enable us to see old and familiar objects in a radically different light. In this way, fiction may help us to notice qualities of, or relations between, objects, persons, and events where these were previously unnoticed.

Finally, fiction often enables its readers to acquire beliefs about, indeed knowledge of, what it feels like to be in certain complex and demanding situations. Empathic beliefs and knowledge of this sort are derived from, and have to be explained in terms of, our awareness or experience of what is sometimes termed a direct object. A feature of such awareness is that it is irreducibly nonpropositional, in the sense that it cannot be captured or adequately conveyed in linguistic descriptions. For instance, no matter how precise and vivid my descriptions are, they will never acquaint you with my feelings as an orphan, or with the strains of Mozart's *Te Deum*, K. 141, or with the anguish of a moral dilemma. In these cases we often say that one can come to know Mozart's music only by listening to it, or that one does not know what it feels like to be bereaved until one has, in one way or another, experienced bereavement.

I have already explained how our imaginative involvement in fiction allows us to respond emotionally or feelingly to the tribulations and triumphs of creatures of fiction.[6] It is as a result of these experiences, I can now add, that we often come to hold certain beliefs about what it must feel like to occupy situations akin to those of our favorite heroes and heroines. Such beliefs are invariably nonpropositional. They are derived from felt experience and are about the felt nature of the experiences which we can expect to have in certain other situations. Consequently, if I am right, they cannot adequately be conveyed by description. This is not to say that such experiences are never brought under concepts. It is only to say that the expression of such concepts in language will not serve to convey beliefs about what it actually feels like to have these experiences. It is such beliefs that I have dubbed empathic, and if they turn out to have some basis in, or to cohere with, our future or past experiences, they will pass as empathic knowledge.[7]

It would seem, then, that we learn many different things from fiction. We acquire factual beliefs, propositional knowledge, values, attitudes, and skills of one sort or another, as well as empathic beliefs and knowledge. The task which now falls to hand is that of explaining how all this is possible. Before doing so, however, it is necessary to say something more about the fictional worlds from which we learn, and the relation in which they stand to the real world.

Fictional Worlds and Resemblance

In composing a fictional work, an author imagines certain characters, events, and states of affairs as enjoying certain properties and as standing in specific relations to each other. Any such coherent group of imaginings is what I have called a fictional world, and it is, of course, part and parcel of novel writing that an author will attempt to "capture" or describe this world in a natural language. On reading these descriptions, a reader may derivatively imagine this world, and when doing so will often assert certain resemblances between the imaginary world of the novel and the actual world.

The mere mention of a resemblance between the fictional world of a novel and the real world may well be a source of skeptical misgivings.[8] These misgivings usually arise in the context of discussions about the picturing relation, for it is sometimes held that while we can and do have pictures of fictional entities such as Pickwick and Santa Claus, these pictures cannot properly be said to resemble their subjects. The reason, presumably, is that we cannot discern a resemblance—visual or otherwise—between a material object (the picture) and something which is entirely immaterial (a fictional entity). "When the painting is fictive," Max Black writes, "there can be no question of placing it side-by-side with its subject to check off 'points of resemblance.' "[9] And Joseph Margolis supports this view when he asks, "How can there be a resemblance, an independently discernible resemblance, between an actual object and an intentional, fictional or imaginary object?"[10]

The force of this argument is far from clear. What is abundantly clear, however, is that we commonly assert, and take ourselves to discern, visual resemblances between fictional and nonfictional entities. A portly, ruddy, and white-whiskered individual will readily be said to resemble Santa Claus, and I can easily dress a horse up to look like Pegasus. According to Kendall Walton, a "skinny rhinoceros or a papier-mâché unicorn may quite properly be said to resemble or look like a unicorn, though there is no unicorn which it resembles."[11] This seems perfectly obvious. Why, then, do Black and Margolis deny it?

The simple answer is that they do not altogether deny it. Black merely raises a doubt about the propriety of asserting a resemblance between Pickwick and his portrait, whereas Margolis seems to subscribe to the view that such assertions, while they undoubtedly occur, are not assertions of genuine or actual resemblances. On his view, "where there are no actual

X's, there is no actual resemblance."[12] As a result he contends that the "best we can do with imaginary entities is to hold that they resemble actual entities because, and only in the sense that, their *descriptions* entail that we take them to resemble actual entities."[13] This, we are assured, does nothing to establish that visual resemblance is required for picturing. Quite the contrary, it is taken to establish that pictures of fictional entities need not genuinely resemble what they picture. The mark of a genuine resemblance, presumably, is that it can be "independently" discerned.

What exactly does this demand for independence amount to? And why should anyone think that there are no independently discernible resemblances between Pickwick and actual persons, or between Pickwick and his picture?

One answer often given is that Pickwick, far from being an actual material object, is an intentional object. He is the product or creature of Dickens's fertile imagination. Assertions of resemblance between a picture and its subject, we are told, "must always presuppose the material existence of whatever is represented. For, obviously, a picture *P* cannot resemble *x* if *x* is not an object with a visible appearance; but having a visible appearance presupposes having material existence."[14]

According to this view, since Pickwick is an intentional and not a material object, he cannot have a visible appearance. Moreover, since fictional entities have the properties that they do have only in virtue of the ways in which we describe, imagine, or think of them, they do not really have these properties at all, and so cannot genuinely resemble anything in virtue of them. It is in this sense, presumably, that there can be no "independently discernible" resemblance between a fictional and an actual entity.

But this argument altogether misconstrues the nature of a fictional entity. It is well known that in order to create a fictional object—whether it be a fictional character or a fictional world—an author must imaginatively impute certain properties to an imagined subject. In creating Fagin, for instance, Dickens imagines a person who is greedy, cruel, and exploitative: a calculating, wheedling, and acquisitive person who helps transform Oliver Twist's London into a cold and hostile world. But the cruelty and greed, the exploitation and hostility, are not properties of a different order from those found in the actual world. Rather, Dickens conceives of and describes Oliver's world as having precisely those properties of hardship, squalor, and greed which are to be found in the actual world. And since fictional worlds, like fictional characters, are created by imaginative fiat, the world of Oliver Twist must have certain properties in common with the actual world.

The mere fact, therefore, that Dickens has created an imaginary or fictional world does not entail that all its properties are similarly imaginary, fabricated, or fictional. This becomes clearer, I think, when we distinguish between those properties of a fictional object that are invented, and those that, far from being invented by an author, are to be found in the actual world. Thus, for instance, we have no hesitation at all in maintaining that the properties of the beam transporter in *Star Trek* are not to be found in the actual world, but are invented, fabricated, or fictional. It is, of course, true that in inventing such properties an author may imaginatively combine, in rather special ways, a set of properties which are to be found in the actual world. Nonetheless, we would all readily affirm that there is nothing which has the (composite) properties of a beam transporter in the actual world. In other words, the starship *Enterprise* does not resemble the spaceship *Columbia* in this respect. However, to the extent that both are capable of space travel, have heat shields, and are capable of sustaining life in space, they do resemble each other.

It is tempting, but mistaken, to respond to this conclusion by maintaining that a fictional object does not *really* possess the properties that its author imputes to it. The starship *Enterprise*, someone might say, does not really have a heat shield, whereas *Columbia* does. This, it is suggested, is why they cannot properly be said to resemble each other. The trouble with this rejoinder is that it comes from someone who is blinded by the fact that fictional objects do not possess their properties in the way that material objects do. But it is quite wrong, in my view, to infer from this quite uncontroversial claim that fictional objects do not really have properties. Of course they do. Pickwick is fat and jovial; Fagin thin and cruel; Oliver meek and honest. If these fictional characters did not really have properties, we would be unable to distinguish them from one another.

There is a tendency, I think, to use the word "real" to mean nonfictional, so that a fictional entity and its properties are never considered real. This tendency is reinforced by the doctrine of physicalism, which encourages us to link reality with materiality. The result, of course, is that any immaterial object, whether it be Pickwick or Pegasus, is regarded as unreal. But J. L. Austin has done much to expose the fallacies which inhere in this line of argument.[15] According to Austin, the claim "This is real" remains vacuous until we know what is being referred to. For, as he points out, one and the same object may both be a real *x* and not a real *y*—a real decoy and not a real duck. And the reason, of course, is that what makes something a real decoy is not at all what makes something a real duck. This is why it is perfectly in order to speak of a real fictional entity which is not a real material entity. Pickwick, on my view, really is a fiction and really has the properties which Dickens imputes to him. He has these properties because fictional entities actually acquire their properties through authorial fiat. In this respect, of course, fictional entities are very different from material entities, but this is as it should be.

Contrary to some claims, then, Pickwick really does have a visible appearance.[16] The plain fact of the matter is that Sam can see him, just as Pickwick can see and respond to Sam. Certainly *we* cannot see Pickwick. However, we should not be too impressed by this fact, for it is also true that Pickwick cannot see us, and yet this does nothing to establish that we lack a visible appearance. All that it establishes is that there is no peep-hole between Pickwick's world and our own. Indeed, I am inclined to the view that this deficiency is only ever contingent. It is possible, as readers of Kurt Vonnegut Jr. will know, to have a novel in which a fictional character sees and describes the appearance of his author. It is arguable, too, that actors or even puppets on a stage give us access to the visual appearance of certain fictional characters, but I cannot argue this point at present without appearing to beg the question.[17]

There is no reason, then, why Pickwick cannot really have properties, or why these properties cannot be the same as the properties found in our own nonfictional world. Indeed, there is a very strong semantic reason for supposing that they must be the same; a reason that helps undermine the claim that resemblance is invariably a vacuous predicate.

Any reader of fiction knows that language functions within the fictional world of a novel or play in much the same way as it does outside it. When, in *Far From the Madding Crowd*, Gabriel Oak learns that Bathsheba Everdene has married a one-time sergeant, he correctly infers that there is a certain female person who has entered into a specific contract (wedlock) with an ex-soldier. Clearly, many of the conceptual and logical considerations which apply in understanding a linguistic communication of this sort in the real world apply as well in the imaginary world of the novel. Failing this, the novel would simply be incomprehensible. It follows, then, that since the sentence "She has married a man who was once a sergeant" can be used to have the same (or a closely similar) meaning within and without the fictional world of the novel, that world must be conceived of as furnishing the same experiences or possibilities of experience—that is, the same truth conditions—as the actual world. In some respects at least, therefore, the imaginary world of the novel must be conceived of as having properties in common with the actual world. We must think of it as containing the institutions of marriage and the law, people of the male and female sex, armies, ranks, and so on. Without this the sentence would have a different meaning in the fiction from the meaning which it has when used of the inhabitants of our world.

Of course, not every sentence used within a fictional world will have the same meaning when used in a nonfictional context. The sentence "A worm is coming" means something substantially different in Frank Herbert's *Dune* from what it would mean in a conversation between two anglers in our world. The reason, of course, is that the truth conditions for each statement differ from the one world to the other. Herbert conceives of a world which furnishes a range of different experiences from those to be had in our world: it is a world, *inter alia*, of giant sand creatures—so-called worms—that roam arid deserts, and that the natives of Arrakis use as a mode of transport. The experiences, therefore, which make a "A worm is coming" true on Arrakis are quite different from those which make it true on Earth. Needless to say, this cannot be true of all the sentences used in the novel, for if it were there could be no way of knowing the respects in which Arrakis differs from (or is like) Earth. But we do know this, and we know it because certain of the sentences used by Herbert retain their ordinary sense in the context of the fiction. However, as we have just seen, they can only retain their ordinary meaning if the imaginary world of the novel is conceived of as having certain properties in common with the actual world. Add to this my earlier observation that fictional entities acquire their properties by being conceived of in certain ways, and it becomes abundantly clear that the world of *Dune* must have certain properties in common with the actual world.

It follows from this that any two objects (whether or not they are fictional) which conform to the same description must be said to resemble each other in certain respects. But this is a point to which I shall return later on. For the time being, we should notice that resemblances between fictional worlds and the real world usually hold in many perfectly commonplace respects, most of which are assumed rather than asserted. Indeed, the fictional worlds of novels are taken to resemble our world in most respects unless there are explicit or implicit directives to the contrary. We assume, for instance, that the human beings who populate Pickwick's world have two eyes, four limbs, breathe air and eat food—this despite the fact that Dickens nowhere asserts all of this. And it is only because Richard Adams indicates that Hazel can speak that we know that he does not resemble actual rabbits in this respect. The same is true of pictures. Even though a picture of Pickwick affords only a frontal view of our hero, we nonetheless assume that he resembles actual men to the extent that he has a back to his head, a backbone, and buttocks, despite the fact that these are not explicitly sketched. Unless we assume this, we cannot properly maintain that it is a picture of a (fictional) *man*. Again, it is only because Pegasus is sketched with wings that we know that it does not resemble an actual horse in this respect. Clearly, then, the extent of resemblance between fictional worlds and the real world will vary from one fictional work to another. In all cases, though, there will have to be some resemblances if we are to make sense of these fictional worlds.

We now have some reason to suppose not just that there must be resemblances between fictional and nonfictional entities, but that assertions to this effect are by no means trivial or vacuous. According to some who have written on the topic, the concept of resemblance "is so vague that anything can be said to resemble anything else in some way or other. To demand resemblance between a picture and what it represents . . . is therefore quite trivial since the condition will always be satisfied."[18] And John Searle makes a similar point when he says: "Similarity is a vacuous predicate: any two things are similar in some respects or other."[19] One reaction to this view is to "cast resemblance in a predominantly essentialistic mould" by suggesting that there is a fixed set of properties in virtue of which resemblances hold between certain types of objects.[20] On this account it becomes more plausible to assert a resemblance between any two fictional entities in virtue of their shared nonmateriality, than it would be to assert a resemblance between the world of Anna Karenina and nineteenth-century Russia. It is this view, I think, which underlies Nelson Goodman's famous claim that "a Constable painting of Marlborough Castle is more like any other picture than it is like the Castle."[21]

On my view, though, assertions of resemblance between fictional and actual entities are by no means vacuous. Nor are they made in virtue of a fixed set of properties. Rather, as we shall see in more detail later on, resemblance is always asserted or assumed relative to a variable purpose or point; and the properties invoked in asserting the resemblance are selected with this point in mind.[22] In the present case, I have argued, the point is largely semantic. It is because we wish to preserve the standard meanings of the words and phrases used in a novel, and because we wish to understand the arrangement of lines and colors in a picture, that we assume or assert resemblances in virtue of a specific range of properties.

The Recognition of Resemblances

Not only do fictional objects have properties, but we have learned that they must have properties in common with the actual objects of our world. Given this, one might consider my case complete. It would seem not only that fictional objects can resemble, but that they must resemble, the actual world. Nor are such assertions of resemblance trivial, for resemblances, we have seen, are always asserted relative to a certain point; and it is knowledge of this point which informs the assertion.

But a good deal remains to be said. The demand, you will remember, is for an "independently discernible" resemblance between fictional and nonfictional entities, and I have yet to show that this is possible. All that we have so far seen is that we cannot deny this possibility either on the grounds that the properties of fictional objects do not really inhere in them, or on the grounds that these properties are of a "different order" from the properties of material objects.

Nor should we think that the properties of fictional entities, and the resemblances asserted in terms of them, cannot be identified independently of an author's private imaginings. To suppose this is to subscribe to a totally fatuous view of the status of fiction. One has only to point to the fact that it is some time now since Dickens died, and yet we are able to consult our bookshelves in order to ascertain the characteristics of Fagin and his underworld. Creatures of fiction may, and often do, acquire the status of what Karl Popper has called objective knowledge.[23] Their characteristics and peculiarities are recorded in books, pictures, and video cassettes, from which they may be retrieved at will.

Thus construed, there clearly are independently discernible resemblances between fictional worlds and the actual one. For all that, though, it can still be argued that fictional objects only have, and can only be known to have, the properties that they do have, in virtue of the ways in which we imagine, think of, or describe them. Their properties, one might say, are only apprehended under certain descriptions: descriptions which are (for the most part) furnished by their authors. It follows, therefore, that in this sense at least resemblances between fictional and nonfictional entities cannot be discerned independently of authorial descriptions.

Spelled out in this way, it is clear, I think, that resemblances between fictional and nonfictional entities are not independently discernible. One has always to rely on authorial descriptions in order to discern them.

But why, someone might ask, should this very obvious fact be taken to show that there can be no genuine resemblances between fictional and actual objects?

The correct answer is that it does not show this at all. Indeed, it should be clear from what I have already said that all informative assertions of resemblance are made relative to a certain point, and it is our awareness of this point which determines the respects in virtue of which the resemblance is asserted. When these respects or properties are expressed in language, we can correctly say not just that we select the respects in virtue of which to assert a resemblance, but that we do so under a certain description.

It would seem, then, that the discernment of a resemblance is often dependent on certain descriptions. This is not to say that objects do not share properties independently of them. Of course they do. Nor do I wish to deny that we can notice certain likenesses without recourse to description. My claim is only that many genuine resemblances are discerned under certain descriptions, and are only usefully asserted because they are discerned in this way. Thus, for example, the assertion "This leaf resembles the orange," while perhaps true, remains largely vacuous and unhelpful until you know in what respects the assertion is being made: that is, until you know under what descriptions the resemblance was discerned. And it is a description that will vary with one's aims or purposes. A botanist with botanical interests may assert a resemblance in respect of cell structure or the presence of transpiration pores. On the other hand, artists or interior decorators, with their interest in visual appearances, will be much more likely to assert the resemblance in respect of color, or size, or shape.

It stands to reason, then, that those botanists who are interested in finding plants of the same cell structure will examine them under this and related descriptions. Here the discernment of the required resemblance depends crucially on the description under which it is discerned, for it is this description which guides or directs the botanist's eye and gives him or her some idea of what to look for. This is true not only of resemblances asserted by botanists and other scientists, but of almost all the resemblances which we discern and assert in our everyday lives. Familiarity with the objects of our environment and the purposes they serve inclines us to look at them in certain familiar ways and under certain familiar descriptions. This is why when someone says, "Fred resembles an elephant," we normally assume that the resemblance is asserted in certain characteristic respects: in respect, say, of size, weight, and general clumsiness, rather than in respect of skin pigmentation and length of eyelashes.

How we normally look at and describe persons and elephants is very largely determined by the values and interests which we have at any given time. It is true, of course, that these may change. Elephants, for instance, may come to be prized for the quality of their ivory rather than for their immensity and bulk, in which case we will observe and compare them not in terms of size and weight, but in respect, perhaps, of the color and grain of their ivory. It is in this way that our interests and values determine the descriptions under which we discern resemblances. In my view, if a resemblance seems obvious and is discerned, so to speak, at first glance, this is frequently because the respects in which, and the descriptions under which, the resemblance is discerned have become familiar, and are in a sense culturally ingrained.[24]

Like all perception, the perception of resemblances is intentional and depends crucially on the concepts, beliefs, and descriptions that we bring to it. The fact, then, that we cannot discern resemblances between fictional and nonfictional entities independently of an author's descriptions scarcely constitutes a criticism of the view that such resemblances genuinely obtain.

But perhaps I have missed the point. It might be suggested that resemblances between fictional and nonfictional objects are not independently discernible because there is, and can be, no perceptual access to fictional objects. A fictional object simply is not the sort of thing that one can isolate and examine in a laboratory so as to apprehend its properties. In order to do this, one must always rely on the descriptions of some author or other. It is for this reason, then, that there can be no genuine resemblances between fictional and nonfictional entities. The best we can do with fictional entities, Joseph Margolis tells us, is to hold that "their *descriptions* entail that we take them to resemble actual entities."[25]

This view poses peculiar problems. It now appears that fictional entities cannot enter into relations of resemblance because of the way in which they are apprehended; because, that is, of the way in which we come to know them. But this maneuver totally distorts our ordinary concept of resemblance. Whereas resemblances are normally asserted if, and only if, two objects have at least one property in common, we are now told that even if a fictional object has properties in common with an actual one, it still cannot resemble it—this merely because the two objects and their properties are not apprehended in the same way. It would seem, then, that the concept of resemblance has been radically revised, but that no reason has been given for this revision. On the face of it, it remains a perfectly arbitrary move.

If what I have said until now is correct, there is no reason at all why Pickwick cannot properly be said to resemble an actual person in certain respects, or why the world of Raskolnikov cannot be said to resemble nineteenth-century Russia. In my view, the recognition of such resemblances is necessary if we are ever to learn about our world from fiction. This is so for two reasons. First, an awareness of a resemblance between the fictional and the real world is alone responsible for the belief that, even though the fiction does not describe the actual world, it does nonetheless have some "bearing on" or relevance to it. And this sets the stage for learning, for unless readers can discern such a relation, the novel will be regarded as wholly irrelevant to their actual situation, and they will not be able to learn anything about it from the literary work. Second, we have already seen that unless readers recognize certain resemblances between the fictional and the real world they will simply be unable to understand the language of fiction, and so will be unable to learn from it.

Beliefs from Fiction

With all of this in hand, it is at last possible to say something about the ways in which we learn from fiction.

There are, we have seen, innumerable respects in which the imaginary world of a novel can resemble the actual world. Even the least lifelike of novels, whether it be J. R. R. Tolkien's *The Hobbit* or Doris Lessing's *Shikasta*, resemble the actual world in many respects. They describe worlds of hills and dales, of trees, air, and water; of birds, fish, and fowl. Like actual people, their inhabitants have aspirations and ambitions, joys and fears; they can think and plan, they can love and mate, walk and run, talk, sing, laugh, eat.

It was, of course, Socrates who belabored the seductive nature of *mimesis*. And there can be no doubt that the proliferation of lifelike detail in Tolkien's or any other novel can lure readers into the uncritical adoption of certain factual beliefs about human beings. However, it would be quite mistaken to think that we acquire such beliefs simply by noticing resemblances between hobbits and ourselves. In order to notice such resemblances one must *already* know or believe that hobbits and human beings possess specific properties. Simply by noticing such a resemblance, therefore, one does not learn anything new or acquire fresh beliefs about human beings (other, of course, than that they resemble hobbits). But even if we agree with this conclusion, we might still be tempted to suppose that one arrives at such beliefs analogically, inductively — by what John Hospers has called "a kind of transference" from the fiction.[26] The view is that, since hobbits have certain properties in common with human beings, and behave in cer-

tain ways because of these properties, we infer that people who find themselves in a similar situation will behave in the same way. Induction, it is
suggested, is central to the way in which we learn about our world from
fiction.[27]

But this account is wholly inadequate. The trouble is that induction
alone cannot furnish new knowledge or fresh beliefs; of itself, it does not
enable us to learn anything at all. The plain fact of the matter, as I have
already argued, is that induction merely involves the application in new
situations of what we *already* know or believe.[28] When, for instance, I eat a
piece of bread, I unhesitatingly apply my past experience of bread to the
piece that I am about to ingest. I infer that it too will nourish me. Now, if
one believes that one learns from an inductive inference of this sort, one has
to maintain that this inference informs me of something about which I was
previously unaware. But this is odd. It seems obvious that I know, and have
known for a long time, that bread (this piece included) will nourish me. To
suppose that I do not know this is either to suppose that I have good reason
to doubt it—which I do not have; or it is to suppose that anything which
can be doubted cannot be known, in which case we remove all possibility
of empirical knowledge.

Now there may, of course, be cases in which the resemblances between
the imaginary world of a novel and the actual world are regarded as so
clear, obvious, and transparent that inductive inferences about the actual
world are drawn from the novel. Clearly, though, such inferences only
occur because we already know or believe that what we have learned of
fictional situations applies to their actual counterparts. And if we already
know or believe this, then, on my view, we do not learn anything by
inferring inductively from the one to the other.

It is only when there is some doubt whether what we have learned of
the fictional world applies in an actual situation that we are able to learn
about our world from the fiction. In such a case, though, we do not rely on
induction for the acquisition of empirical knowledge or factual beliefs.
Rather, since we doubt the applicability of our past experience (of the
fiction) on this occasion, we must conjecture, imagine, or hypothesize that
our experience of the fictional world applies in an actual situation. It is not
induction, but our ability to hypothesize, which is brought into play.

An uncritical reader may simply assent to such a hypothesis and so
come to believe a certain proposition about our world. This does of course
happen. More critical readers, however, will assess the hypothesis either in
terms of the extent to which it coheres with their established beliefs, or by

tentatively projecting it on to the actual world. If, in the latter case, it is supported by the readers' experiences—that is, if it enables them to negotiate the world more successfully and to make sense of objects and events in their environment—they will adopt it, believe it, and in the light of corroborating experience, will gradually come to regard it as knowledge.

What a rational reader cannot do is appeal to features internal to the fiction in order to justify hypotheses and beliefs about the actual world.[29] This simply because fictional statements are not assertions about the actual world and do not purport to convey information about it. To some this must suggest that fiction does not really *impart* knowledge at all, but only conveys or suggests propositions which have to be independently corroborated. But if this is true of fiction, it must also be true of the humble reference book, for it is clear that a reference book can only be said to impart knowledge about the actual world if we are justified in believing that it is reliable. It goes without saying, though, that our knowledge of its reliability is not acquired from our experience of the book itself. It is acquired from a range of totally different experiences. And yet we readily maintain that reference books impart knowledge. The same courtesy should, in my view, be extended to fiction.

It is plain, I think, that whether or not our readers adopt a critical attitude in assenting to a hypothesis derived from fiction, they will, in each case, have learned something from the fiction. What one learns may, of course, be false, and the great Socratic fear is that the proliferation in the novel or play of lifelike detail will lure the reader into accepting various untested propositions. It is clear from what I have said that this remains a possibility, although it is by no means as inevitable as Socrates at times suggests. Whether a reader adopts a critical attitude to the hypotheses derived from, or suggested by, the work, will depend on a range of social and psychological factors: factors which I cannot consider at present.

Skills from Fiction

It would seem, then, that readers acquire factual beliefs and propositional knowledge from fiction in much the way that scientists gather knowledge about the fabric of the universe. Both rely extensively on hypotheses and their corroboration. The only difference is that scientists can and do invent their own hypotheses, whereas readers of fiction are very much less inventive. They merely borrow the fabrications of authors, and their sole contribution is to conjecture or hypothesize that these fabrications apply to the actual world. This difference aside, though, it would seem that I have reduced the epistemology of fiction to that of science, and that I therefore regard the acquisition of factual beliefs and propositional knowledge in each case as fundamentally similar.

To some this must appear implausible. We learn from fiction, we are told, in a way which is much richer than the mere dispassionate formulation and testing of hypotheses.[30] We become involved in the fiction, "caught up in" it, we "lose ourselves" in the lives and situations of its creatures. We "identify" with them, share their hopes, fears, and joys. This, we are told, contributes to and enhances the learning experience. Since I have so far ignored this dimension, the view is taken that my account of learning from fiction must be inadequate.

Although there is considerable substance to this objection, I want to insist that my account so far is incomplete rather than seriously defective. Until now I have attempted only to explain the acquisition of factual beliefs and propositional knowledge from fiction. These, I have argued, are not acquired analogically or inductively, but are the products of certain speculations induced by the fiction. Now, if one believes, as I do, that a speculative, conjectural, or fanciful element is essential to the growth of our body of empirical knowledge and beliefs,[31] then, in this fundamental respect at least, the acquisition of factual beliefs from fiction will resemble their acquisition in science. If this is what is meant by the claim that I have "reduced the epistemology of fiction to that of science," then I must remain entirely unrepentant.

Nonetheless—and here the objection hints at something important—factual beliefs form only a minor and relatively insignificant component of what we learn from fiction. Fiction is not, for the most part, a source of propositional beliefs and knowledge about the world. We consult encyclopaedias and chemistry, geography, and history books, not novels and plays, when we require such information. Certainly fiction is often lauded as a source of insight and knowledge, but a closer look reveals that it is praised for the practical and empathic knowledge that it affords and seldom, if ever, for propositional knowledge. From fiction, I have said, we may acquire certain strategic and conceptual skills (practical knowledge); and we may learn what it feels like to be caught up in certain situations (empathic beliefs and knowledge). It is when we ask how all of this is possible that we are forced to tell a story which is very different from the one told in the case of factual beliefs and propositional knowledge: a story, moreover, which emphasizes our imaginative and emotional involvement in the fiction.

There can be little doubt that readers often respond to fiction by imagining the various events and situations described by an author. Tolstoy's words, one might say, become the occasion of a reader's imaginative entry into the world of his fictional creatures; one derivatively imagines the world of Anna Karenina by considering Tolstoy's descriptions without a mind to their truth-value. In other words, one considers what it is like to be caught up in Anna's situation, one considers her quandaries, her perplexities and moral dilemmas, and arguably as a result, one is able to experience the dread and hopelessness of her situation. Such a reader may very well acquire certain empathic beliefs about what it is like to be in this or a similar situation. It is partly as a result of these beliefs, I now wish to argue, that the reader is able to acquire certain skills from the work.

How is this possible? Well, consider the following example.[32] Suppose that I want to retrieve a ball which has lodged itself in the upper branches of a walnut tree. I gaze upward trying to fathom which branches will best provide a foothold and which a secure grip. Clearly, if I can imaginatively re-create the situation—that is, if I can "see" myself in my mind's eye moving from this branch to that, holding here and stepping there, and if I can imagine what it feels like to stand on a high, swaying branch while reaching for a ball, I will not only have some idea of, but will have developed what is in effect a complex hypothesis about, what it is like to be in such a situation. To the extent that I assent to this hypothesis, I may be said to have acquired certain empathic beliefs about what it is like to retrieve a ball from the upmost branches of a tree. Not only do these beliefs allow me to construe my predicament in a certain way, but they also allow me to develop plans of action appropriate to it. I will now attend to what I believe are the likely difficulties in the situation, the possible risks, and I will try to conceive of ways of avoiding them.

Of course, the best-laid plans can and do go awry, and in this case I could break my neck simply because my imaginings, and the empathic beliefs derived from them, are wayward and inaccurate. As a result I acquire a range of inappropriate expectations about my task, and this, of course, is the key to failure. Usually, though, our imaginings are guided and constrained by what we already know, and if the resultant empathic beliefs cohere with present or past experiences, we will be tempted to rely on them. They will be used as a foundation on which to base our understanding of, and our actions in, the situation. Those of us, therefore, who have climbed the masts of sailing ships, or have clung to a rope off the Caroline Face of Mount Cook, are better placed to gauge the accuracy of beliefs about what it is like to retrieve a ball from the upmost branches of a tree. Such persons can claim a certain insight into the situation—an understanding bred both of their imaginative involvement in it, and of their past experience.

My claim, of course, is that much the same thing happens when we respond imaginatively to fiction. Readers of *Anna Karenina* do not only imagine or re-create the heroine's quandaries, but given sufficient interest, they actually ponder and explore them. They imagine what it is like to be assailed by such problems, they feel the fright and despair that accompany them, and, arguably as a result, they are able to discern their overwhelming complexity.

Clearly, then, those readers who are curious enough will have at hand a set of hypotheses about what it is like to be ensnared in a situation akin to Anna Karenina's. Like all hypotheses, these may tentatively be projected on to the world, and if they enable us to make sense of specific events and situations, they will most likely be adopted or believed. Empathic beliefs of this sort will no doubt be assessed in terms of the extent to which they cohere with our past and future experiences. If they do cohere with our past experience, with what we already know or believe of people in similar nonimaginary situations, we will not only regard the action of the novel as plausible, but we might even claim to know what it would be like to be in a situation such as Anna's. Still more, empathic beliefs of this sort will mediate a reader's assessment of the risks involved in the heroine's various responses to her predicament, and from time to time such readers will no doubt offer solutions of their own, which are then tentatively imposed on the fictional situation in order to assess their adequacy. As we saw in the case of our vagrant ball, readers who engage in this imaginative activity acquire what might be termed a set of practical hypotheses: that is to say, they have at their disposal a range of possible ways of responding to, or negotiating, a certain sort of problem.

Needless to say, though, not all of these envisaged responses will be adequate to the problem. Indeed, some may be rejected without ever being tried in practice; rather in the way that, after further consideration, one rejects potential moves in a game of chess. Others, however, will be put to the test. If found wanting, they will simply be abandoned, but if they are helpful they will be tried on successive occasions, will eventually come to be relied upon, and will be adopted as proven strategies.

Clearly, then, if the problems which confront fictional characters are seen to arise in the actual world, any reader who has acquired empathic beliefs pertinent to such problems may well be more aware of, and hence more sensitive to, the difficulties involved in solving them. If this turns out to be the case, we are justified in saying that the fiction has imparted empathic *knowledge* of the situation, that it has given readers a "pretty good idea of," or enabled them to know something about, what it feels like to be ensnared in such a situation.

It is interesting to notice, though, that although fictional literature deals extensively with the quandaries of creatures who are not unlike ourselves, it does not always arrive at or even suggest definitive solutions to these problems. Indeed, it is partly because we regard Anna Karenina's final response to her unhappy situation as wildly mistaken that the novel is both poignant and deeply tragic.

In the light of this it might be considered a curious fact about human beings that they find fiction interesting. After all, the best fiction seldom offers solutions to pressing practical problems, but merely explores and elaborates human predicaments and frailties. Why, someone might ask, do we find this so absorbing? Why do we bother with it? Part of the explanation, I think, is to be found in a well-known, but philosophically neglected, feature of human nature. People are deeply and persistently curious about each other. They long for and often pursue the details of one another's lives. Such knowledge may, of course, be profoundly useful, for in discovering how others manage their affairs, conduct their lives, and tame their environment, we can learn from both their successes and their failures. And we often respond benevolently to such knowledge either by lauding success or by helping people when they fail and are in distress.

There is, unfortunately, a darker side to such curiosity. At times we hunt out the minutiae of private lives, speculate and gossip about them. Sometimes we gloat at the disgrace of others, and in a variety of subtle ways help to perpetuate it. It is for this reason, I think, that people are generally shy of the interest we take in them, and shun our curiosity.

Either way, whether our curiosity about others is benevolent or malicious, it is seldom dormant. We are, I think engaged in a protracted quest to satisfy a seemingly insatiable interest: a quest by no means confined to back-fence chatter and the public lounge, but alive and well, I am sure, in the more hallowed preserves of the University Club and Bellamys.

It is alive, too, in libraries everywhere. On my view, we read and are intrigued by fiction because we are, at root, profoundly interested in people. Whereas actual people throw cloaks of secrecy about themselves and are hostile to prying eyes, their imaginary counterparts are unoffended by our curiosity. It is this, I would venture, which inclines us to embrace fiction as one legitimate source of intimate knowledge about people. After all, it is not as if creatures of fiction are unlike the flesh-and-blood people who populate our world. They are, it is true, the offspring of the imagination, but it is an imagination guided by an author's experience of actual people. And as long as some of these experiences coincide with our own, we will, to that extent, find the characters plausible and may become imaginatively "caught up in" their trials, quandaries, and perplexities. My argument has been that it is our imaginative participation in the fiction which furnishes us with empathic beliefs, and, partly as a result, with a set of practical hypotheses for tackling similar quandaries in the actual world. Such hypotheses may amount either to possible ways of *considering* such problems, or they may amount to possible ways of *tackling* them. Either way, they help furnish practical rather than purely propositional knowledge and belief.

Cognitive Skills and World Views

Not that this is the only way of acquiring skills from fiction. What I have called cognitive or conceptual (as opposed to strategic) skills are acquired in a very different way: a way which often depends on the prior acquisition from the fiction of factual beliefs. Suppose, for example, that because of Raskolnikov's folly in *Crime and Punishment* one comes to believe that human reason is weak and that faith in Christ will alone solve mankind's problems. As a result, one may be more inclined to think of philosophers as fundamentally misguided, self-deceived, and even as bent on their own destruction. Similarly, if, in the light of Jane Austen's *Emma*, one comes to believe that pride breeds self-deception, one may come to look for, and for the first time notice, the respects in which proud people are self-deceived. Again, if because of Dostoyevsky's novel one believes that human selfishness is frequently lost in times of ordeal, one may come to think of ordeals not just as a threat to human life and limb, but as a way of overcoming one's self-centerdness.

Clearly, then, the factual beliefs which we acquire from fiction may challenge and undermine our normal ways of construing the world and understanding ourselves. They may furnish us with new ways of articulating our experiences, and with new ways of classifying and relating the objects and affairs which surround us. As a result we may come to perceive qualities of, and similarities between, objects and events, where these were previously unnoticed. It is in this way that fiction at times enables us to "re-arrange" our world, to "re-model" it and fashion it anew.

Of course, the mere acquisition of factual beliefs will not ensure the acquisition of corresponding conceptual or cognitive skills. Indeed, no number of factual beliefs, whether true or false, can ever guarantee the acquisition of a skill. For even if all the facts of, say, plumbing were made known to me, I would still at the very least have to try them in practice before I could be said to have mastered the skills of plumbing. Similarly, it is only by applying or trying to apply the factual beliefs acquired from fiction in looking at or thinking about the world that a particular *way of looking* or *way of thinking* can become an acquired skill.

In the present instance, then, readers can only acquire conceptual or cognitive skills from fiction by tentatively projecting the factual beliefs gleaned from the work on to the world about them. They try to see specific objects, events, and relationships in terms of these new beliefs, and they attempt to rethink, perhaps to explain, what was previously baffling or bewildering. If their application of these beliefs is met with obvious rewards, if it helps them to dispel puzzles and doubts, to make sense of or come to terms with enigmas of one sort or another, they are likely to adopt these ways of thinking and observing. And when once adopted and entrenched, they can correctly be described as acquired skills.

However, if readers find that their application of such beliefs is unhelpful, they are hardly likely to adopt the resultant ways of thinking about or looking at the world. Thus, for instance, one might be tempted, in the light of Raskolnikov's behavior, to think of human reason as peculiarly flaccid and fallible. But if this is not borne out by one's experience, or if it does not help to explain why reason often enables us to solve problems in a way that unreason does not, one is hardly likely to adopt this way of thinking. In other words, if a particular factual belief acquired from fiction and tentatively projected on to the world does not enable us to negotiate the world the better, we will reject this mode of thinking and observing.

I make no claims for this being the only way in which conceptual or cognitive skills are acquired from fiction. It seems obvious that they can also be acquired with the help of metaphors, and it is arguable that metaphors invite us to look at things in a new way without first imparting factual beliefs about those things. Precisely how metaphors work is a vast and important question that properly forms part of this study. It is a question that will occupy us for the next three chapters. The crucial point to be noticed at present, however, is that there clearly are many different ways in which we learn from fiction, and hence from the products of the fanciful imagination. Conceptual and strategic skills, we have seen, are not learned in the same way, and both, of course, are acquired in ways other than the way in which we glean factual beliefs and propositional knowledge from fiction.

The Exploration of Values

And what of values? At least part of the charm and fascination of fictional literature resides in the fact that it forces us to look anew at, and to reconsider, certain of our attitudes and values. All sorts of values are up for scrutiny—economic, ecological, intellectual, architectural, religious, and moral values are only some that become candidates for exploration and reassessment. Nonetheless, moral values enjoy a certain primacy, and it is these that I am concerned with at present.

Fiction, I think it true to say, often explores, teases, and tests our moral standards and attitudes. Occasionally a work will undermine attitudes, confound our moral beliefs, and instill new or different moral values. And in such situations a reader can properly be said to have learned something from the fiction. No doubt there will be those who think that the acquisition of values never amounts to the acquisition of knowledge, and that such learning can therefore have little to do with the topic of this chapter—fiction and the growth of knowledge. But such an objection is premature. Even though I cannot argue the case here, it seems that we can know that certain actions are right or wrong. Certainly we often claim to know this, just as we often claim to know how we ought to behave. Equally important for my argument is the fact that we can and do come to know that to make a moral decision in a certain situation is often complicated and difficult. We can come to know, too, that we are no longer as certain as we once were about our moral attitudes; and, of course, we can come to know that we have revised these attitudes. Such knowledge, I now want to argue, is often acquired from fiction, and is acquired in a number of different ways.

First of all, we know that factual beliefs are often integrally related to values, so that to acquire a factual belief from fiction is, on occasions, to acquire a value of one sort or another. If, as a result of seeing Athol Fugard's *Marigolds in August*, I come to believe that the South African political system dehumanizes black people, I thereby acquire a certain moral attitude toward that system. I think of it as wrong, iniquitous, or unjust. As a result I now know that I have a particular, perhaps a revised, moral attitude toward the South African political system.

There is, though, an altogether different way of acquiring values from fiction. Suppose, for instance, that in the light of Defoe's *Robinson Crusoe*, I come to think of isolation no longer as unproductive and arduous, but as a spur to human resourcefulness. Now, if I set great store by the latter, if I value it highly, I am very likely to place a similar value on isolation, which I now see as promoting human resourcefulness. Of course, such a transfer of values need not always be something of which I am aware. I might simply discover that my attitude toward isolation has changed, and, on reflection, I might locate *Robinson Crusoe* as the source of that change. It should be stressed, too, that I need not transfer my values in this way at all, and that whether I do will depend on what I happen to know or believe. Thus, for instance, if I believe that isolation is responsible for much human suffering, or that it is inconducive to good mental health, I am hardly likely to value it very highly, no matter how highly I regard human resourcefulness.

There clearly is a sense, then, in which *Robinson Crusoe*, rather than pontificating on the virtues and ills of human loneliness, invites us to reconsider, explore, and test our current attitudes to isolation. The best fiction, or at least the fiction which earns the most praise, seldom pronounces decisively on moral issues. It does not offer dogmatic or authoritative solutions to problems of value. Rather, as we shall see, fiction is often at its most exciting, and instructs us most adequately in matters of value, when it explores moral problems and brings its readers to see them in their fullness and complexity. And this brings us to a third—perhaps the most important —way of acquiring values from fiction.

The comprehending reader, I suggested earlier, imaginatively re-creates the fictional world delineated by an author, and in so doing "enters into" the life of that world. We consider what it is like to be faced with the problems which confront the hero, the villain, the school master and his mistress. We share their fears, elation, and sadness, and the tears that we shed are bred of a close and intimate understanding of their situation.[33] Step by step we explore their quandaries, their dilemmas, the consequences of their untoward actions, and, as we saw earlier, the resultant empathic beliefs and knowledge enable us to develop strategies for negotiating similar situations in the actual world. Not only this, for readers are also in a postion to grasp the extent and force of the moral problems that assail fictional characters ensnared in such situations. They are able, for instance, to appreciate the extent to which Raskolnikov becomes a victim of circumstance, and they are made acutely aware of Anna Karenina's anguish in having to choose between alternative courses of action.

It is plain, I think, that when once we involve ourselves imaginatively in Anna Karenina's world, we become acquainted not only with the complexities, but also with the exigencies, of her situation. As a result we are brought to consider the extent of her duties and obligations, and in so doing we invariably ponder the moral question, "How ought she to behave?" It is in attempting to answer this question that our own values are held up for scrutiny and reassessment, and it goes without saying that our answer to the question will determine whether we retain these values.

Clearly, then, whatever the values extracted from the fiction, it is not as if Tolstoy instructs us in morality or imposes his own moral values on us. Rather, he brings us to reconsider our existing values and attitudes by tempting us to apply these to a complex and very lifelike situation, which he has sketched in abundant detail and with consummate skill. If a reader believes that his or her values are adequate to the fictional situation, they will merely have been reinforced by the novel and will remain unaltered. At times, though, one may come to believe, indeed know, that one's attitudes are unsatisfactory: that they do not do justice to the complexity of the situation. As a result there is a shift or alteration of values. One might acquire new, very specific, moral principles, or, rather more likely, one may modify existing principles or their application in the light of the fiction. Thus, for instance, one may now believe, even know, that adultery is not always as wrong as one had previously supposed; or one may believe that one ought always to acquaint oneself with the facts of an adulterous situation before venturing to judge it.

Of course, fiction is not the only source of new or altered values. Actual experience of the real world can have a similar effect, for when one is ensnared in a morally complex and demanding situation, one's attitudes and values are invariably called into question. The difference is that fiction allows us to do so with minimal cost to ourselves and others. Our vicarious concern for a favorite heroine, the moral judgments we make about her and the moral decisions we take on her behalf, the scorn and derision, the praise and blame that we heap upon her, can all occur without the anguish and painful consequences that are often attendant in the actual world. We acquire moral insights without having to live in the situations which occasion them. What is more, they are insights which are often more easily acquired from fiction than from their actual counterparts. A narrative sequence can be so designed as to give us much more knowledge about a complex fictional situation than we could reasonably hope to attain if ensnared in its nonfictional equivalent. Thus, for instance, when reading *Crime and Punishment* we do not only see matters from Raskolnikov's point of view, but from that of Sasha and Razumikhin as well. It would, of course, be very difficult for a man guilty of a crime such as Raskolnikov's in the actual world to adopt so broad a perspective.

There clearly are a number of different ways in which we acquire values from fiction. In my view, it is when readers become imaginatively "caught up in" the fiction that it best allows them to explore and reassess their values. And this, it seems, is an important aspect of fiction, for in fostering reasoning of this sort, fiction helps sharpen our sensitivity to moral issues and increases our awareness of the sorts of quandaries and difficulties encountered by people who would otherwise be the victims of ill-considered judgments. Good fiction, it is sometimes said, explores the human condition, but this, Hilary Putnam correctly contends, is just another, somewhat more pretentious, way of saying that it explores the moral problems and dilemmas which many of us experience in our actual lives.[34] Its worth here is to be found not just in imparting values, but in getting its readers to grasp the difficulties involved in adequately judging certain human situations.

Conclusion

In all, there is no one way in which we learn from literary works of art. There is, rather, a *pot-pourri* of ways, a veritable medley of methods, for acquiring beliefs, knowledge, skills, and values of one sort or another. Each of these methods needs careful scrutiny, and while I take myself to have pointed to some of their salient features, much work remains to be done.

One thing that must now be apparent is that propositional beliefs and knowledge form only a fragment of what is learned from fiction. Still more, they are by no means the most useful aspect of what is learned. The practical knowledge acquired from a fictional work, as well as one's empathic knowledge or beliefs about the situations akin to those in which fictional creatures find themselves, is, we have seen, profoundly useful. And yet, such knowledge is not scientific.

This is important, for as I said at the outset of this chapter, philosophers have tended in the wake of the Enlightenment to the view that because propositional knowledge and belief are the stuff of science, they alone constitute the province of epistemology. Much of this chapter may be seen as antidote to that view: one which is bred of my attempt to resuscitate a romantic epistemology.

SEVEN

The Problem of Metaphor

The fanciful imagination is never more obviously at work than when it coins a good metaphor.

This is why Enlightenment thinkers choose to denounce metaphor, and why the later romantics glorify it. To the romantics, metaphor turns out to be a kind of salvation: it is the incarnation of many of their claims about the powers of the imagination. The creativity of metaphor, its cognitive and affective powers, leads some to the view that metaphor constitutes the fabric of our world: that it permeates all experience, molds our language, and shapes our thought. It is a view that is most cogently stated by Nietzsche when he tells us that

When we talk about trees, colours, snow and flowers, we believe we know something about the things themselves, and yet we only possess metaphors of the things, and these metaphors do not in the least correspond to the original essentials.[1]

On his view, metaphor is not primarily a linguistic phenomenon. It is the imaginative process of coming to make sense of the world. The "creator of language," we are told,

calls to his help the most daring metaphors. A nerve stimulus, first transformed into a percept! First metaphor! The percept again copied into a sound! Second metaphor![2]

And from all of this he concludes, as I pointed out earlier, that truth is no more than "a mobile army of metaphors" that "after long usage seem to a nation fixed, canonic and binding."[3]

According to Nietzsche, then, there is nothing at all to be said in favor of the Enlightenment emphasis on the literal truths of science as the key to an otherwise elusive reality. Science itself is a bundle of metaphors, and there is no literal truth or literal meaning. To think that there is such a thing is either to ignore or else to forget the origins of our language and experience in metaphor. Science, according to this view, does not guarantee truth. It is, rather, a self-deluded attempt to assure ourselves of order in a disordered universe.[4]

But romantic thought has not found favor everywhere, and to some these claims on behalf of metaphor must seem nothing less than the height of extravagance. As lords of the Enlightenment, Thomas Hobbes and John Locke led devastating attacks on metaphor. According to Hobbes, the primary function of language is to communicate our knowledge about the world. Since this can only be achieved with the help of literal truths, whenever we "use words metaphorically; that is, in other sense than that they are ordained for; and thereby deceive others," we do not only fail to convey genuine knowledge, but we subvert reason and are guilty of "sedition" and "contempt."[5] Locke agrees, and in a well-known passage denounces both the fanciful imagination and its progeny. On his view,

Since wit and fancy finds easier entertainment in the world than dry truth and real knowledge, *figurative speeches* and allusion in language will hardly be admitted as *an* imperfection or *abuse* of it. I confess, in discourses where we seek rather pleasure and delight than information and improvement, such ornaments as are borrowed from them can scarce pass for faults. But yet, if we would speak of things as they are, we must allow that all the art of rhetoric, besides order and clearness, all the artificial and figurative applications of words eloquence hath invented, are for nothing else but to insinuate wrong *ideas*, move the passions, and thereby mislead the judgement, and so indeed are perfect cheat; and therefore . . . wholly to be avoided and, where truth and knowledge are concerned, cannot but be thought a great fault either of the language or person that makes use of them.[6]

The same mistrust of metaphor is to be found in this century—most obviously in the work of the logical positivists. Their rigid distinction between the cognitive and emotive functions of language led them to banish metaphor (as a typically unverifiable utterance) to the wastebin of emotive utterances. Thus, for instance, A. J. Ayer seems to agree that if a poet's statements "have no literal meaning, they are not subject to any criteria of truth and falsehood: but they may still serve to express or arouse emotion."[7] In point of fact, Ayer tells us, it is

very rare for a literary artist to produce sentences which have no literal meaning. And where this does occur, the sentences are carefully chosen for their rhythm and balance. If the author writes nonsense, it is because he considers it most suitable for bringing about the effects for which his writing is designed.[8]

On Ayer's view, metaphor is no more than a variety of nonsense, congenitally incapable of bearing a meaning or enjoying cognitive content. Metaphors have an affective dimension, but according to him they have nothing to say, no message to impart.

Although logical positivism has long since been discredited, its view of metaphor still survives. So, too, does the romantic glorification of the trope. It is hardly surprising, then, to find that current theorizing about metaphor moves in two very different directions. In the one direction lies the romantic view that all language, and hence all meaning, is metaphorical; in the other lies the view, bred of empiricism and the Enlightenment, that there is no such thing as metaphorical meaning. Both of these positions are ably and persuasively presented in the work of major contemporary philosophers. The first—that all meaning is metaphorical—is, I shall contend, basic to deconstruction, and is to be found in the writings of Jacques Derrida. The second—that there is no such thing as metaphorical meaning—is to be found in a widely acclaimed article by Donald Davidson. Both views are influential, both mistaken.

In order to discuss these positions adequately, it is necessary to begin by considering a widely held view—some might say a commonsense view—of the relation between metaphorical and literal discourse. It is one to which I certainly subscribe, and one, moreover, which gives considerable impetus to both Derrida's and Davidson's writings on metaphor. Derrida reacts negatively to it; Davidson appears to embrace and elevate it. Both use it as a springboard for their theories. It is with an explanation, elaboration, and partial defense of this view that I shall begin.

The Literal and the Metaphorical

On the commonsense view, metaphor is first and foremost a linguistic phenomenon. It involves the use, in a specific context, of a sentence or set of sentences in a way which encourages us to think of something or other in terms which are appropriate to something else.

We can recognize that an utterance is a metaphor only if we know from its context that it should not be taken literally, and this, of course, requires familiarity with the literal meanings of at least some of the words and phrases deployed in the utterance. Equally obvious is the fact that we cannot understand or be appropriately affected by a metaphor unless we are acquainted with the literal meanings of the terms used within it. Were this not so, one could replace any word in a metaphor with any other, and still not alter the meaning and effect of the utterance. But this clearly is not the case. When Mark Antony cries despairingly, "Authority melts from me," we cannot substitute the word "leaps" for "melts" without affecting the meaning and effect of his utterance. And this, it would seem, can only be explained in terms of the fact that the literal meaning of "leaps" is different from that of "melts."

It is not just my contention, but it is held almost as a matter of commonsense, that metaphor and its comprehension depend crucially on literal discourse. But this does not tell us very much at all, for it merely assumes, but does not explain, the distinction between literal and nonliteral discourse. In this respect I am in good company, for most philosophers who insist on a contrast between metaphorical and literal discourse fail to offer any account of the literal use of language. It is not that they are unable to offer such an account, but that they merely assume it. It will be instructive in the present context to explain what it is that they assume.

Let us begin with the observation that it is normally and very generally assumed that words in a natural language are not used randomly. On this view, if language is to fulfill its communicative function, the words and expressions which form part of it must be applied in a regular and systematic way. Thus, for instance, anything properly described as an elephant must manifest certain features which are widely regarded by the members of a given community as the "marks" or criteria in virtue of which one applies the word "elephant." To apply this word in the absence of these features and in the presence of others, or to apply the word "airplane" in virtue of these features, is to use these words inappropriately. One may say of such people that they have either ignored, or are otherwise ignorant, of the established "program" for the use of the words "elephant" and "airplane."

Anyone who is acquainted with such a "program," who knows the conditions for the appropriate use, say, of the word "elephant," will also know what features these animals are generally supposed to have: features, one might say, which mark the concept "elephant," and which serve to distinguish elephants from other objects. Not only this, for anyone in possession of the "program" for the use of the word will also know how to combine it, in well-formed sentences, with other words and phrases. This, then, is my view—the usual view—of what it is to be able to use the word literally.

Literal discourse consists of nothing other than the use of words and phrases in accordance with the established "programs" for their use. Such "programs" may tie the use of words to certain observable features of objects, but they need not. They may instead give rules for combining certain words with others in meaningful sentences. But whatever the case, to be acquainted with the "program" for the use of the word "truth" or "elephant" in a given community is not just to know the literal meanings of these terms, but is also to possess the concept of an elephant or the concept of truth which prevails within that community. For this reason, literal discourse always reflects the conceptual *status quo*. It should be stressed, however, that the *status quo* may alter. What a speech community regards as the distinguishing features of elephants may change as the communal body of knowledge grows, or as beliefs and theories pertaining to elephants alter. When, where, and of what we apply the word "elephant" depends very largely on these beliefs and theories; and the same is true of any other word or expression which is used to mention an object, event, or state of affairs.

This account clearly assumes that we do have access to a world "out there"; a world, moreover, which constrains our use of language. Hence it might be thought that I have begged the question against those, like Derrida or Nietzsche, who would deny us access to a real world, and who insist instead that we are confined to our own systems of signs or metaphorical constructions. But I have not begged the question. I have already shown that Derrida fails to give us any convincing and sustainable arguments against the metaphysics of presence, and that we have no reason, as a result, to maintain that we cannot have access to a real world which guides and constrains our use of language.[9]

One consequence of my account of literal discourse is that any figurative, and in this sense nonliteral, utterance involves deviating in some measure from the established "program" for the use of at least some of its constituent words and phrases. Of course, not all deviations will result in malformed sentences or defective utterances. There is nothing defective about the utterance "He is hot"; although if made of a person in virtue of temperament rather than temperature, it will deviate from the established "program" for the use of the word "hot." This suggests that by itself, standing free of any context, a sentence or sentence-type cannot properly be said to be a metaphor. There are no syntactical or grammatical markers which declare a sentence metaphorical. This must always be discerned in context. Even those sentences which are commonly deemed by philosophers to be paradigmatic examples of metaphors ("Man is a wolf"; "The chasm yawned below him") are properly so regarded only because we imagine certain contexts in which they are used metaphorically. But we could equally imagine contexts in which they are used literally to state either falsehoods or truths.

One can therefore have metaphorical utterances which are neither grammatically nor syntactically defective but which nonetheless involve deviations from the established "programs" for the use of their constituent words. Not all such deviations, it must be stressed, amount to the nonliteral or figurative deployment of language. Some may be accidental, others born of ignorance; and in such cases a break with the established "program" for the use of a word or phrase will result either in idiomatic infelicities or in varying shades and degrees of nonsense. But neither errors of idiom nor gibberish can properly be regarded as instances of figurative or nonliteral discourse. Deviation from the established "program" for the use of a word is necessary, but is never sufficient, for the nonliteral, figurative, or metaphorical use of that word.

But how, you may ask, are we to know whether a deviation of this sort is to be construed as a metaphor? Why shouldn't we regard it as a mistake or a howler? It is no use arguing that we come to know that it is a metaphor by looking for and discerning the speaker's meaning. For even if the speaker's meaning is discernible, and even if it is different from, and does make more sense than, the literal meaning of the sentence, this is what we should expect to find in most, if not all, cases of linguistic incompetence. Those of us who are polite always try, and are often able, to understand what an incompetent speaker means by a deviant or defective utterance, but no matter how worthy the meaning this does not make a metaphor of his or her semiarticulate fumblings.

The matter is complicated by the fact that what is deemed an incompetent utterance on the lips of one speaker may well be regarded as a metaphor when voiced by another. So, for instance, the inarticulate foreigner at London Zoo may say of a lion that it is delicious — meaning, perhaps, that it is hungry, or angry, or fat. And in such a situation it would, of course, be perfectly appropriate, if a little rude, to correct this usage. More to the point, we can easily conceive of a situation in which the use of the same sentence — "The lion is delicious" — would pass as a metaphor, and here it would be quite inappropriate to correct the speaker. This because the only alternative to construing the utterance figuratively is to construe it as a mistake. Hence if we do construe it metaphorically we must believe that it was not made by mistake, and so cannot venture to correct it. For this reason, if our foreigner's defective utterance should turn out to have the same meaning as the utterance when construed metaphorically, this would entail not that the foreigner, in the fullness of ignorance, had coined a metaphor. For, as we know, the foreigner spoke in error, and used the word "delicious" believing it to have a literal meaning which it does not have.

Clearly, then, metaphors are not made in error. We assume that those who coin them are perfectly familiar with the literal meanings of the words they use nonliterally. In a nutshell, we must assume the linguistic competence of the speaker whose utterance is construed as a metaphor. Of course, a speaker may coin a metaphor unintentionally, and in such a case there is a sense in which the metaphor was made in error.[10] But even though a metaphor has been unintentionally coined, we can attribute it to the speaker only if he or she is familiar with the literal meaning of the utterance, for otherwise it remains a simple mistake. It is in this sense that metaphors are not made in error and always require the linguistic competence of those who coin them. For this reason, signs of linguistic competence or incompetence will serve as clues or pointers as to how to construe certain utterances. Well-known authors, like respected teachers and orators, will be considered less prone to mistaken usage than, say, a schoolboy or a foreign student of the English language. Here our knowledge of, or beliefs about, the linguistic prowess of certain speakers facilitates our construal of their utterances.

All of this, then, gives us an idea not just of what we normally mean when we speak of literal discourse, but also of the quite radical dependence which metaphor is normally considered to have on the literal use of language. I do not, of course, wish to suggest that my account is in any sense complete, but I do wish to suggest that it captures some very fundamental aspects of our discernment of, response to, and talk about metaphor.

To insist, as I have done, that metaphorical discourse is dependent on its literal counterpart, is not, of course, to deny that metaphors can and do contribute importantly to literal discourse. However, mistakes arise when theorists become overly impressed by the formative influence and vast scope of metaphor, and declare in consequence that language is essentially and primordially metaphorical. This certainly is what I. A. Richards means when he declares that "metaphor is the omnipresent principle of language."[11] This same view, I shall contend, is to be found (in a rather special form) in the deconstructionist writings of Jacques Derrida. It is to these that I shall now proceed.

Derrida on Metaphor

If Derrida is to be believed, we can never have access to a real world, to a set of brute facts which constrain, guide, and regulate our use of language.[12] This is why he regards my commonsense view of literal discourse as entirely without substance. It is not just logocentric in character, but is clearly bred of the metaphysics of presence, which, as we learned earlier, he regards as totally untenable. According to Derrida, we need to remind ourselves that language proceeds as the unconstrained play of signs, an "arche-writing," a system in which each sign gets its meaning not by referring to some "transcendental signified" but contextually—in virtue, that is, of its relations to other signs within the system. Moreover, since the ways in which signs interact within any given text may be seen to vary, one cannot think of a text, a discourse, or its signs as possessing a settled or determinate meaning. Any attempt to uncover determinate meanings is no more than a distortion which represses the actual nature of language. It conceals the fact that language is a free play of signs which cannot be constrained by an extra-linguistic reality.

Hence on Derrida's view, what we regard as literal meaning is always a function of the use to which we *choose* to put our words.[13] We willingly interrupt the play of language, artificially restrict the sense of certain signs, constrain them to our purpose, and give to them the honorific title of *literal truth*. Each such "literal" use, though, when pressed to its origin, is grounded in the free and unconstrained interaction of signs—in that system of differences that Derrida calls "writing." When once we freeze this play, when once we speak determinately, we are, according to Derrida, speaking metaphorically. For this is a linguistic artifice: we have imaginatively, but artificially, carved out a sphere of use for the signs in question. We have arrested the free play of signs, and we have come, as Nietzsche said, to treat their new contrived use as "fixed, canonic and binding."[14] Elsewhere Derrida tells us that this sort of artificial restriction placed on the scope of a sign, and more particularly, on the word "writing," is "named by metaphor." To give the literal meaning of this word is, he maintains, to speak metaphorically, and he contends that "it is not a matter of inverting the literal meaning and the figurative meaning of 'writing' but of determining the 'literal' meaning of 'writing' as metaphoricity itself."[15] Clearly, when once language becomes intelligible, when once it appears to have determinate meanings, those meanings, on Derrida's view, are invariably metaphorical: there simply is no literal meaning.[16]

What Derrida has done, of course, is to deconstruct the "hierarchical opposition" *literal/metaphorical*, but it is clear that he can do so only because he takes himself to have previously dismantled the metaphysics of presence on which this opposition depends. With all of this behind him, he believes himself able to dismantle philosophy's pretensions to the truth, and he does so by treating philosophy as a variety of literature. Normally we think of literature as the realm of fancy, rhetoric, figurative embellishment, and fiction, while philosophy is privileged as the realm of argument, evidence, and literal truth. But according to Derrida, his arguments show that there simply are no grounds for this view of philosophy. Since nothing is ever present to us, there is no "transcendental signified" which can constrain the play of language. Consequently, philosophy is as much an invention and fiction as literature is. It is as much a product of rhetoric and metaphor, and is similarly concerned with style and effect. Moreover, like literature, it too is concerned to change our view of the world, but unlike literature it does so by claiming an authority that it cannot possess and to which it has no title. For whereas literature is honest and modest enough to admit its origins in fancy and metaphor, philosophy disguises or represses its origins, and pretends instead to latch on to the real nature of things.[17]

This helps explain Derrida's seemingly perverse claim that "it is not so much that metaphor is in the text of philosophy . . . rather, these texts are in metaphor."[18] We can now understand why deconstruction often points to what it regards as the metaphorical origins of literal discourse, and why it attempts to "unpick the elements of metaphor . . . at work in the texts of philosophy."[19] This is done not merely to expose contradictions in our thinking, but, more particularly, in order to show that there is an alternative to the metaphysics of presence and the logocentrism which it encourages.[20]

It should be clear from this that Derrida does not offer a theory of metaphor comparable to those, say, of Aristotle, Max Black, or Donald Davidson. It is no part of his aim to explain how metaphors work or what they mean. His is the largely Nietzschean view that the order we impose upon the world, the sense we see in it, is a construct—one, moreover, which, according to Derrida, is produced only through the artificial constraints which we place on the play of signs. Hence, on this view, what we take to be the literal truth is bred of linguistic artifice or metaphor, so that all determinate meaning turns out in the end to be metaphorical.

The trouble, of course, is that we cannot take Derrida's view seriously unless he is able to offer arguments which can dislodge us from the metaphysics of presence. For until we have reason to suppose that there is no real world present to us in experience which constrains the "play of signs," his assault on the commonsense view of literal discourse fails to get off the ground. Hence, if his arguments fail, he can have no reason either to treat the notion of literal meaning as "metaphoricity itself," or to assert the omnipresence of metaphor.

Earlier, however, we saw that Derrida is simply unable to produce a convincing argument against the metaphysics of presence.[21] In the end, and by his own admission, he does no more than present us with a literary invitation to look at language differently. His "arguments," he says, are no more than "an adventure of vision,"[22] and one is, of course, at liberty to reject the vision, to decline the invitation, and to persist in thinking of language as a more or less efficient instrument for negotiating a nonlinguistic world. Since this view of language is positively helpful, since it can be stated consistently, there is very good reason to accept it. On the other hand, Derrida has given us no reason at all for accepting his picture of language.

But Derrida does have a powerful ally. Friedrich Nietzsche, as I have said, also contends that literal meaning is an illusion and that everything that passes for it is at root metaphorical. However, the similarity between Nietzsche and Derrida on the issue of metaphor is, in a sense, superficial. Nietzsche does not regard metaphor as essentially linguistic. It is a process which begins with the act of perception itself, and involves moving from one distinct sphere (a nerve stimulus) into another (an image): it involves "equating the unequal."[23] This linking in the mind of wholly discrete entities is, Nietzsche assures us, a product of the fanciful imagination. These are metaphors "pouring forth as a fiery liquid out of the primal faculty of human fancy."[24]

Even if we grant (as I have done) that our initial acts of cognition are imaginative and fanciful, it is difficult to see why Nietzsche should regard them as metaphors. He appears to confuse the process of coining a linguistic trope with a similar but different process which, as I argued in Chapter Two, is basic to the acquisition and growth of all knowledge. It is a confusion which trades on an unwillingness to acknowledge a distinction between necessary and sufficient conditions, for whereas the exercise of the fanciful imagination certainly is necessary for metaphor, it is not sufficient. To treat it as sufficient is simply to distort the ordinary meaning of the word "metaphor," for in so doing we come to regard any fanciful concatenation of objects—whether it be a masterfully designed building or a highly imaginative Lego or Meccano construction—as a metaphor. And this seems perverse.

Perhaps because of the influence of the romantics, Nietzsche is much too impressed by the role of the fanciful imagination in the acquisition and growth of knowledge. He clearly thinks that how we construe the world is simply "up to us," and that almost any fanciful construal will do as well as any other—the only problem being that of bringing others to see the world as we do. On his view, there is no Truth—if by that we mean correspondence to the facts; this because there can be no knowledge of the facts, of the brute, unchanging realities which are described as "things themselves." Nietzsche's use of the word "metaphor" seems designed to emphasize the extent to which our view of reality is a product of the imagination, and hence the extent to which it is under our control. We all know that metaphors are figures of speech which *we* coin. To suggest, then, that our picture of a stable and well-ordered world is just the product of someone's fanciful metaphors is to suggest that we can easily abandon this picture, that we can coin and adopt alternative metaphors and so see the world and reality differently.

Nietzsche, it seems to me, is not intent on developing a theory of *metaphor* at all. He uses the word "metaphor" rhetorically in order to drive home the lesson that our so-called literal truths are all the product of the fanciful imagination. If I am right, one can concede the latter point without wishing to describe every act of fancy as a metaphor, or every item of knowledge as a product of metaphor. Still more, as I argued earlier, it does not follow from the fact that all our knowledge and all literal truths are bred of the fanciful imagination that we have no access to a real world, or that it (the real world) is merely a figment of the imagination.[25]

Davidson on Metaphor

We have, as yet, no grounds at all for supposing that language is essentially metaphorical. On the contrary, if my arguments in the section "The Literal and the Metaphorical" are correct, we have considerable reason to insist on the distinction between metaphorical and literal discourse. For there I argued that our acquaintance with the literal meanings of words and sentences is crucial both to the discernment and the comprehension of metaphor.

This, of course, is reminiscent of Donald Davidson's well-known account of what metaphors mean,[26] for like myself, Davidson seeks to explain this by appealing to the literal meanings of words. But here all similarity ends, for on Davidson's view a metaphor has no meaning apart from its literal meaning; there simply is no such thing as metaphorical meaning. Metaphors, he tells us, "mean what the words in their most literal interpretation mean, and nothing more" ("What Metaphors Mean," p. 30). On his view, we have to distinguish "between what words mean and what they are used to do"; and metaphors, he contends, belong "exclusively to the domain of use" (p. 31). How they work is food for pragmatics, not semantics; for it is the imaginative *use* of literal sentences that "nudges us into noting" similarities which were, perhaps, previously unnoticed (p. 36). Not only this, for Davidson also advances the related thesis (p. 44) that metaphors have no special message or cognitive content apart from their literal meaning. They do, of course, have cognitive effects, but these are just the effects of the imaginative deployment of certain sentences which enjoy nothing more than a literal meaning.

But Davidson's arguments for this view are strained and unconvincing. He offers at least three distinct arguments, the first of which proceeds as follows:[27] It is "trite and true," we are told "that a metaphor makes us attend to some likeness" (p. 31). Literal similes, of course, do the same, but we are not at all tempted in their case to posit some second meaning (over and above their literal meaning) that is responsible for this effect (p. 38). Why, then, should we be tempted to do so in the case of metaphor? Why can't we simply allow that metaphors draw our attention to likenesses, and do so with the help only of the *literal meanings* of the words that they contain?

The answer to this question is easily come by. For even if it is true that metaphors invariably draw our attention to likenesses, it seems plain that they frequently do a good deal more than this. Thus, for instance, when Antony tells Enobarbus "Authority melts from me," he does not just draw Enobarbus's attention to certain likenesses. He also *asserts* a supposed fact about his powers of command and thereby informs Enobarbus about a specific state of affairs. But when once we construe this metaphor as an assertion, we can make sense of it only if we do not ascribe a literal meaning to it, and hence to all of its constituent words as used on this occasion. For if we did, we should have to assume that Antony is either demented or stupid, since when construed literally what he says is either absurd or else plainly false. Here, then, to answer Davidson's question, is why we assume that metaphors have a second (metaphorical) meaning over and above their literal meaning.

Davidson can avoid this conclusion by insisting that metaphors never assert anything. And there is some evidence to suggest that this is indeed his view. At one point he contends that "a metaphor merely nudges us into noting" the likenesses that "a simile tells us" (p. 36). And earlier he maintains that "a metaphor doesn't *say* anything beyond its literal meaning (nor does its maker *say* anything, in using the metaphor, beyond the literal)" (p. 30; emphasis added). But if this really is Davidson's view, it is simply at loggerheads with the facts. For it is plain that all sorts of illocutionary acts can be, and are, performed with the help of metaphors. Thus, for instance, I could ask of a trained accountant, "Does he still chew numbers for a living?" and in so doing I clearly use a metaphor to ask a question. Similarly, my emphatic "Kill it!" when I want my children to stop fooling around is both a metaphor and a command; while Antony's "Authority melts from me" is a metaphor which, in context, clearly asserts something about Antony's inability to command his soldiers. If construed literally, each utterance fails to make proper sense; and this is why we are led to suppose that certain words are not being used (on this occasion, and in this context) to have their literal meaning. Certainly such metaphors may "nudge us into noting" specific similarities, but this is better regarded as one of the (perlocutionary) effects of these (metaphorical) speech acts, and it seems entirely gratuitous to suppose that this is all that a metaphor can achieve.[28]

There is, I think, another reason for supposing that there are metaphorical meanings. For if it is true, and I certainly think that it is, that metaphors "nudge us into noting" a range of likenesses, it is also true that not every likeness that we notice on account of a metaphor need be appropriate to it. It is not enough to say that the literal content of the utterance determines which likenesses should be noticed and which not, for it is easy to think of appropriate responses to the literal meanings of the words used in a metaphor that would not constitute appropriate responses to the metaphor itself.[29] Thus, for instance, were Enobarbus to rush Antony into a cool room in order to stem the melting of his authority, we would rightly contend that he had not noticed an appropriate likeness between authority and things that melt; that he had not responded appropriately to the metaphor. It is no use appealing to the context in which the word "melts" is used in order to determine what would, and what would not, be an appropriate response to the metaphor, for to do so is in effect to try to ascertain what meaning *other than* its literal meaning the word is being used to have on this occasion. Although I cannot argue the matter here, an appeal to context in such a case amounts only to an appeal to the nonliteral, perhaps the metaphorical, meaning of certain words (and hence of the utterance) in order to determine what will and what will not count as an appropriate response to the metaphor.[30]

To talk of metaphorical meanings in this way is not, contra Davidson (p. 41), to suggest that such meanings attach themselves permanently to the words deployed in a metaphor. Rather, metaphorical meaning has to be explained as the somewhat special sense which certain words acquire because of the way in which they are intentionally, yet deviantly, used in a specific context. Davidson's mistake, I think, is his belief that words retain their literal meanings on all occasions of use (pp. 31, 38, 41). But this must be wrong if, as I have contended (and as Davidson himself suggests in his account of radical interpretation), their literal meaning is ultimately a function of use. On my view, it is always possible to know the literal meaning of a word, and to know that it is not being used to have its literal meaning on this occasion. It is, in part, Davidson's unwillingness to countenance this possibility that leads him to reject the notion of metaphorical meaning.

Davidson's second argument against metaphorical meaning is equally unconvincing. He rightly wishes to distinguish learning the use of a word with a known and established meaning from learning an entirely new use for the same word (p. 35). And it is his contention that any theory of metaphor that allows the notion of metaphorical meaning will undermine this distinction. He asks us to imagine a Saturnian who is trying to master the English language, and who takes your metaphorical use of the word "floor" literally by supposing it to be "drill in the use of language" (pp. 34–35). "What difference," Davidson asks, "would it make to your friend which way he took it?" And his answer is that if one subscribes to the theory of metaphorical meaning it will make very little difference, "for according to that theory a word has a new meaning in a metaphorical context," and consequently "the occasion of the metaphor would . . . be the occasion for learning the new meaning" (p. 35).

This argument does little for Davidson's case. For one thing, it suggests that the theory of metaphorical meaning is committed to the view that some words in a metaphor acquire permanently changed meanings. But this, we have seen, is by no means the case. Still worse, it does not follow from the claim that metaphors always introduce new meanings that it makes "little difference" to our Saturnians whether they take your utterance as drill in the use of language or as a metaphor which involves a new, nonliteral, meaning. It is of course true that since our envisaged Saturnians are not competent speakers of the English language, they can have no way of telling whether your use of the word "floor" is metaphorical. Even so, provided that they have the least conception of what it is to learn a language, it cannot be a matter of indifference to them whether they take the utterance as a metaphor or as a lesson in the literal meanings of words. For should they take it as a lesson, they would simply be mistaken, and the mistake would be an impediment to the mastery of the language. In this sense, it makes a considerable difference to our Saturnians whether or not they take the utterance as a metaphor. So even if we allow that each metaphor introduces a new, nonliteral, meaning, it does not follow from this that there is no difference between a metaphorical utterance and an utterance intended as "drill in the use of language." The latter clearly instructs a speaker in the literal meanings of words, phrases, sentences in an extant language. Metaphorical utterances do not.

Davidson's armory is not yet exhausted. "If words in metaphor bear a coded meaning," he now argues, "how can this meaning differ from the meaning those same words bear in the case where the metaphor *dies?*" (p. 43). The dead metaphor "Donald is hot under the collar" simply means that Donald is angry; but this, according to Davidson is not what an audience would have pictured when it first encountered the metaphor. The audience would have pictured a person discomforted by anger—with steam, so to speak, puffing about his ears. And on this point Davidson may well be correct. However, the fact that a metaphor no longer has the *effects* that it once had hardly establishes that there is no such thing as metaphorical meaning. One can allow that a newly coined metaphor has certain effects bred of its freshness and the element of surprise, and one can concede that its literalized counterpart must lack these effects. But having said this, one can quite consistently maintain that *the meaning* of "hot under the collar" in our dead metaphor is precisely what it was in our once fresh metaphor, and that this meaning differs from the then-literal meaning of the phrase. For when used literally at that time, the truth conditions of the utterance "Donald is hot under the collar" would have been given in terms of a certain temperature range; but it is apparent that the truth conditions of the now dead metaphor will bear little relation to Donald's body temperature, and will have much to do with his emotional state. What has happened, of course, is that the phrase has become literally ambiguous: it has acquired a second literal meaning. But how, we can now ask Davidson, is it possible for this phrase (the so-called dead metaphor) to have a new literal meaning, if that meaning was not the once fresh metaphor's metaphorical meaning?

Davidson's arguments do little to convince. One can agree with him that metaphor is not merely a play on words or a kind of pun; and one can agree, too, that metaphor must be a matter of use. However, as Janet Soskice points out, his resistance to a semantic account of metaphor has some very odd consequences. Davidson, as we know, believes that a metaphorical utterance nudges us into noting similarities, and is more like a bump on the head or a jolt than the expression of a proposition. But metaphor, Soskice rightly observes, is importantly different from nudges, jolts, and bumps on the head. While all three may make us see similarities, metaphor "does so as a form of language use and as such must involve some inference from the speaker's utterances." [31]

Davidson would most probably agree that we have to draw inferences from the metaphorical utterance, but he is adamant that these inferences are not part of what the metaphor means. This, as Soskice points out, suggests that his argument amounts to no more than a stipulation as to the way in which the term "meaning" is to be used; a stipulation that, while perhaps of value within his wider theory, is unduly restrictive within an account of metaphor. Soskice illustrates the point graphically by asking us to imagine the following conversation:

DAVIDSON: He is a jackal.
INTERLOCUTOR: You mean he is a coward and a scrounger?
DAVIDSON: No, although I am committed to regarding him as a coward and a scrounger and although I intended by my utterance to make you see him thus, I only said and I only meant "He is a jackal." [32]

Put thus, Davidson's claims about metaphorical meaning begin to look decidedly odd. He would, as Soskice contends, have been in a stronger position had he distinguished between what a sentence means and what a person means in uttering it.[33] But Davidson disallows this move by maintaining that "a metaphor doesn't say anything beyond its literal meaning (nor does its maker say anything, in using the metaphor, beyond the literal)" (p. 30).

Meaning, Radical Interpretation, and Metaphor

Whatever else it is designed to do, Davidson's account of metaphor clearly is meant to show that metaphor need not be an embarrassment to his views about meaning. He does this via the simple expedient of denying that there is such a thing as metaphorical meaning, and hence by denying the possibility of a semantic account of metaphor. Even so, a close look at his theory of meaning and the account of radical interpretation based on it suggests that the latter can be adapted both to explain how people make sense of metaphor and to preserve the notion of metaphorical meaning.

Davidson, it is well known, means to provide a theory for the semantics of natural languages: a theory which will give the meaning of every meaningful expression in a natural language.[34] If such a theory is to be non-circular, it must of course proceed independently of the concept of meaning and its cognates—that is, independently of all intensional concepts such as "meaning," "intention" and "belief"; and this, Davidson believes, will best be achieved by developing a theory of truth for the natural language in question. Such a theory, he maintains, will give us "the meanings of all independently meaningful expressions on the basis of an analysis of their structure."[35]

All that Davidson requires by way of a theory of truth is "a set of axioms that entail, for every sentence in the language, a statement of the conditions under which it is true."[36] To this end he proposes to adopt and adapt Tarski's Convention T, so that, on Davidson's view, we can take as axioms (or as theorems[37]) all sentences of the form "*s* is true if and only if *p*," where "*s*" is to be replaced by a description (in the meta-language) of a sentence, and "*p*" by that sentence (in the object language).[38] Such axioms are what Davidson calls T-sentences, and he believes that by giving T-sentences of this form we will be able to give the truth conditions for, and so the meaning of, every sentence *s* in a natural language. He writes:

A theory of truth entails, for each sentence *s*, a statement of the form "*s* is true if and only if *p*" where in the simplest case "*p*" is replaced by *s*. Since the words "is true if and only if" are invariant, we may interpret them if we please as meaning "means that". So construed, a sample might then read " 'Socrates is wise' means that Socrates is wise."[39]

This, of course, does not entail that all that can be learned from a theory of truth about the meaning of a particular sentence is somehow contained in the biconditional of the T-sentence. Rather, Davidson insists that we learn about the meaning of the sentence in "the proof of such a biconditional"—or, which is the same thing, in the construction of the appropriate T-sentence.[40] These are the same because the sorts of considerations which constitute "the proof" of the biconditional will be the same as those which ought ideally to be taken into account when constructing the

T-sentence. In constructing such a proof (or T-sentence), we will have to show not only "how the truth value of the sentence depends on a recursively given structure,"[41] but we will also have to take into account "the fact that many sentences vary in truth value depending on the time they are spoken, the speaker, and even perhaps the audience."[42] And this is accommodated "either by declaring that it is particular utterances or speech acts, and not sentences, that have truth values, or by making truth a relation that holds between a sentence, a speaker and a time."[43]

Despite this, Davidson insists that by formulating a theory of truth for natural languages he is able to establish that natural languages constitute formal systems. They are, however, formal systems in a relatively weak sense of this term—in the sense, that is, "that every true expression may be analysed as formed from elements (the 'vocabulary')," a finite supply of which, in combination with a finite supply of rules, are sufficient for the language in question.[44] Natural languages certainly are not logical systems, for, as we have now seen, what counts as a true utterance within the system, and hence what counts as the meaning of that utterance, must depend on a host of contextual contingencies. By Davidson's own admission, therefore, and despite what he says earlier, it will not be possible to give a purely structural analysis of the meaning of meaningful expressions. Contextual features will have to be taken into account. So while natural languages are formal systems of a sort, the construction of T-sentences for utterances within such systems is anything but a formal procedure. It relies on our apprehension of the contexts in which speakers find themselves, their relations to such contexts, and their beliefs about them.

According to Davidson, we can furnish the appropriate T-sentence for an "uninterpreted utterance" such as "Die hond blaf," and in this way come to give its meaning, only if we have reason to impute certain beliefs to the speaker.[45] The trouble, of course, is that if all we have to go on is the honest utterance of the speaker, we cannot infer his or her beliefs without knowing the meaning of the utterance. And there is no chance of inferring the meaning without knowing the belief.[46] Davidson proposes to solve this problem by assuming that the speakers' beliefs are usually correct, and that they speak the truth more often than not. For if we cannot assume beliefs on the part of the speaker "which are consistent and true by our own standards, we have no reason to count that creature as rational, as having beliefs, or as saying anything."[47]

What is more, if Davidson is right there is a good deal of evidence which may be had independently of interpretation to the effect that the speaker intends to state a truth. In the present case such evidence may include the fact that a dog is barking near the speaker at the appropriate time; that the speaker earnestly asserts "Die hond blaf"; that the speaker prefers this proposition in these circumstances to some other.[48] All of this, says Davidson, should be taken as evidence for the T-sentence:

"Die hond blaf" is true for a speaker (of Afrikaans) at a certain time t, if and only if the dog is barking (near the speaker at t).

Of course, such evidence is by no means conclusive and can be supplemented. According to Davidson, the method of supplementing it "is one of getting the best fit"—that is, of maximizing agreement "in the sense of making the speaker (and others) right, as far as we can tell, as often as possible."[49] Thus conceived, interpretation is holistic in nature—which is to say that our choice of interpretation for the above sentence does not just involve that single sentence, but involves the systematic assignment of truth conditions to the widest possible range of utterances in the language. For, as Davidson argues, our interpretations must be consistent with all the other interpretations that we offer of sentences within that speech community.

It matters little at this stage whether or not we agree with Davidson. More to the point is the fact that what he says would seem to be applicable to metaphor. Metaphors, I have argued, can be used in assertions which are puzzling if taken literally, and to this extent they demand interpretation. Certainly such interpretations will not be radical in Davidson's sense, for both he and I agree that they must depend on our knowledge of the literal meanings of the words and phrases used in metaphors. For all that, though, metaphors do require interpretation, and Davidson gives every appearance of telling us what such an interpretation must look like. So, for instance, when Antony declares "Authority melts from me," Enobarbus may well be puzzled by the utterance. He knows that Antony is not stupid and does not believe that his authority is literally melting. There is contextual evidence to the effect that Antony wishes to say something about his authority, and that what he wishes to say is not adequately captured by the literal meaning of the sentence that he uses. What is more, the evidence suggests that Antony believes that what he is saying is both important and true.

We know that Davidson deems such evidence sufficient for the construction of T-sentences in all cases of radical interpretation, so why not in the case of metaphors too? The fact that this metaphor does not involve Enobarbus in *radical* interpretation just makes the process of getting the right (holistic) fit, and so of furnishing the appropriate T-sentence, that much easier, and certainly does not constitute any objection to this mode of coming to understand it. So it seems open to a puzzled Enobarbus, on the basis of the evidence available to him, to construct the T-sentence:

"Authority melts from me" is true (in English) for Antony at time t, if and only if Antony is gradually losing his authority at or about time t.

An ability to furnish the correct T-sentence, Davidson tells us in a different context, ensures that one has an adequate grasp not only of the appropriate entailment relations between this and other sentences, but also of its truth conditions, and hence its meaning.[50] Consequently, if Davidson's program works at all, the above T-sentence (or some version of it) must give us the meaning of Antony's utterance: a meaning which is metaphorical inasmuch as it differs from the literal meaning of the sentence Antony uses. By recognizing its metaphorical status, one effectively acquires the best holistic fit for the interpretation, for, as we shall see in more detail presently, it can now be used to help compute the meanings of other sentences in the language.[51]

Perhaps the most serious objection to this application of Davidson's program is that it fails to grasp and acknowledge the fact that T-sentences are supposed by Davidson to be theorems or axioms. They are theorems which, if he is right, are capable of giving the conditions under which every sentence in a natural language is true. Like all other theorems, these must be fully extensional; and this is important, for, as we have seen, it is part and parcel of Davidson's aim to provide a semantics for natural languages *independently* of intensional concepts. But if T-sentences are wholly extensional theorems, then, like all other theorems, they too must admit the substitution of coextensive expressions. So, for example, when once we know that two right angles are equal to 180°, we can infer from the Euclidean theorem:

The three angles of a triangle are equal to 180°

that

The three angles of a triangle are equal to two right angles.

The same, it is thought, must apply to any genuine T-sentence. Take, for instance, the T-sentence:

"The man is crying" is true for a speaker (of English) at time t, if and only if the man is crying at t.

If it is true that the predicate "is crying" is coextensive with the predicate "is weeping," then (the argument goes) "is weeping" can be substituted for "is crying" to the right of the biconditional without altering its capacity to give the truth conditions and hence the meaning of a certain utterance in the English language. But this, the objection continues, is precisely what we cannot do when we attempt to offer a T-sentence for metaphorical utterances. Consider here Romeo's famous declaration "Juliet is the sun."[52] According to this objection, if we try to construct a T-sentence which gives the putative meaning of Romeo's utterance, it will look like this:

"Juliet is the sun" is true for Romeo at time t, if and only if Juliet is the sun at time t.

However, we also know that "is the sun" is coextensive with "is a body of hot gases at the centre of the solar system." But we cannot substitute the one for the other to the right of the biconditional in the above T-sentence without radically altering what we intuitively take to be its (metaphorical) meaning—namely, that Juliet is an outstanding person, unequaled by her peers. Hence it is concluded that in this case we do not have a genuine T-sentence; indeed, that it is not possible to construct T-sentences for metaphors since such sentences could never admit the substitution of coextensive expressions, and so cannot serve as theorems in a formal system.

This objection will work only if it is true that genuine T-sentences are always extensional. A closer look at the objection, and at what Davidson actually says, suggests that T-sentences cannot be extensional in the required sense, and so fail in the round to qualify as theorems. Part of the difficulty is that central to the very notion of a T-sentence is the idea of an utterance being *true for a speaker,* and it seems entirely clear that an utterance will be true for a particular speaker only if that speaker believes the proposition expressed by the utterance. The concept of belief is an ineliminable part of any T-sentence, and Davidson does not dispute this. It is tempting, therefore, to conclude that given the T-sentence

"The man is crying" is true for a speaker (of English) at time t, if and only if the man is crying at t

it does not follow that "The man is weeping" will also be true for, and so believed by, the speaker in question unless he or she knows that "is weeping" and "is crying" are coextensive predicates. And this, of course, suggests that T-sentences are not, after all, the fully extensional theorems that the objection supposes them to be, since they do *not* admit the substitution of co-extensive predicates.

Davidson anticipates and attempts to forestall this sort of rejoinder. On his view, when constructing a T-sentence for an utterance, we can tell from the evidence available to us that the speaker assents to a particular sentence and accepts it as true. "This," he concedes, "is a belief, but it is a single attitude applicable to all sentences, and so does not ask us to be able to make finely discriminated distinctions among beliefs."[53] According to Davidson's account, therefore, the evidential base available to us in a certain context allows us to grasp the fact that a speaker regards an utterance as important and true; and we can therefore recognize that the speaker believes what was uttered, even though, as interpreters, we do not know what it is that is believed. All that the T-sentence does, therefore, is record the fact that the speaker believes the utterance in question: it gives us the speaker's attitude to it. Since it does not attribute a particular propositional belief to the speaker, the question of referential opacity does not properly arise.

But this, if true at all, is true only of the construction of the first part of a T-sentence: that which falls to the left of the biconditional. Any T-sentence is constructed around the T-sentence frame:

'. . . .$^{(1)}$. . . .' is true for a speaker of a given natural language at t, if and only if . . . .$^{(2)}$. . . .

In constructing a T-sentence for the utterance "The man is crying" all that we initially have is the utterance of this sentence in a certain context. If the evidence gleaned from the context is such as to make us believe that the utterance is held to be true by the speaker, we can complete (1) of the sentence frame without at this stage having enough evidence to complete (2). At this point we know that the speaker holds the utterance true and believes it, but we do not of course know what he or she believes until we are in a position to complete (2). However, when once we complete (2) on the basis of the contextual evidence available to us, we thereby give (the supposed) meaning of (1) and so attribute a specific belief to the speaker at t—namely, the belief that the man is crying. Since we now know (or take ourselves to know) that the speaker believes that the man is crying, we cannot substitute "is weeping" for "is crying" in (2) without attributing a different belief to the speaker. Belief contexts are referentially opaque. Consequently, even the most central and obvious examples of T-sentences are not extensional and so cannot be regarded as theorems in any ordinary sense of this word.

So it is no objection to my attempt to apply Davidson's interpretation program to metaphor that the resultant T-sentences are not extensional. T-sentences in general, we have now seen, are not extensional; nor are they theorems or axioms in any ordinary sense of these words. And this fact, I think, takes ample care of the objection at hand. The objection arises, so it seems, because there is a tendency to emphasize the formal constraints that Davidson attaches to his theory of interpretation at the expense of what he calls the evidential constraints.[54] While it is undoubtedly true that the formal constraints on his theory are intended to make it possible for him to give a structural and recursive account of the meaning of all sentences in a particular natural language,[55] it is also the case that the content of any interpretation is importantly determined by contingent features of the context of the utterance—that is, by what Davidson refers to as the "evidential base" for the interpretation.[56]

There seems to be no reason, then, why we cannot use Davidsonian semantics in order to furnish a T-sentence which will give us the meaning of a metaphorical utterance. Such a procedure, it is worth emphasizing, need not be incompatible with Davidson's avowed aim of giving a systematic and structural account of the meaning of all meaningful expressions in a natural language. The resultant T-sentence does not only give the truth conditions for the metaphorical utterance, but it also helps explain the entailment relations between it and all other meaningful expressions in English—although, as with all T-sentences, it does so only after achieving the right "fit" with the interpretation of other utterances in the language. In achieving the appropriate holistic fit for Antony's utterance, one comes, of course, to recognize its metaphorical status; to recognize, that is, that its words do not all bear their literal meanings on this occasion of use. This knowledge not only facilitates the interpretation of other sentences in the English language, but also helps explain the relation of this utterance and its use of particular words to other utterances and words in the language.

To object to this procedure on the ground that it is impossible to provide an adequate paraphrase of a metaphor merely begs the question against any attempt to apply Davidson's program to metaphorical utterances. Certainly it is true that Antony's use of "melts" may have connotations which are not captured in Enobarbus's T-sentence, but this is a problem with all translation and is by no means peculiar to the interpretation of metaphor. The translation, for instance, of the Afrikaans "Jy is 'n lafaard" with the English "You are a fool" comes very close to the meaning of the original, but, as any Afrikaner will tell you, it does not capture all the nuances of the word "lafaard." But this deficiency is entirely contingent. For all we know, there may be sentences or words in the English language that will suit, but even if there are not, it is always possible for the language to develop in ways which will eventually allow us to furnish an adequate translation (interpretation) of the utterance. The same, I would venture, is true of metaphor.

Perhaps the objection is better cast in Davidsonian terms, for he maintains that "the statements of truth conditions for individual sentences should, in some way yet to be made precise, draw upon the same concepts as the sentences whose truth conditions they state."[57] In other words, one might think that the very same concepts which somehow appear on the left of the biconditional in Enobarbus's T-sentence ought to be expressed on the right. Since the phrase "gradually losing his authority" does not appear to "draw upon" or express the same concepts as "authority melts from me," someone might object that the T-sentence does not provide an adequate interpretation of Antony's (metaphorical) utterance; and, moreover, that this will be true of any T-sentence which we construct for a metaphor that does not actually repeat the utterance to be interpreted.

But any such conclusion is much too hasty, and seems, in any event, to be unwarranted. We know that we can use different words in the same language, or, indeed, in different languages, to express the same propositions and the same concepts. When, in one context, I say, "He is not very tall," and in the same (or very similar) context I say, "He is rather short," I use different sentences and words to express the same propositions and concepts. It is arguably the case, therefore, that the sentence to the right of the biconditional in Enobarbus's T-sentence does "draw upon the same concepts" as the sentence to the left of the biconditional. In any event, Davidson does not clarify what it is for two sentences to "draw upon the same concepts," and until he does, this sort of objection seems to lack substance.

It is possible, of course, that some metaphors—what Max Black calls *resonant* metaphors—will have multiple meanings or an indefinitely large number of connotations.[58] But this does not pose any particular difficulty for Davidson's program, for we often find nonmetaphorical utterances which also "allow a high degree of implicative elaboration." Hence, if Davidson's program applies at all, it ought to be able to cater for any resonant utterance, whether or not it is a metaphor. Again, while it is true that the T-sentence offered in interpreting a metaphor almost always lacks its impact, vigor, and vivacity, this is of no real consequence for the applicability of Davidson's program. For the impact, like the vigor, of a metaphor belongs to the pragmatics, not the semantics, of the utterance. Consequently, a metaphor may be *emphatic*—in Max Black's sense that the producer will not countenance any substitute for the words used—without this affecting the fact that its meaning (but not its effects) can be given with the help of a T-sentence.[59]

It is true that metaphors are not always assertions, and so cannot always be said to have truth conditions. But this cannot be Davidson's reason for refusing to apply his truth conditional theory of meaning and interpretation to metaphor. There are many literal utterances—whether they be commands, prayers, promises, or the expression of wishes or desires—which are not assertions and cannot be said to be true or false. Presumably, though, Davidson considers that his account of meaning can handle such cases—perhaps by following John McDowell's suggestion and by introducing force indicators which enable us to derive a suitably related indicative sentence (capable of bearing a truth-value) from any utterance.[60] There seems to be no reason, then, why Davidson cannot make the same sort of adjustment in the case of metaphor—thus preserving the notion of metaphorical meaning.

Conclusion

This application of Davidson's program, I have said, will not preserve the freshness, shock, or surprise of an effective metaphor, but to regard this as counting against metaphorical meaning is to confuse the meaning of an utterance with its effects. Our problem, then, is undiminished, for we still need to know what good reasons Davidson has for resisting this attempt to salvage the notion of metaphorical meaning. Those of his objections that I have so far considered do not appear to help, but there is, perhaps, a further objection—a variant of the Saturnian case—which should be considered. This objection is especially important since it allows us to see Davidson in relation to Derrida.

Davidson could very well object that if his account of meaning and interpretation is made to apply to metaphor, it would be possible for people to understand Antony's metaphor despite the fact that they are entirely ignorant of the literal meanings of the words and phrases used within it. And yet this would contradict his earlier and very plausible contention that a grasp of the literal meanings of the words used in a metaphor is necessary if we are properly to understand it. Perhaps, then, it is the threat of this supposed inconsistency which explains Davidson's reluctance to apply his account of meaning to metaphor.

This threat should not be taken too seriously. While it is true that people who are wholly ignorant of English may, on Davidson's theory, successfully interpret Antony's utterance, they are nonetheless initially unable to recognize that the utterance is a metaphor. And to this extent they do not properly understand it. The discernment of a metaphor, I argued earlier, is always a function of one's knowledge of the literal meanings of the words used within it. So while radical interpretation cannot at first afford a proper understanding of metaphor (where this involves recognizing its metaphorical status), there is every reason to suppose that interpretation which is nonradical (in the sense that it is not entirely "from scratch") will enable us to recognize its metaphorical status. It therefore still seems possible, despite Davidson's supposed reservations, to apply his account of meaning and interpretation in a way which preserves the notion of metaphorical meaning.

And yet, by disposing of the objection in this way, we arguably ignore Davidson's deeper worry. For is it not true that, if my position is the correct one, all utterances, whether literal or metaphorical, would be capable of being interpreted in the same way? And if so, the distinction between literal and metaphorical meaning seems to be an artificial one. The upshot is that Davidson opts for literal meaning as the only type of meaning that can "explain what can be done with words" ("What Metaphors Mean," p. 38); and he does so, I suspect, not because metaphorical meaning cannot explain what can be done with words, for in a certain sense it clearly can. One appeals to metaphorical meaning to explain away the apparent absurdity, falsehood, or triviality of a metaphorical utterance, and to do this *is* to "explain what can be done with words." It seems that in treating literal meaning as the only type of meaning, Davidson wishes to avoid the unpalatable romantic alternative of maintaining that all meaning is metaphorical.

Of course, everything that I have said so far suggests that this worry, if it is indeed Davidson's, is groundless. For if he allows that interpretation is not always "from scratch," is not always radical, then it is possible for Enobarbus to provide a T-sentence which gives us the metaphorical meaning of Antony's utterance. Still more, on my understanding of Davidson's interpretation program, Enobarbus can eventually come to discern the metaphorical status of Antony's utterance even if, to begin with, he is entirely ignorant of the English language. He will do this, as I have said, by getting the right "fit" for his interpretation—by seeing, that is, that it coheres with all or most of the other interpretations that he offers of English utterances. Precisely how Enobarbus constructs the appropriate T-sentence, is, of course, an important question; and, as I shall show in the following chapter, any answer to it which is compatible with the holistic nature of Davidson's theory will also accord with Max Black's interaction theory of metaphor.

We now have some reason to suspect that Davidson has more in common with Derrida than at first meets the eye. Initially they appeared to hold radically divergent views about metaphorical meaning; but in the end this difference amounts only to a refusal in each case to countenance the distinction between metaphorical and literal meaning. And if what I have said above is correct, each rejects the distinction because he conceives of *all* meaning in a single way—neither has any room in his account for different types of meaning. Of course, Derrida's emphasis is different from Davidson's; in talking about metaphor, he is concerned with the *genesis* of determinate meaning, whereas Davidson is concerned with the *interpretation* of utterances. Both, however, offer holistic accounts. Derrida does so because he believes that our use of language is never constrained by a nonlinguistic reality. Davidson does so for exactly parallel reasons since he believes that our interpretations can never be guided by nonlinguistic entities—by events, physical objects, or experiences which may have been the referent of the native utterance.[61] At this point, and in this way, both Derrida and Davidson reject the "metaphysics of presence."

It would be wrong, though, to regard Davidson as a closet deconstructionist, for he does allow the possibility of correct interpretation. But Derrida also seems to allow this possibility—with the proviso, of course, that an interpretation can be correct only within a particular "language game." And here lies the rub, for this proviso clearly echoes Davidson's holism: his insistence, that is, that any T-sentence which is to serve as an interpretation of a given utterance within a certain language community must preserve the truth of, and so be consistent with, all the other assertions which are held to be true in that community. This, however, does not make Davidson an advocate of deconstruction. The aim of deconstruction is to show that the "language games" we play are not inevitable: that we can at least partially shake off the conceptual structures which mold our thought. But here Derrida and Davidson part company. Davidson is adamant that if interpretation is to take place at all, it must be in terms of the interpreter's beliefs and concepts. There is no other possibility because, as he argues elsewhere, there are no alternative conceptual schemes.[62] Derrida, I suspect, would reply that interpretation does not really take place: that it is just another of the games that we play with language, and that a "really" adequate "interpretation," a deconstructionist interpretation, would show this to be the case.

There remains one last trivial respect in which Derrida and Davidson are at one. They both offer accounts of the relation between metaphorical and literal discourse which turn out, on inspection, to be unacceptable. Their mutual failure does not establish that my common-sense account of this relation is correct. It does, however, establish that we have, as yet, no good reason to doubt it.

EIGHT

Another Look at Metaphorical Meaning

The claim that there is no such thing as metaphorical meaning is puzzling.[1] It is puzzling not just because it appears to deny the obvious, but also, as we learned in the previous chapter, because its foremost proponent, Donald Davidson, has developed an interpretation program which gives every appearance of applying to metaphor in a way that generates metaphorical meanings.

But appearances are not enough. It still remains to explain precisely how Davidson's interpretation program can be used to construct a T-sentence that gives the meaning—the metaphorical meaning—of a metaphor. My task in this chapter is to furnish such an explanation.

We know, however, that Davidson's interpretation program can properly apply to metaphorical utterances only if they are capable of bearing truth-values. But this, we have already seen, poses no real difficulty. Metaphors are used in the performance of many different illocutionary acts. They are used when we ask questions, issue commands, warnings, threats, and also, of course, when we make assertions. If this is so, and there seems to be copious evidence to support the claim, then like all assertions, metaphorical ones will be either true or false. On my view, if we know their truth conditions, we know their meaning: a meaning, moreover, which will be distinctively metaphorical inasmuch as it differs from the literal meaning of the sentence used on this occasion.

For any illocutionary act whatsoever, whether it be a question, a command, or a warning, we can derive a suitably related indicative sentence capable of bearing a truth-value.[2] Consequently, Davidson's interpretation program would seem to be applicable to all metaphorical illocutionary acts, and will involve constructing a T-sentence which gives the truth conditions for, and hence the meaning of, any given metaphor. On this view, the metaphorical utterance is always the primary bearer of metaphorical meaning. However, by working "backwards" from the T-sentence which gives its meaning, we may impute nonliteral or metaphorical meanings to individual words when it becomes clear that they cannot bear their literal meanings on this occasion of use. The difficulty, of course, for anyone interested in the problem of how we discern metaphorical meaning is to know how to construct the appropriate T-sentence. Don't we first have to know what the speaker believes, or at any rate what is intended by the utterance? And how can we possibly know this if we do not already know the meaning of the utterance?

This, we have seen, is precisely Davidson's formulation of the problem of radical interpretation.[3] The difficulty with metaphor, though, is not nearly so profound since its interpretation *qua* metaphor is never entirely radical, but always depends on our knowledge of the literal meanings of the words used within it. Indeed, we cannot so much as recognize that an utterance is a metaphor unless we know that some of the words and phrases deployed within it are not being used to have their literal meanings; and this, of course, requires knowledge of those meanings. To know the literal meaning of a word, I argued earlier, is just to know how it is standardly used: the conditions under which it is used, and how it can be combined with other words and phrases in well-formed and meaningful sentences.[4] Put differently, we can say that to know the literal meaning of a word is just to be acquainted with the established "program" for its use; and this "program," I shall now argue, plays a crucial role in the construction of any T-sentence which gives the meaning of a metaphor.

An Interpretation Program for Metaphor

Suppose that Bill Brandt comes across a well-known politician in a compromising situation, photographs the scene, and says: "I have locked you into my picture."[5] It is reasonable to suppose that what Brandt says must have some meaning, but taken literally, the metaphor makes no clear sense: it is either absurd or else patently false. In such a case we must either assume that Brandt is radically confused, or that he is fully cognizant of the fact that what his utterance means on this occasion does not coincide with the literal meaning of the sentence that he uses. Let us assume, then, that Brandt is not confused, and that his utterance, taken in context, does make some kind of (nonliteral) sense. Our problem is to know how to discern this sense.

If Donald Davidson's program is anything to go by, we are required not just to attend to the context of utterance, but to assume that Brandt's beliefs about this context are, for the most part, the same as our own. Failing this, says Davidson, we will have no reason to suppose that the speaker is fully a person, let alone a rational person.[6] It follows from this, I think, that we must initially assume (on the basis of our construal of the contextual evidence) that Brandt believes that what he is saying is both important and true. If we add to all of this the requirement that we should attend to the literal meanings of the words used on this occasion—in the belief, of course, that Brandt believes that his audience is acquainted with these meanings—then we can interpret the metaphor by constructing the following T-sentence:

> "I have locked you into my picture" is true for Brandt (in English) at time t, if and only if the speaker has indelibly recorded (on film) the visual image of some or other person in a way which accurately reveals certain aspects of the situation, at t.

Here our knowledge of the literal meanings of the words used in Brandt's utterance facilitates the process of arriving at an interpretation which has the "right holistic fit"—that is, which coheres with all or most of the other interpretations that we offer of utterances in the English language. An ability to produce this T-sentence, I would contend, shows not only that one has grasped the implicative relationships between the use of this sentence and other sentences in the English language, but also that one has grasped what the sentence *means* on this occasion.[7]

Of course, as it stands this T-sentence may very well fail to capture all the connotations and implications of the metaphor. However, there is no reason why it should not be further amended and refined until it does capture all of these. So, for instance, it might fail to capture some of the connotations of the verb "to lock." We all know that locking *limits* human mobility, that it places people under the *control* of others, that it renders them *vulnerable*, that it is achieved *mechanically*, that it is a *sudden* action, that it involves manipulating *levers*, often with the help of a *key*, and so on.

Max Black is entirely correct when he observes that metaphors are sometimes "suggestive" in just this way.[8] Often such metaphors are "emphatic" in the sense that their speaker will not allow any change to the words used, and are "resonant" insofar as they support "a high degree of implicative elaboration."[9] These are what Max Black calls "strong" metaphors, and his aim is to give a functional analysis of them, to show how they work, by applying and supplementing his earlier interaction theory of metaphor. It is perhaps because strong metaphors are always emphatic that Black is reluctant to apply Davidson's translation program to metaphor. For in his reply to Davidson, Black insists that we must "not mistake an explication of a metaphor's meaning for a translation";[10] although he argues convincingly against Davidson not just that there is such a thing as metaphorical meaning, but also that metaphors can "say" something, can have an illocutionary force, and (it would seem to follow) can be the bearers of truth-values.[11]

There is, however, no need for Black to resist the application of Davidson's program to metaphor, since the T-sentence that I have given can be progressively refined to incorporate any one, or all, of the connotations that I have mentioned, and may, of course, be extended well beyond that. This is not to say that the meaning of a metaphor is either inexhaustible or ineffable; nor is it to say that it must be indeterminate. For it seems plain that considerations of context will determine which of the implications or connotations form part of its meaning—its metaphorical meaning; and it is *this* meaning that Davidson's program seems eminently able to uncover.

It is true, of course, that resonant metaphors are semantically over-endowed, so that they are bound to have more than one meaning. "Ambiguity," as Max Black puts it, "is a necessary by-product of a metaphor's suggestiveness."[12] But this in no sense undermines my attempt to apply Davidson's program to metaphor, for the T-sentence offered by way of interpreting a resonant metaphor will always reveal this ambiguity (and will do so by incorporating the appropriate disjunctions or conjunctions). This is a positive virtue of the program, since it preserves and renders explicit what we know to be true of many metaphors—namely, that they are the bearers of multiple meanings.

There is no reason, then, why we cannot construct a Davidsonian T-sentence in order to give the meaning, the *metaphorical meaning* of Brandt's metaphor. Of course, such a T-sentence will not capture the effects of the metaphor: the fact, for instance, that the politician is upset or threatened by Brandt's utterance, or that (in Davidson's words) he is "nudged into noting" certain likenesses between photographs and prisons.[13] The reason, quite simply, is that these effects are not properly part of the meaning of the utterance, and so cannot be captured in a T-sentence which is intended to do nothing other than reveal that meaning.

The trouble, though, is that we prize and value metaphorical language precisely for its effects. It is because metaphors are particularly *effective* ways of speaking that they figure so prominently, not only in everyday discourse, but in the literary arts as well. This being the case, one might be inclined to think that if Davidson's T-sentences cannot capture these effects, we have no good reason to apply his program to metaphor. But we would be wrong to think this. For one thing, the effect that Brandt's metaphor has on our politician depends in part on the politician's emotional, cognitive, and attitudinal states at the time—and no T-sentence can be expected to capture this. However, the effect which the metaphor has will also depend on the politician's grasp of its meaning; and we have seen that Davidson's interpretation program furnishes us with this meaning. Not only this, for I shall now argue that the program also furnishes us with a means of understanding how metaphors achieve certain of their effects.

Construing a Metaphor

In order to see that this is so, it is necessary to attend very closely to the way in which one constructs a T-sentence for a metaphor. It is the process of constructing the T-sentence, we should notice, rather than the T-sentence itself, that furnishes a model in terms of which we can explain how we come to understand and respond to a metaphor.

Davidson, you will recall, lists three initial requirements for the construction of T-sentences in the case of radical interpretation. The first is that we should attend to the context of the utterance; the second, that we should assume that Brandt shares most of our beliefs about that context; and the third, that we should assume that he wishes to say something both important and true about it. To this I added the further requirement for the interpretation of a metaphor, namely, that we should attend to the literal meanings of the words used by Brandt. This is essential, for once we assume that the utterance is a metaphor, we must also assume that Brandt is acquainted with the literal meanings of the words that he uses, and that he believes his audience to be similarly acquainted. It is, then, the interplay between our knowledge of the context of use and our knowledge of the literal meanings of the words used that allows us to construct a T-sentence which furnishes the meaning of the metaphor. But how, exactly, you will ask, does this "interplay" take place?

In order to answer this question we need to remind ourselves that literal discourse consists of nothing other than the use of words and phrases in accordance with the established "programs" for their use within a given speech community. To know the "program" for the use of the word "picture" is, among other things, to know what features these objects are generally supposed to have. It is to be acquainted with a range of communal beliefs about pictures. Of course such beliefs can and do change. What a given community regards as the distinguishing features of pictures may alter as the communal body of knowledge grows, or as theories pertaining to pictures develop and change. Bearing this in mind, we may say that to know the literal meaning of the word "picture" is to be acquainted with a network of beliefs which are associated with that word in a given speech community—beliefs which constitute the established "program" for its use. This network of beliefs is what Black has called "the system of commonplaces associated with the word";[14] what he later calls its "implicative complex".[15]

Now, if we follow Davidson's requirements for the construction of a T-sentence, and if we know the literal meaning of the verb "to lock," then we are forced to assume that Brandt is not using the word to have its literal meaning on this occasion. For we know that pictures are not cages and that people cannot be locked into them. Moreover, since we believe that Brandt also knows this, we are bound to assume that when he says "I have locked you into my picture," he is not asserting that people can *literally* be locked into a picture.

The problem, of course, is to furnish the nonliteral meaning of Brandt's utterance. And since Brandt not only knows, but believes that we know, the literal meaning of the verb "to lock," it seems entirely reasonable to explore the "program" for the use of this word in order to ascertain which of the many standard beliefs about locking Brandt exploits (or covertly appeals to) in his utterance. But we can do this with a reasonable chance of success only if we bear in mind the fact that this metaphor has two subjects: that a person is said to have been *locked* into a *picture*. In order to understand what is being said, therefore, it seems reasonable to consider not only the beliefs enshrined in the "program" for the use of the word "locked," but also the beliefs reflected in the "program" for the use of the word "picture." And we need to relate these two sets of beliefs tentatively to one another. We need, provisionally, to "project" or "map" the one "program" or network of beliefs on to the other, and so "filter" the one through the other.[16]

And this, of course, is strongly reminiscent of Black's interaction view of metaphor. Unfortunately, though, these metaphorical ways of speaking, while suggestive, tend to hide rather than expose the ways in which we construct the appropriate T-sentence.

We can remedy this by looking more closely at the interaction between the sets of beliefs which constitute these "programs." Those of us who know the literal meaning of the word "lock," and so possess the "program" for its use, believe that the word is appropriately used of certain actions which

(a)   are achieved mechanically;
(b)   limit human or animal access to objects, places, or other people;
(c)   confine objects or people to certain spaces (cupboards, lockers, cages, drawers);
(d)   provide security for people or valuable objects;
(e)   may involve the use of keys;
(f)   enhance one's control over the objects, animals, or people thus confined.

And in a similar way, there is a network of beliefs associated with the word "picture." We use this word of objects which

(a′)   are two-dimensional arrangements of lines and colors;
(b′)   record visual appearances;
(c′)   are often framed;
(d′)   may "freeze" the pictured subject in pictorial space;
(e′)   are indelible;
(f′)   may be mechanically produced with the help of cameras.

Both "programs" can, of course, be extended indefinitely, but our apprehension of the context of the utterance, and, more particularly, the speaker's deliberate exploitation of that context, will direct our attention to only a few aspects of the respective "programs."

Thus, for instance, we know—and Brandt assumes that we know— that given the context of the utterance it would be entirely inappropriate for us to construe its meaning in terms of our shared belief (e) that locking may involve the use of keys. For exactly the same reason, our belief (a′) that pictures are two-dimensional arrangements of lines and colors cannot plausibly be taken to have any bearing on the meaning of Brandt's utterance. To a very large extent, then, Brandt relies on what he takes to be our shared knowledge of the context of the utterance in order, as it were, to subvert possible misconstruals of its meaning, and to restrict quite severely the range of plausible interpretations that we can offer of it.

This same knowledge prompts us to single out more likely beliefs in terms of which to construe the utterance. It seems more appropriate, for instance, to try to construe its meaning in terms of the beliefs (c), (b), and (f): the beliefs, namely, that by locking people up one confines them, limits their freedom, and enhances the control that others have over them. But why, you will ask, should these beliefs be thought to apply to pictures? The short answer is that they are not thought to apply. They are thought only to be potentially applicable in this context to a subset of pictures—namely, photographs; and as a result they are tentatively projected on to certain of our beliefs about (photographic) pictures in order to ascertain whether this sheds any light on the meaning of the utterance. And it is the form and context of Brandt's pronouncement, as well as the fact that we are puzzled by it, which encourages us to do so.

Suppose, then, that our beliefs (b), (c), and (f) are projected on to certain of the beliefs that we associate with the word "picture": the beliefs (b') and (e'), that (photographic) pictures record visual appearances, and that they do so indelibly. The resultant ways of thinking of the indelible and recording properties of pictures (that they confine us, limit our freedom, and enhance the control that others have over us) is then tentatively entertained in order to ascertain whether it enables us to make better sense of the photographer's utterance. If it does, we may decide that this construal helps furnish the truth conditions for Brandt's utterance, and hence that it gives us the meaning, or part of the meaning, of the metaphor. But even if we do think this, we may continue to cast around in a similar fashion in order to ascertain whether the meaning of the utterance can plausibly be construed in additional or alternative ways. So, (c) may be projected on to (c'); (a) on to (f'). As a result, we will tentatively think of the frame of a picture (c') as a way of confining the pictured subject (c); or of the click of a camera shutter (f') as the act of turning the key in a lock (a). My guess is that in this context we will think of the former rather than the latter as part of what Brandt's utterance "I have locked you into my picture" means; although this is a point to which I shall return later on.

This, then, is the way in which we come to construct a T-sentence for Bill Brandt's metaphor. The process, I have said, involves projecting certain of the beliefs associated with the verb "to lock" on to those associated with the word "picture," and vice versa. The metaphor of *projection*, however, should not be allowed to hide the tentative and exploratory nature of this activity. To some it might suggest that the process is well regulated—a suggestion which altogether ignores its imaginative dimension. It is, one might say, a process of imaginative aspection in which we are successively brought to entertain, consider, and in this sense "see" various aspects of pictures through the medium of beliefs which pertain to the action of locking, and various aspects of locking through beliefs which pertain to pictures.

Certainly our knowledge of the context of the utterance will influence which beliefs are eventually adopted as relevant, and which rejected as irrelevant, to our construal of the meaning of the utterance. This is why I have described the construction of a T-sentence for a metaphor as a function of the interplay between our knowledge of literal meanings on the one hand and context on the other. "Interplay" should be construed as what Kant would call a kind of "free play"; for the process, although constrained by our knowledge of the context, remains fundamentally tentative, and is one in which construals are adopted or abandoned more or less at will. There are no set moves, no procedures to be followed. The most that we can do is reconstruct the course of our imaginings, but we cannot lay down rules that, if followed, will invariably unlock the semantics of metaphor.[17]

On my view, then, we construct a T-sentence for Brandt's metaphor by proceeding imaginatively—and this is what we are forced to do in any case of interpretation or translation.[18] The trouble, though, is that Davidson also insists that:

The evidence for the interpretation of a particular utterance will . . . have to be evidence for the interpretation of all utterances of a speaker or a community.[19]

In the light of this, it is objected that insofar as the T-sentence for Brandt's metaphor does not impute literal meanings to its constituent words, the evidence for its correctness cannot count as evidence for the interpretation of literal utterances in Brandt's language. And this, it is suggested, is why Davidson's interpretation program cannot properly be made to apply to metaphor.[20]

But this objection is misplaced. For, as we have seen, the evidence for the T-sentence that we offer of Brandt's metaphor *will* furnish evidence for the interpretation of other utterances in the language provided that the interpreter either knows, or assumes, or (in the case of a non-native inter-preter) eventually reaches the conclusion that Brandt's words do not bear their literal meaning on this occasion of use. Since the interpreter who recognizes the metaphorical status of Brandt's utterance will know that his (Brandt's) words do not bear their literal meaning, there is no reason why the evidence for the T-sentence offered on this occasion cannot be used to compute the T-sentences for other utterances in Brandt's language. After all, if the interpreter knows that the verb "to lock" is not being used literally, then the very same evidence which counts toward the interpretation of Brandt's metaphor could count as evidence for an interpretation of the literal utterance "You cannot lock people into pictures."

The problem is greater in the case of the non-native interpreter. Such an interpreter will not initially recognize the metaphorical status of Brandt's utterance, and, as a result, the evidence for its interpretation will not initially count as evidence for the interpretation of other utterances in Brandt's language. The non-native interpreter will soon find that the T-sentence offered, in the light of this evidence, for the literal utterance "I will lock you up" is inadequate and generates inconsistent interpretations within the language. In such a case, the non-native interpreter plainly has a long and tedious row to hoe, but will, after a series of failures, discover the way in which the evidence for the interpretation of Brandt's metaphor can serve as evidence for the interpretation of other utterances in the language. In effect, this involves coming to recognize the metaphorical status of the utterance. The process, although long and difficult, must be possible if Davidson's arguments against conceptual relativism are correct.[21]

From Meaning to Emotion

It is the imaginative play involved in interpreting a metaphor, I shall now argue, which is in large measure responsible for the affective dimension of Brandt's metaphor.

We know that as our politician casts around for suitable construals of the metaphor, certain contextually selected beliefs about locking are tentatively mapped on to other similarly selected beliefs about pictures (and vice versa). Each such construal is considered, and will be abandoned if it does not help furnish the meaning of Brandt's utterance. Thus, for instance, our politician may, in pondering the utterance, tentatively project the belief (a) that locking is achieved mechanically, on to the belief (f′) that pictures may be mechanically produced with the help of cameras. Photographic pictures, the politician might be led to think, are mechanically contrived snares.

In context, of course, it seems unlikely that this is part of what the utterance means. For all that, though, this way of thinking about pictures will very likely set up a chain of associations. The shutter of the camera becomes a device for "shutting" or entombing our politician: it "shuts" him up—and does so in more than one sense. It becomes a window "shutter"—a barrier with horizontal prison bars. In this way, we move randomly or at will from association to association. None of this, I emphasize, need be part of the meaning of Brandt's utterance; whether it is must depend on whether or not Brandt can reasonably be expected to share these associations. If not, then they will not find their way into our T-sentence. However, they may still form part of that fanciful process of elimination whereby the T-sentence comes to be constructed, and if they do, then, provided that we have certain values and concerns, they will become the object of a range of emotions. Our politician may quite understandably become frightened by these ideas; and recognizing his own fear and his helplessness in the face of it, he finds a new object of emotion and is angered, or frustrated, or self-pitying.[22] As sympathetic bystanders, we may feel similar emotions, or we may take an altogether less sympathetic view and delight in the politician's discomfort.

What emerges, then, is that each tentative construal of the meaning of the metaphor, as well as the associations and elaborations that it encourages, can become the object of a cluster of emotions. This, of course, is integral to the affective dimension of metaphor, and, on my view, is properly discerned only when an audience attempts to construe the meaning of a metaphor. To this someone will no doubt object that the very same range of emotional effects could be produced without anyone trying to locate the (metaphorical) meaning of Brandt's metaphor. Why, it will be asked, can't the literal meanings of the words in this metaphor alone prod us into the chain of associations and elaborations responsible for these emotional effects? And this, of course, is precisely Donald Davidson's point.

Nor is Davidson's position without substance. For it is true that our knowledge of the literal meanings of the words used in a metaphor can itself produce a variety of associations, elaborations, and emotions. In this respect the objection is entirely correct. There is another respect, however, in which it is deficient. For although Davidson allows, correctly, that our knowledge of the literal meanings of the words used in a metaphor can set off an indefinitely large chain of associations and subsequent emotions, he fails to recognize that not all of these will be appropriate to the metaphor. Indeed, if one is to be able to talk informatively of the affective power of Brandt's metaphor, one has to be able to tell which of these (sometimes highly idiosyncratic) associations and emotions are appropriate to it. But in order to do this we have first to ascertain which of our many commonplace beliefs about the subjects of the metaphor Brandt is exploiting. It is clear, though, from what I have already said, that once we do this we are, in effect, attempting to uncover the (metaphorical) meaning of Brandt's utterance. This is why I have insisted that the affective dimension of a metaphor is only properly discerned relative to its (metaphorical) meaning. It is only when we know the meaning of Brandt's utterance—no matter how vague or multifarious it may be—that we can know which responses to it are appropriate, which inappropriate.

By this stage it should be abundantly clear that Davidson's interpretation program can be applied to metaphor in a way which helps us explain not only how we arrive at the meaning of a metaphor, but also how we come to be moved by it. Still more, it can, I think, facilitate an account of the cognitive effects of metaphor, for by entertaining various imaginative construals of the meaning of Brandt's metaphor, one may come to think of pictures differently, and to notice or invent relations between them and other objects which were previously unremarked. Our imaginative elaborations and the various associations which they conjure up may forge new conceptual connections, and this is best regarded as a cognitive effect of the metaphor. As a result of Brandt's utterance, for instance, our politician may come to think of cameras, say, as tombs. And he may continue to think of them in this way even though there is no temptation on his (or anyone else's) part to think either that this is part of what the metaphor means, or that it is in any way a function of the metaphor's meaning.

Such a response is, of course, inappropriate. It has little or nothing to do with the meaning of the metaphor, but depends instead on our politician's idiosyncratic and largely subjective associations. Certainly such a response can be regarded as a cognitive *effect* of the metaphor, but it is not properly a part of the metaphor's cognitive *content*. The reason, quite simply, is that unless the cognitive content of a metaphor is thought of as a function of the metaphor's meaning, it is difficult to think of it as properly attaching to, and so as being part of the content of, the metaphor. But although a function of meaning, cognitive content should not be confused with it; nor should it be regarded as a kind of message.[23] The meaning of an utterance, like a message, is (as Davidson observes) always propositional in character. Its cognitive content, by contrast, need not always be, but may instead involve the acquisition of conceptual skills of one sort or another. As a result of the cognitive content of a metaphor, one may come to see the world differently, or to think differently about it—where these metaphorically induced skills are irreducibly nonpropositional and so cannot be identified with either the meaning or the message of the metaphor.

Conclusion

Contrary to Davidson's view of the matter, the fact that metaphors can have an indefinitely large number of emotive and cognitive effects in no way militates against the possibility of metaphorical meaning.[24] Indeed, by using his interpretation program we have found that it is not especially difficult to uncover the meaning of a metaphor. And once this has been ascertained, it becomes a comparatively straightforward and eminently rational matter to decide which responses to the metaphor are appropriate, which inappropriate.

Davidson seems to think that we only ever *imagine* that metaphors have a meaning or a message, and that we do so because "all the while we are in fact focussing on what the metaphor makes us notice."[25] But in this he is wrong. Certainly metaphors can jolt and prod us into noticing a great many things, not all of which will be propositional. Nonetheless, I have shown that metaphors do have nonliteral meanings which must be sharply distinguished from their cognitive and affective dimensions. Indeed, a grasp of a metaphor's meaning will alone enable us to tell which of our many responses to it are appropriate. Not all will be, and Davidson seems unable to distinguish between those that are and those that are not. He certainly cannot appeal to the literal meaning of the metaphor as a criterion of appropriateness, for we know that when construed literally the metaphor makes no proper sense.

As I have explained it, it is only after we have discerned a metaphor's meaning that we can tell which of our very many responses to it are apposite, and which not. The aim of this chapter has been to defend the possibility of metaphorical meaning, and, by invoking Davidsonian semantics, to show in some detail how it may properly be discerned. What we have found is that an application of Davidson's interpretation program to metaphor results in an account of metaphorical meaning which is not very different from Max Black's interaction theory of metaphor. Far from such a theory, ignoring the affective and cognitive dimensions of metaphor, I have shown that it is able to account fully and handsomely for both.

NINE

Metaphors of Fiction

It is wrong to think of the language of fiction as radically different from that of nonfiction. For, as we have now seen, unless fiction preserves most of the logical and conceptual connections of nonfictional discourse, we will simply be unable to comprehend it.[1] It is to be expected, therefore, that any viable account of how ordinary, nonfictional metaphors work will apply equally to the metaphors of fiction. Despite this, it seems obvious that the metaphors of fiction are often more powerful, more suggestive and effective, than those of nonfictional discourse. This needs to be explained, and contrary to Donald Davidson and those who follow him, I shall argue that such an explanation is forced to rely on the notion of metaphorical meaning, and is, moreover, fully compatible with the interaction theory of metaphor.[2]

Since literary fictions are invariably the offspring of an author's imaginings, the language of fiction is often more contrived, more deliberately, cleverly, and precisely arranged, than that of nonfictional discourse. Our descriptions of the actual world, even when couched in metaphor, are constrained by our experiences of the world, and we have relatively little control over the contexts in which they are construed. In fiction, by contrast, the constraints of experience are less direct and much less obvious. To a very large extent it is simply up to the author to delineate a world of his or her invention; and it is a world whose language can be, and usually is, designed to highlight certain events, emphasize certain values and attitudes, display certain insights, and create certain effects.

Metaphors, it is well known, prod and nudge us into noticing certain likenesses; they launch us into chains of associations—and in this sense at least are often highly suggestive. Whether or not we are emotionally affected by any of these likenesses or associations, and the extent to which we are moved by them, will depend on our values and concerns at the time. Consequently, if an author can construct a narrative in a way which encourages certain concerns and cultivates certain values, the metaphors of the text which exploit any of these will usually have greater affective force than a metaphor which occurs in a context over which the speaker has relatively less control. For in the latter context it is less likely that the appropriate values and concerns will be before the audience's mind in the way that they are made to be in a fictional context. My claim, then, is that metaphors are very much more effective in contexts especially designed for them. In all other contexts, the speaker can usually only assume, but usually has no direct input into, or control over, the listener's immediate concerns and concomitant values.

It would be convenient at this point to give an exhaustive classification of the many ways in which authors contrive to enhance the metaphors of their texts. But to do so *a priori* seems impossible. The most that we can do, I think, is to confine ourselves to certain examples. This will not only enable me to defend what I have said so far, but will also go some way toward explaining the lately unfashionable notion of a literary symbol which Nelson Goodman and others so studiously avoid.[3]

Sentential Metaphors of Fiction

Let us take, as our first example, a metaphor from James Joyce's *A Portrait of the Artist as a Young Man*. At a certain point, Joyce writes: "The air was soft and grey and mild and evening was coming."[4] Let us consider the metaphor "The air was soft." If one is not acquainted with the context within which this metaphor occurs, then my bet is that it will appear to be an especially limp and flaccid example, one without punch or vigor. Indeed, taken out of context, one might consider it a dead metaphor, or one fast approaching that state. But when we reconstruct its context, the metaphor takes on an entirely different hue.

The context of its occurrence is complicated. Stephen Dedalus, a sensitive and lonely child, is sent away from the mother and family he loves to a Jesuit boarding school. He is bewildered by this new, hostile world, and after accidentally breaking his glasses is unjustly beaten and made to kneel in front of the class by the prefect of studies:

—Lazy idle little loafer! cried the prefect of studies. Broke my glasses! An old
schoolboy trick! Out with your hand this moment!
Stephen closed his eyes and held out in the air his trembling hand with the palm
upwards. He felt the prefect of studies touch it for a moment at the fingers to
straighten it and then the swish of the sleeve of the soutane as the pandybat was
lifted to strike. A hot burning stinging tingling blow like the loud crack of a
broken stick made his trembling hand crumple together like a leaf in the fire: and
at the sound and the pain scalding tears were driven into his eyes. (*Portrait of the
Artist*, pp. 50–51)

Frightened and not a little upset by this injustice, Stephen seeks redress
from the rector, and walks through the long, dark, gloomy corridors of the
school seeking directions to the rector's study.

By this stage the reader is rightly apprehensive, for it seems plain that
the rector could easily compound the injustice. Happily he does not do so,
but chooses instead to trivialize the incident, and to regard the beating as
the result of a simple misunderstanding. After an overwrought and tearful
encounter, the small boy eventually emerges into the evening air relieved
and euphoric. And Joyce writes: "The air was soft and grey and mild and
evening was coming." Our skillfully nurtured concern for the boy and for
the sanctity of his innocence furnish the values in terms of which we respond to the metaphor. The "softness" of the air is thought of as a balm to
the boy. We are happy that he is healed, and we are suffused with feelings
of relief at his misplaced but welcome euphoria.

It seems clear from this that authors can and do control the contexts in
which metaphors of fiction occur. Our awareness of that context, as well as
our imaginative participation in it, heightens the affective power, and directs
the suggestiveness, of the metaphor. Consequently, what at first seems a
half-dead metaphor when taken out of its literary context, becomes, if not
a lively metaphor, at least a powerful and highly suggestive one when taken
in the context designed for it by Joyce. There can, of course, be no assurance
that Joyce's manipulation of the context will instill the appropriate concerns
in the reader. This must depend on the reader's initial values. A sadist will
be delighted by Stephen's beating, and such a reader will not be affected by
the metaphor in anything like the way that I have suggested. It is nonetheless
the case that Joyce can reasonably assume certain initial values on the part
of his readership; and it is with these in mind that he constructs the scene.

It is true, of course, that in this context a reader will not usually have
to compute the meaning of the metaphor in the way suggested, say, by Max
Black or John Searle.[5] And it is true, too, that one misses the point of this

metaphor if one dwells extensively on the meaning of the word "soft" in this context. The point of the metaphor is plainly affective. Even so—and contrary to what Donald Davidson and Stein Haugom Olsen suggest—it does not follow from this that the word "soft" bears its literal meaning on this occasion of use. Those who argue that it does appear to believe that the literal meaning of the word can summon up all sorts of associations and emotions in the reader, and that it is these, rather than an ineffable metaphorical meaning, which are responsible for the affective dimension of the metaphor. But this suggestion at once poses the problem, to which our attention was drawn in the previous chapter, that not all of the associations and emotions conjured up by the literal meaning of the word will be appropriate to the metaphor, and that the reader has to have some way of deciding which are appropriate and which are not. No doubt Davidson, like Olsen, would contend that it is the context of the metaphor which helps us to discern this, but such a move, as we shall now see, immediately commits them to the notion of metaphorical meaning.[6]

This requires an explanation, and a good place to start is with the commonplace observation that when used literally, the words "air" and "soft" are applied in regular and systematic ways in accordance with certain of our beliefs about air and softness. Air is something you *breathe*, it is *life-sustaining*, it is *gaseous*, it can be *still* or in *motion, cold* or *warm, refreshing, transparent*, and so on. Something that is soft, on the other hand, may be *malleable, manipulable, solid* yet *yielding, smooth* and even *quiet* (i.e., *not loud*). As we saw earlier, these beliefs about the subjects of our metaphor are what Max Black calls their "associated commonplaces," and on his version, like most versions of the interaction theory, any metaphor such as Joyce's invites us to "look at" or think about one subject of the metaphor in terms of beliefs associated with, and appropriate to, the other.

It is, however, immediately apparent from the context of Joyce's metaphor that not all of these beliefs will be of equal use; that when he writes "The air was soft" he does not wish us to think of the air as *malleable* or *manipulable*; still less that softness should be "looked at" as *transparent* or *gaseous*. Were we to consider the subjects of the metaphor in these ways we would no doubt have whole trains of associations and a host of emotional responses consequent upon them, but not one of these would be appropriate to the metaphor. It seems obvious, though, that in the context created by Joyce, we are being invited to project a range of different beliefs about air (that it is *life-sustaining* and *refreshing*) on to very specific beliefs about softness (that soft things may be *smooth, yielding, quiet*). In this way we are brought to think of the softness of the air as a balm, a restorative, which helps banish Stephen's fears and heal his pain.

When once we discern this we have at our disposal a means of telling whether any given emotional or associative response to Joyce's metaphor is appropriate. Clearly, though, we can only do so because we have already ascertained which of our beliefs about air and softness Joyce appeals to or exploits on this occasion. But to say this is just to say that we have already ascertained what the word "soft" means in this context. Moreover, since what is meant (that the air is *healing* or a *balm*) is at odds with any of the literal meanings that "soft" can bear, it seems reasonable to suppose that the word has a nonliteral, figurative, or metaphorical meaning on this occasion of its use. It is true, of course, that in this context any competent reader will discern this meaning without conscious effort and certainly without having to engage in any lengthy computations. The fact that the metaphor is somewhat hackneyed makes the process of discernment all the easier, and ensures that whatever its point, it cannot be cognitive.

If anything at all is now clear, it is that the literal meaning of the word "soft" can produce indefinitely many affective responses, not all of which will be appropriate to Joyce's metaphor. Any attempt to appeal to the context of the metaphor in order to ascertain the appropriateness of a response to it, is, we have now seen, an attempt to show which of our many commonplace beliefs about air and softness Joyce means to exploit on this occasion. But once we do this, we are in effect trying to show what "soft" means in its metaphorical setting. We are appealing to its metaphorical meaning, not its literal meaning.

There is a further reason why we cannot appeal to the literal meaning of the word "soft" within this context if we are ever to grasp Joyce's metaphor. The fact of the matter is that the word has several literal meanings, and there is no way of knowing which of these it bears in the context designed for it by Joyce. We simply cannot tell whether the word "soft" means *malleable* or *manipulable* or *weak* or *smooth* or *quiet* or *yielding*. Indeed, if we could glean any of these meanings from the context of the metaphor, we would have to allow that the literal meaning thus discovered was appropriate to that context — for how otherwise could the context be a clue to its meaning? But when once we believe that "soft" bears an *appropriate* literal meaning in this context, what possible reason can we have for thinking that "The air was soft" is a metaphor?

It is for all of these reasons, then, that one cannot consistently maintain

(1) that metaphors bear only the literal meanings of their constituent words, and (2) that we can appeal to their contexts in order to discover which among many possible affective responses to them are appropriate.

So while it is true that the point of Joyce's metaphor is neither cognitive nor semantic, but is plainly affective, we can only tell which affective responses to it are appropriate once we have discerned its metaphorical meaning. My argument, therefore, threatens Olsen's suggestion that the interaction theory of metaphor, insisting as it does on metaphorical meaning, is unable to account for certain literary metaphors.[7] This, we are told, is true of "ornamental metaphors": metaphors, that is, which are purely decorative and have "no cognitive content except that presented by the literal meaning of the expression" ("Understanding Literary Metaphors," p. 42).

An example of an ornamental metaphor, Olsen maintains, is to be found in Oberon's well-known speech:

> I with the Morning's love have oft made sport,
> And like a forester, the groves may tread
> Even till the eastern gate all fiery red,
> Opening on Neptune, with fair blessed beams
> Turns into yellow gold his salt green streams.

(*A Midsummer Night's Dream*, III, ii, 390–94)

The claim is that the expression "the eastern gate" is an ornamental metaphor which does not, in this context, possess a metaphorical meaning. The reader, we are told, "recognizes the referent of the metaphorical expression," but does so without recourse to a metaphorical meaning. The metaphor, it is contended, is "not an invitation to compute a speaker's meaning, but to visualise" (p. 42).

Even if we agree, and I certainly do, that it would be a mistake to dwell on the meaning of this metaphor, we are still left with the problem of explaining how we know what should or should not be visualized in response to it. It seems clear that one should not visualize the sun creeping through a wicker or a wrought-iron gate; still less through a garden or a city gate. It seems altogether more appropriate to visualize a blazing sun at dawn rising over a "yellow gold" sea. But how can we know that this is more appropriate? Only, I have shown, because we know that "gate" does not bear its literal meaning on this occasion of its use. Contrary to what Olsen says, it is clear from the context created by Puck's and Oberon's interchange that "gate" means something like *beginning* or *daybreak*—for

Shakespeare here exploits the temporal beliefs which attach to a sunrise (the east "all fiery red") in order to convey the idea that the gate is where the day *begins*. For this, of course, is where the sun *enters* our world and *starts* its journey across the sky. Hence by using the interaction theory of metaphor it becomes possible to explain not only how the word acquires this meaning in the present context, but also why a specific response to the metaphor is either appropriate or inappropriate. And it is the all but spontaneous grasp of this meaning in the context created for it by Shakespeare that directs the reader's visual imaginings.

My argument so far stresses the importance of literary contexts in determining the effectiveness of metaphors of fiction. It is the context of the metaphor, I have shown, which in a sense controls or manipulates the reader's values, and, by enabling us to grasp its figurative meaning, directs the reader's response to it. But the story does not end here. For it seems plain that such contexts will also determine how important or central a metaphor (or set of metaphors) is to the fiction. Metaphors can be more or less strategically situated and, in a manner of speaking, can become structural devices which bear a great deal of the thematic "weight" of the fiction. Such metaphors will not only have an affective dimension, but will also possess considerable cognitive value.

This emerges quite clearly in *A Portrait of the Artist as a Young Man*. The novel teems with metaphors of light which, if taken out of context, would at times appear senseless, at times hackneyed and dull. In context, though, they can be seen to develop, embellish, and sustain the theme of the novel. Consider this extended metaphor near the beginning of Chapter Three. Stephen is staring at an equation on the page of his scribbler that begins "to unfold itself" and to "spread abroad its widening tail." And Joyce writes:

It was his own soul going forth to experience, unfolding itself sin by sin, spreading abroad the bale-fire of its burning stars and folding back upon itself, fading slowly, quenching its own light and fires. They were quenched: and the cold darkness filled chaos. (p. 103)

Taken out of context, the metaphor of his soul "spreading abroad the bale-fire of its burning stars" makes little sense, and it is, of course, quite impossible to gauge its import in the novel as a whole.

But this is easily remedied, for when once we read the opening paragraphs of this chapter, the metaphor does begin to make sense. In the very first paragraph we are apprised of the dullness, the routine, and the confinement of Stephen's school life:

The swift December dusk had come tumbling clownishly after its dull day and, as he stared through the dull square of the window of the schoolroom, he felt his belly crave for its food.

It is all dull and routine; except, that is, for the "swift December dusk," for we are told:

It would be a gloomy secret night. After early nightfall the yellow lamps would light up, here and there, the squalid quarter of the brothels. He would follow a devious course up and down the streets, circling always nearer and nearer in a tremor of fear and joy, until his feet led him suddenly round a dark corner. (p. 102)

The secrets of the night, the yellow lamps, the brothels, attract Stephen as a moth to a flame ("circling always nearer and nearer in a tremor of fear and joy"); and we are reminded at this point (as at many others) of Stephen's namesake—the other Daedalus—who in his attempt to escape the dullness of interminable imprisonment in the Labyrinth of Crete, flies, together with Icarus, toward the sun.

In addition to this, earlier chapters will have brought the reader to suspect that Stephen is impatient of the ideological fetters that he is made to bear; that although he is imprisoned by them, he seeks to shake them off and to achieve a degree of enlightenment. And so we understand what is meant when Joyce writes: "It was his soul going forth to experience." But not all experience, the reader realizes, is of equal value, and at this point the "stars" of enlightenment seem less attractive to Stephen than the "yellow lamps" of the brothels. It is in this context—in the context, that is, of what precedes (and, eventually, what proceeds from) the extended metaphor of Stephen's soul "spreading abroad the bale-fire of its burning stars," that we can begin not just to make sense of it, but to gauge its importance in the work as a whole.

The metaphor clearly exploits a whole range of commonplace beliefs about light, fire, stars, and darkness in a way which enables us to grasp its meaning, and thereby the allusion to the flailing Icarus. That the metaphor is of more than passing importance is clear from its location in the novel. It not only articulates some of our earlier concerns and insights regarding Stephen, but it anticipates others. It is a metaphor that is reinforced and enhanced by related metaphors of light and darkness, which abound both at this point and elsewhere in the work. When, toward the end of the novel, we read "his soul was waking slowly. . . . It was that windless hour of dawn when madness wakes and strange plants open to the light and the moth flies forth silently" (p. 216), we are reminded of the earlier metaphor, which informs, and is informed by, the present one. The novel, one could say, takes its form around this cluster of interrelated metaphors of light, which, far from being idly repetitive, enrich one another, and enhance the reader's grasp of the entire work.

In such cases it is the literary context of the metaphor which determines its scope and thematic importance within the work. There are, of course, degrees of both, and it seems safe to say that most metaphors of fiction will be less pivotal than the metaphors of light in Joyce's novel. Some will have a purely decorative function, others will be cognitively valuable but scarcely pivotal, and a few will be quite central to the work. On my view, it is always the context of the metaphor (and, of course, the way in which we interpret that context) that determines a metaphor's scope and function within a work. One could put this differently by saying that it is misleading to suppose that there are settled *kinds* of literary metaphors. It is altogether more appropriate to think of metaphorical expressions as having different, contextually determined, functions. Thus, for instance, the expression "the eastern gate" could assume a function (in a speech other than Oberon's) which affords it much greater scope in a particular context than it has in the context designed for it by Shakespeare. And there will, of course, be as many functions for metaphors of fiction as an author can invent. It is for this reason that we can hardly hope to give an exhaustive classification of literary metaphors.[8] Nor can such a classification ever be based on the syntactic features of the metaphorical expression, but must, instead, be based on its function in a given literary context.

Juxtapository Metaphors of Fiction

There are many, perhaps infinitely many, ways in which an author can construct contexts for metaphors of fiction, and we cannot pursue all of these here. More important at this stage is the fact that not all metaphors of fiction share the same structure, for not all are sentential in form. Some involve the stark and incongruous verbal juxtaposition of two or more subjects and their associated ideas without any explicit predicative relationship between them. These I shall call juxtapository metaphors. A clear example of one can be found in the passage from Joyce I cited earlier, for he there aligns soutane and pandybat in a way which invites the reader to think of those who wear soutanes in terms of the violence and pain of the descending pandybat. And this may very well test or tease or shape the reader's attitude to the priesthood.

It seems quite clear, then, that this juxtaposition is not merely contrastive in function. For in this case some of our commonplace ideas and beliefs (what Max Black calls "associated commonplaces") about one of the subjects somehow informs our notions about, and attitudes toward, the other. And this, in part, is why we regard it as a metaphor. There are many other juxtapositions in Joyce's novel which do not invite such a transference and which we do not regard as metaphorical. Thus, for instance, we find as part of the very same incident that the calm air of evening is juxtaposed with Stephen's ordeal, but we do not regard this as a metaphor. Its function is contrastive, for it breaks the tension of the narrative by a sudden, contrasting, and lyrically measured change of scene. The context is such that there is little point in transferring any of our ordinary beliefs about the approach of evening to Stephen's ordeal, or vice versa. As a result, our beliefs about the respective poles of the contrast do not interact with or inform one another. The case is plainly different with soutane and pandybat, for we know from our reading that the novel is concerned, among other things, with the influence and power of the priesthood. Rich in this knowledge, we are virtually forced to think of the soutane, and hence (through a metonymic transfer) the priesthood, in terms appropriate to the pandybat.

This example demonstrates quite clearly that juxtapository metaphors do occur, and, moreover, that they can occur in a single passage and at a single point within the unfolding of a narrative. Much more significant, though, is the fact that a particular juxtapository metaphor can pervade an entire work, and in some sense signal its theme. In George Eliot's *The Mill on the Floss*, for instance, Maggie Tulliver's life is lived out alongside the river Floss; and from time to time throughout the novel some of our beliefs about the irreversible flow, the life-sustaining force, and the capriciousness of the river inform our view of her. If I am right, we can properly regard the river Floss as a metaphor for the sustenance and bounty, the capriciousness and danger, which infuse the action of the novel. Much the same, I think, is true of the railway in *Anna Karenina*. Nowhere in the novel does Tolstoy predicate the attributes of rail travel to Anna's life; and yet, as a result of their juxtaposition in the novel, the railway "comments" on her life, and can be regarded as a metaphor for the echoes of fate which haunt the narrative.

Metaphors of this sort abound in fiction. Of Franz Kafka's *The Castle* it could well be said that the castle broods over the action of the novel, and becomes a metaphor for the unknown, the impregnable, and the oppressive. The whale in *Moby Dick*; the fox in D. H. Lawrence's short story of that title; the storm in *King Lear*, like that in Thomas Hardy's *Far from the Madding Crowd*, are all arguably juxtapository metaphors which comment on aspects of the narrative.

Literary critics often attest to the presence of, and take some delight in discovering, such metaphors. Sandra M. Gilbert argues for "transvestism as metaphor in modern literature." Quoting from Virginia Woolf, she tells us "it is clothes that wear us and not we them," adding that "we may make them take the mould of arm or breast, but clothes mould our hearts, our brains, our tongues to their liking."[9] And using this as her model, Gilbert goes on to show how transsexual dress functions as a metaphor in the works of Joyce, D. H. Lawrence, T. S. Eliot, and Virginia Woolf.[10]

And writing of *Anna Karenina* in an article entitled "Tolstoy's Metaphor," the critic Anatole Broyard construes the death of Vronsky's horse in the steeplechase as a metaphor which comments on Vronsky's treatment of Anna.[11] Of the last jump in the race, Tolstoy writes:

She flew over it like a bird, but at the same instant, Vronsky, to his horror felt that he had failed to keep up with the mare's pace, that he had, he did not know how, made a fearful, unpardonable mistake in recovering his seat in the saddle.

The horse falls, and Tolstoy continues:

She fluttered on the ground at his feet like a shot bird. The clumsy movement made by Vronsky had broken her back.[12]

According to Broyard, what Vronsky has done is to break Anna's back, too. "His 'clumsy movement' was in encouraging her to leave her husband when she was already at the limit of her strength."[13]

Critics plainly do allow that there are metaphors of (what I have called) a juxtapository sort. However, to my knowledge these critics are altogether silent about the ways in which they differ from ordinary sentential metaphors. Up until now I have characterized this difference in terms of the absence of explicit predication, saying that a juxtapository metaphor involves only the alignment of two incongruous subjects without predicating the one of the other. But this is not entirely accurate. Take, by way of example, John Irving's *The World According to Garp*. In this novel, Garp the growing youth and writer is starkly juxtaposed with Garp the wrestler, so that his wrestling can be seen to inform his struggle to grow and to write. The trouble, though, is that although a juxtapository metaphor, Irving does describe Garp the writer as a wrestler. He writes:

In that first wrestling season at Steering, Garp worked hard and happily at learning his moves and his holds. . . . He knew that he had found his sport and his pastime; it would take the best of his energy until the writing came along.[14]

Garp the writer is said to be a wrestler. Predication does take place, albeit in a somewhat roundabout way. And yet, if I am right, we have a juxtapository, not a sentential, metaphor. Why is this so?

A first point to notice is that Irving's description of Garp as a wrestler makes perfectly good sense when construed literally. It lacks the absurdity, or else the falsity, or else the triviality, of a literally construed sentential metaphor. Second, even though Irving's description is neither absurd, nor false, nor trivial, it does seem to be *odd* that a sensitive youngster, an aspirant writer, should want to be, and should become, a wrestler. Our many preconceptions about wrestlers and writers make it difficult for us to align the two. It is this incongruity which prompts us to try and make sense of aspects of Irving's novel by viewing the one activity (writing) through the medium of beliefs commonly associated with the other (wrestling).

So although it is characteristic of a juxtapository metaphor that it does not involve explicit predication, this is by no means a necessary feature of such metaphors. What is necessary is that such predication, when it occurs, should make good literal sense, for otherwise we would be left with nothing more than a sentential metaphor. Also necessary is a degree of incongruity. It should at the very least appear to be of interest, and thereby at odds with our conception of the normal course of things, that Lear is in a storm, that a fox is in the chicken run, that the river Floss figures prominently and forebodingly in the background to Maggie Tulliver's life, that Vronsky kills his mare, and that Garp is a wrestler. In each of these cases, though, we can properly speak of a juxtapository metaphor only if we make sense of the incongruity in the way that we normally make sense of sentential metaphors —that is, by thinking of, or "viewing," the one subject in terms proper to the other. For unless we respond to the juxtaposition in a way reminiscent of our response to the more central cases of metaphor, we will have no grounds at all for regarding the juxtaposition as a metaphor.

These observations go some way toward distinguishing juxtapository metaphors from their sentential cousins. But a good deal more remains to be said. Part of the problem is that not everyone will find the same juxtaposition incongruous, for what we regard as odd varies with our knowledge, beliefs, and attitudes. Consequently, if we treat incongruity as a necessary condition for such metaphors, it turns out that whether or not a particular alignment of subjects in a novel counts as a metaphor must depend on the reader, and not, as one might have supposed, on the author. And if this is right, it must be inappropriate to praise an author for the juxtository metaphors in his or her text. This, of course, seems odd and is in need of resolution. A parallel problem arises when we reflect on the fact that not everyone will consider the same subjects in a novel to be juxtaposed or aligned. Why, someone might ask, should we think that the death of Vronsky's horse Frou-Frou is juxtaposed with the fate of Anna Karenina? Why not treat this as just another event in a long and complex novel? Isn't it possible that Broyard just *invents* the juxtaposition? Then, again, why should we think the juxtaposition incongruous? Wouldn't one expect a Russian cavalry officer of the nineteenth century to ride a horse in a steeple-chase? Much worse, if it is true that Broyard invents the juxtaposition, and if he alone finds it incongruous, in what sense is he justified in speaking of it as "Tolstoy's Metaphor"?

One must, of course, concede that not everyone will find the same juxtaposition incongruous—and that whether or not one does, depends on one's knowledge, beliefs, values, and expectations. Some readers may think the juxtaposition of Frou-Frou's death and Anna's life entirely congruous, since the one (they might say) clearly resembles the other. In such a case, though, if one cannot attribute incongruity to the juxtaposition, it would be inappropriate to regard it as a metaphor at all. We would do better to regard it as a juxtository simile, or, as we shall see presently, as a literary image.

Even though people do not find the same juxtapositions incongruous, it does not follow from this that incongruity in a work is a function simply of the reader's cognitive state. Nor does it follow that juxtository meta-phors depend on the reader to the exclusion of the author. Earlier in this chapter I said that authors can and do justifiably assume specific values and beliefs on the part of their projected readership. They can do this because they usually have a considerable grasp of the cultural milieu of those for whom they write. As a result authors are bound to have a pretty good idea of what their readers will consider unusual or odd, commonplace or boring, and they will structure their narratives accordingly, and so create literary contexts which highlight certain incongruities. It follows that we can, in-deed must, credit the author of a work with those incongruities that can properly be discerned within it. Of course, not every reader will find the same event incongruous. Readers can and do have different values and expectations. However, anyone who is acquainted with the relevant aspects of the culture within which the work was produced will be able to tell what is, and what is not, properly regarded as incongruous within it. In saying this, I do not wish to suggest that the acquisition of such knowledge is unproblematic. There are important, at times insurmountable, difficulties involved in acquiring knowledge of this sort. However, as I argued earlier, these difficulties are always contingent, so that it remains in principle possible to acquire knowledge of one's own and other cultures.[15]

The problem of what is to count as the juxtaposition or alignment of subjects in a literary work is now easily settled. It is true, of course, that we can so trivialize the notion of juxtaposition that all events and objects in a given novel turn out in the end to be juxtaposed. But this ignores the element of deliberation and care which properly enters into the process of aligning or juxtaposing two subjects within a work. Authors rightly see themselves as responsible for the structure of their narratives, and it is not surprising, therefore, that they should strive to achieve certain literary effects. At times this involves aligning two subjects in a way which (so the author believes) will be regarded by the reader as significant rather than as merely incidental to the drift and development of the narrative. But how, you will ask, are we to distinguish between the two? How are we to tell that two subjects or events are significantly aligned rather than incidentally located in the same novel? On my view, it is when the presence of the two subjects in a meticulously designed literary context, is considered to be of interest—perhaps because it is out of the ordinary, unusual, strange, or jarring—that the reader will suppose the two subjects aligned, and will begin to search for the point or significance of the juxtaposition. And we have already seen how authors use their knowledge of the readers' values and beliefs in order to achieve this end.

There are, of course, many different ways of doing this, and I cannot hope to describe all of them here. By way of a single example, however, let us return to the question which I raised earlier about the death of Vronsky's mare. Why, I asked, do we not treat this as just another event in a long and complex novel? Why should we regard it as juxtaposed with the fate of Anna Karenina?

My answer trades on the commonplace observation that our construal of any one aspect of a literary work depends greatly on our grasp of other aspects, their interconnections, and the whole which we (as attentive and knowledgeable readers) take them to comprise. Put differently, how we construe the death of Vronsky's mare will depend on our grasp of the literary context within which it occurs. It is, of course, Tolstoy who is responsible for this context, and given some knowledge of it on our part, we are forced to choose between treating Frou-Frou's death as merely tangential to the story—as a decorative embellishment, so to speak; or treating it as somehow aligned with the central concerns of the work. We know from our reading that Vronsky cares for his horse. He also cares, so we believe, for Anna. It is, I would contend, because the reader wants to be able to trust Vronsky in the way that Anna does, it is because we hope that he will give her the security and the solace that she needs, that his mistake and the consequent death of Frou-Frou stand so uneasily with what has gone before. We hope for a gentle, carefree, considerate Vronsky, but the accident highlights his fallibility. And this, Tolstoy anticipates, will be of concern to his readers. It portends Anna's fate, and it would be an insensitive reader who considered the death of the mare a mere flash of adventure and excitement reflecting solely on Vronsky's horsemanship. In this carefully constructed context, the reader is bound to feel a profound unease at the accident, and is virtually compelled to see Frou-Frou's failure at the hurdle as aligned with the course and the "hurdles" that Anna must run.

Of Literary Symbols

One can, I think, treat the death of Vronsky's horse as symbolic: as a literary symbol which somehow captures or alludes to the character of Anna's relationship with Vronsky, as well as to her imperiled situation and likely fate. Of course, this is a symbol in a very special sense of the word, one of which critics and philosophers are sometimes shy.[16] Nelson Goodman rightly points out that there are at least two senses of the word "symbol."[17] In the first sense—the sense with which he is concerned—anything at all that refers or denotes is a symbol. Words are symbols, pictures are symbols, and all representational works of art are symbols. In its second sense, the word "symbol" applies only to some words, phrases, and descriptions within a given work of art, liturgy, ritual, or practice. In this sense, to say of a word or phrase that it is a symbol is to say that it is being (or has been) used in a highly suggestive way to inform and even arouse an audience by conveying a certain insight, a certain mood, a certain feeling. When such symbols occur in literature, I shall call them *literary symbols*—thereby distinguishing them from those symbols which are purely referential and which merely stand for or denote other objects.

How literary symbols work is generally regarded as something of a mystery. In what follows, though, I shall argue that the mystery dissolves when once we realize that a literary symbol is a kind of metaphor—a juxtapository metaphor. By ignoring purely referential symbols, I do not, of course, intend to suggest that these symbols are artistically unimportant or that they have no place in literary works of art. My aim for the moment is only to keep the two kinds of symbol distinct, and in this way to avoid a host of possible confusions.[18]

Although theorists sometimes hesitate to speak of literary symbols, their reluctance, I shall now contend, is largely misplaced. There are, as far as I can see, two dominant reasons for their timidity. The first is the difficulty of explaining what a literary symbol is and how it works. The word "symbol," we are told, is used in many different ways.[19] As a result the notion is far from clear, and until clarified it cannot be used as an explanatory device. The second reason has to do with a recent, somewhat fashionable, view of artistic creation. The belief seems to be that any artist who deploys literary symbols in a work displays a certain "heavy-handedness," a lack of spontaneity, and produces contrived and labored artworks. The popular view enounced by Mary McCarthy is that of the symbol-monger—a simple-minded stylist who first writes the story and then proceeds "to put in the symbols."[20] It is a view which derives some currency from the New Criticism, for the fear must always be that the presence of a literary symbol in a work will invite the inference that the author must have *intended* to symbolize something or other.[21] It is perhaps because of this that the critic Humphrey House scruples to ascribe the use of literary symbols to Coleridge, and insists that if there are any symbols in "The Rime of the Ancient Mariner" they must all be unconscious.[22]

It is, of course, true that a writer need not deliberately and painstakingly devise literary symbols for later insertion in a work. Just as some metaphors are coined without effort, so too are some literary symbols. But even if an artist does strive to coin a metaphor, invent an epigram or a literary symbol, this will not of itself detract from the merit of the resultant work. The ideal of spontaneity in the arts is but a recent one. It finds its origin in the eighteenth-century romantic movement, and was taken to its extreme, and disposed of, in the Dadaist movement of the 1920s. Many brilliant artists attest to the intense labor and self-conscious inventiveness of artistic production; few, if any, speak of it as spontaneous.

Nor are the fears engendered by the New Criticism of any real substance. That there are literary symbols is beyond contention, and one can easily grant (as Monroe Beardsley does) that they do not work just because somebody *willed* them to work.[23] One can agree, too, that we do not normally consult the author's intentions in order to understand a symbol. There clearly are conventional and structural devices which facilitate the comprehension of a symbol, although to say this in no way entails that the author did not intend the symbol, or that literary symbols must be unconscious. There may be some such symbols, but there is no reason to suppose that they must all be of this sort.

So far as I can see, then, there are no grounds for being suspicious of literary symbols. Such suspicion, I have tried to show, is bred of a partial, historically located view of artistic creation, as well as of the misguided application of certain doctrines of the New Criticism.

Rather more important is the objection that talk about literary symbols is inherently unclear, and will remain so until we are able to produce an account of the nature and workings of such symbols. It is my contention, though, that my earlier account of juxtapository metaphors offers considerable insight into the nature and workings of literary symbolism. This stands to reason if, as I have intimated, any juxtapository metaphor can be regarded as a literary symbol, and any literary symbol as a juxtapository metaphor.

That literary symbols should be regarded in this way begins to be apparent when we attend to what is perhaps the most obvious feature of a literary symbol—namely that it always involves the "transference" of certain ideas, feelings, and values from one subject to another. This feature is often remarked upon. John Hospers contends that with the help of symbols "our thoughts, attitudes and feelings are *transferred* from one thing to another and become, so to speak, 'cross-fertilized' by the intertwining."[24] He gains support for this view from Isabel Hungerland, who speaks of literary symbols as involving "a transference of trains of thought and the accompanying attitudes and feelings . . . from one object to another."[25] And concurring in this belief is Melvin Rader who tells us that literary symbols draw our "attention to the interrelatedness of things."[26]

This feature of literary symbols is easily explained if we regard such symbols as juxtapository metaphors. For it is then a matter simply of applying the interaction theory of metaphor in order to explain the power of a symbol to transfer certain of our ideas and feelings from one subject to another. Put differently, we can explain it in just the way that we earlier explained the transference of "associated commonplaces" in metaphor.

Even so, the identification of literary symbols with juxtapository metaphors seems strained. Some literary symbols, it will be said, do not embody incongruities in the way that juxtapository metaphors do. Rather, they work iconically—with the help of similarities or resemblances. These, we are told, are not referential symbols, for they do not refer to anything beyond the text. They are genuine literary symbols which resemble other events or processes in the narrative: in the way, say, that the moth-around-the-flame resembles aspects of Stephen Dedalus's life in *A Portrait of the Artist as a Young Man*. On my view, though, while there can be no doubt that there are such literary devices, it is mistaken to regard them as literary symbols. Since they depend for their effect on their congruity rather than their incongruity, we would do better, as I said earlier, to mark this distinction by regarding them as juxtapository similes, not metaphors; hence as literary images rather than literary symbols.

There is, however, a further reason for questioning the identification of literary symbols with juxtapository metaphors. The trouble, we are now told, is that juxtapository metaphors always involve two or more subjects, whereas a literary symbol is invariably a single entity. Consequently, we are left with the problem of deciding which of the subjects of a juxtapository metaphor is the literary symbol. But this, as we will see, is not a particularly pressing problem. We have already learned that it is the apparent incongruity of two juxtaposed subjects in a literary work which inclines the reader to treat the juxtaposition as a metaphor. To this I can now add that it also inclines the reader to treat the more incongruous, and hence the more prominent, of the two subjects (what we would call the "focus" of the metaphor) as a literary symbol. However, it would be mistaken to infer from this that literary symbols are single or unitary entities, for it seems plain that what is commonly regarded as a literary symbol achieves its prominence, and allows the transference of ideas from one subject to another, only by being juxtaposed with some or other subject.

It is, of course, the literary context of the juxtaposition that determines (in all manner of ways) which of the juxtaposed subjects is the more unusual, and hence the more prominent. Occurring where it does in the novel, the death of Frou-Frou is much more startling, and hence much more prominent, than the gradual unfolding of Anna's relationship with Vronsky. It is, of course, true that in nineteenth-century Russia adultery would be a much more unusual occurrence, and the focus of much more attention, than a horse's death. But at this point in the novel, and in this skillfully contrived context, it is the horse's death which is forced upon our attention. And this is why we are inclined to treat it as a literary symbol.

We are also inclined to treat the river in *The Mill on the Floss* as a literary symbol, and yet it must be obvious to everyone that the horse's death and the river do not enjoy the same sort of prominence in their respective novels. The death of Frou-Frou jars heavily and immediately with the reader's knowledge of Anna's trust in Vronsky. The river Floss, on the other hand, is not at odds with anything in George Eliot's narrative. Repeated mention of it, however, and its gradual, yet constant, intrusion into the narrative, give it a prominence that engages the reader's interest. In this minimal sense, it too achieves a degree of incongruity that inclines the reader to treat it symbolically. As a result, certain of its characteristics are transferred to Maggie's life, and we say of the Floss that it is a metaphor for, or that it symbolizes, the unrelenting forces of life and death integral to the heroine's fate.

In much the same way, the activity of wrestling in *The World According to Garp* may be said to symbolize Garp's struggle to develop as an individual and as a writer; while the pandybat in the hand of Joyce's priest may be said to symbolize the hurtful power of the priesthood in Ireland. There are, I think, countless examples of similar juxtapository metaphors that may be regarded as literary symbols, and literary symbols that can profitably be treated as juxtapository metaphors.

And yet, if this is so, why is it that Broyard speaks of Tolstoy's *metaphor*, and not of Tolstoy's *symbol*? And why does Robert Penn Warren speak of the symbols rather than the metaphors in "The Rime of the Ancient Mariner"? [27] Is this merely a matter of convenience and usage? To a very large extent it is. We have already seen that the word "symbol" has suffered a curious reversal of fortune in some quarters and has earned a good deal of abuse. For this reason the word "metaphor" may be considered to have the respectability and persuasive force that "symbol" lacks. Then again, the mere fact that there is a tradition in literary criticism of describing Coleridge's albatross as a symbol militates against Robert Penn Warren's now designating it a metaphor.

There is, though, another, not unfamiliar, reason for refusing to allow that some of the symbols which occur in literary works are actually metaphors. The word "symbol," I have just said, is ambiguous as between symbols which merely *stand for* other entities, and symbols which involve a sort of allusion, and hence a transference of ideas and feelings. Our concern has been with symbols of the latter sort, and it is these, I have suggested, which are always properly regarded as juxtapository metaphors. The problem is that literary works, like paintings, often contain symbols not just of the first, but also of the second variety. Thus, for instance, the water-snakes in "The Rime of the Ancient Mariner" are sometimes said to symbolize "all happy living things," but this means no more than that the water-snakes *stand for* them.[28] In such cases, one clearly cannot substitute the term "metaphor" for "symbol," but in all other cases one can.

It would seem, then, that there are excellent grounds for identifying juxtapository metaphors with literary symbols. This, as we have just remarked, is not to deny that there are very many symbols in literature which cannot plausibly be construed as juxtapository metaphors. These, however, are always Goodmanesque in character: they *stand for* something or other, but do not involve the transference of ideas and feelings from one subject to another. My claim, however, is that it is only when a symbol in a literary work brings about such a transference because of its incongruity that we can properly speak of it as a *literary symbol*. And it is only then that we can correctly regard it as a juxtapository metaphor.

If I am right, the nature and functioning of all literary symbols can be exhaustively explained in terms of the account that I have given of juxtapository metaphors. This approach has a certain virtue, for unlike the explanations of symbolism offered by Monroe Beardsley and John Hospers, it encourages us to preserve the distinction between purely referential symbols on the one hand, and literary symbols on the other. Beardsley tends to assimilate the two.[29] He contends that there are three cardinal relationships in virtue of which one thing can symbolize another. First, there may be a natural similarity between the symbol and the symbolized. This he calls the *"natural basis* of the symbolism." Then, too, there may be a *conventional basis*: some "agreement or stipulation" according to which one object will symbolize something else. Finally, and most important of all, there is what Beardsley calls "the *vital basis* of the symbolism"—a history whereby it becomes plausible for a word or an image or an object to be used as a symbol. Thus, for instance, the history of the Christian cross makes it a suitable symbol for Christ's suffering, and the way in which cages and prison bars have traditionally entered into our lives makes it plausible for them to be used as symbols of, say, human bondage.

The trouble with this explanation of the dynamics of symbolism is, as I have suggested, that it tends to obscure certain important distinctions between symbols. Beardsley assumes that to say of X that it symbolizes Y is just to say that X stands for Y. It is, therefore, the relation of *standing for* that he seeks to explain in three different ways. Consider, for example, what he has to say about the barbed wire of a concentration camp, which is said to symbolize "the barbarity of totalitarianism or man's inhumanity to man" (*Aesthetics*, p. 288). "The barbed wire," he writes, "does not stand for totalitarianism because anyone willed it to; there is a natural basis for the symbolism; a totalitarian state is *like* barbed wire in certain ways. And there is, of course, a considerable vital basis" (p. 291). If Beardsley is to be believed, therefore, both the vital and the natural basis allow the barbed wire to be used to symbolize, and so to *stand for*, totalitarianism.

This, however, suggests that we are dealing with a purely referential symbol. That we are not becomes clearer once we realize that what Beardsley calls the natural and the vital basis of this symbol really consists in a range of commonplace beliefs and feelings about barbed wire which are bred of our knowledge of it and of the way in which it has traditionally entered into our lives. The symbol works not by standing for anything, but by transferring certain of these beliefs and feelings about barbed wire to the system which allows its use. As a result we can say that it symbolizes the cruelty, inhumanity, and savagery of totalitarianism, but this is not to say, as Beardsley does, that it *stands for* totalitarianism.

There is only one basis mentioned by Beardsley that can account for purely referential symbolism. It is, of course, the *conventional* basis, for we can always stipulate or agree that a particular object—say, a piece of patterned cloth—will stand for, and so symbolize, a certain country. And whenever X symbolizes by convention, fiat, or agreement alone, it is a purely referential symbol. It is true that with the passage of time such symbols may cease to be purely referential. The swastika, for instance, started out in this manner in recent German history, but the way in which it affected people's lives led to an accretion of beliefs about, and feelings toward, it. The result is that the symbol can be used in fiction to function as a literary symbol—as a juxtapository metaphor whereby certain of our beliefs and feelings are transferred from the swastika to some other subject within the fiction. Beardsley's *natural* and *vital* bases help explain how such beliefs and feelings accrue, but what Beardsley's account does not explain is the transference involved in the literary symbolism. It is a virtue of the account that I have given in terms of juxtapository metaphors that it is able to do so.

Conclusion

Why, I asked at the outset of this chapter, are metaphors of fiction so much more effective, powerful, and suggestive than the metaphors of ordinary, nonfictional discourse? The clue, we have now seen, is to be found in the fact that authors can devise and so control the contexts within which metaphors of fiction appear. This allows the author to cultivate certain beliefs, values, and concerns in the reader which a well-placed metaphor can, and usually does, exploit. Although this context is often such as to make the meaning of the metaphor obvious to an attentive reader, I have argued that we should not be tempted on this account to suppose that metaphors of fiction lack a metaphorical meaning. Such a meaning, I have shown, is essential if we are to be able to ascertain which, if any, of the many affective responses to a metaphor are appropriate.

A grasp of the appropriate literary context not only enables us to comprehend and respond to a metaphor, but also determines its function and scope within the literary work. On my view, metaphors of fiction may have indefinitely many functions and can enjoy varying degrees of importance within the work—all of which can properly be discerned in context. And this is why it is mistaken to suppose that we can furnish an exhaustive classification of all possible literary metaphors in terms of their diverse functions. Products of the imagination are not made to a blueprint, and this being so, it is unrealistic to suppose that literary metaphors will always fit neatly into a pre-existing classificatory scheme.

Finally, we have seen that not all metaphors of fiction are sentential in form. Indeed, many of the metaphors approvingly referred to by literary critics involve the incongruous juxtaposition of two or more subjects, usually without any explicit predicative relationship between them. In this case, the metaphors of fiction are plainly different from those of nonfiction, for our ordinary discourse does not appear to leave very much room for juxtapository metaphors. This is so because such metaphors can work only in a carefully contrived context, and it seems clear that speakers do not usually have sufficient control over the contexts of their everyday nonfictional utterances to be able to bring this off.[30] The juxtapository metaphors of fiction, we have seen, can properly be identified with literary symbols, so that my analysis of juxtapository metaphor goes some way toward resuscitating and explaining the currently unfashionable notion of a literary symbol.

Metaphor, I have said, is the progeny of the fanciful imagination. My aim in the last three chapters has been to explain how metaphor works, and in this way to defend the romantic view that metaphors are cognitively significant: that, in addition to their affective dimension, they can impart conceptual and cognitive skills and so bring us to see the world differently. In so doing, I have tried to resist the more extravagant romantic claims made on behalf of metaphor by Nietzsche and Derrida, while refusing to succumb, in the way that Davidson has, to the lure of positivism.

TEN

Literature, Imagination, and Identity

The case for a romantic epistemology is all but complete. There is much, I have tried to show, that can be said in favor of the view that the fanciful imagination, fiction, and metaphor are a vital source of knowledge about, and understanding of, our world. But the story does not end here, for despite the best efforts of latter-day literary critics, there still exists the widespread belief that literary works of art can afford considerable insight into the culture, or period of the culture, in which they were produced.[1] Against this view, the autonomism of the New Critics, and the antirealism of the structuralists and deconstructionists, count for very little indeed.[2] The popular and dominant view is that there exists an "intimate and inevitable" link between literature and a national or cultural identity.[3] And it is this view that is reflected in the fact that people often look to a body of literature in order to discover the special and distinctive features of their culture. Their demand, it seems, is that a chosen body of literature should help furnish them with a distinctive cultural identity.

That people often favor literature with these demands seems clear enough. What is perfectly unclear, however, is the precise nature of the demand. The concept "culture" is murky, and talk of cultural identity doubly so. We need to know both what is to count as a distinctive culture, and what it is that one searches for when one sets out in pursuit of a cultural identity. Only by answering questions such as these will we be able to make any sense at all of the perennial search for cultural distinctiveness and identity through literature.

I shall begin, therefore, by explaining the concept "culture," for without such an explanation, we cannot hope to understand what it is to search for a cultural identity. The thought that literature can furnish us with such an identity finds its origin in the romantic nationalism of the nineteenth century, and it is no doubt the widespread influence of romantic theory which makes this view seem reasonable. I shall argue that when construed in a rather special way, this view is indeed reasonable—although there are once again romantic excesses, this time Hegelian in character, which should be avoided. My explanation trades on the romantic epistemology which I developed earlier (Chapter Two), and will be used to explain the philosophically neglected and frequently overlooked fact that literature (and the fanciful imagination generally) helps furnish us not just with a cultural, but also with an individual, identity: with particular ways of looking at, and thinking about, ourselves as individuals. And the importance of this, I shall argue, cannot be overestimated.

Geist, Volksgeist, and Culture

Let us begin with the obvious. It is plain, I think, that one can know that a country or a group has a distinct culture, a culture peculiar to itself, only if one also knows that the culture is not held in common with any other country or group of people. But this poses a vital problem, for how are we to tell that any two people, or groups of people, belong to the same or different cultures? The temptation is to appeal to what are normally regarded as cultural phenomena: to language, dress, political and economic systems, ideologies, bodies of belief and knowledge, moral and artistic values, religion, and so on. And it seems reasonable to suppose that the extent to which people agree or disagree in such matters is a measure of their common culture.

But if this is our measure, and I certainly think it a plausible one, it tends to convert culture into a somewhat unwieldy beast. The French, the Germans, the English, and the Italians speak and behave differently: they have different customs, different manners and modes of dress. And it is presumably in virtue of such considerations that we speak of distinct French, German, English, and Italian cultures. However, a closer look shows that there are also similarities of language, customs, and modes of dress, and when we attend to these the people of Europe seem to cluster under the general umbrella of Western culture. Still worse, it appears that people can have cultural similarities without actually sharing a culture. The English and the Irish speak the same language, share much of their history, and have even had monarchs in common, but despite this English and Irish cultures remain distinct. While one may insist that religion helps differentiate the two, the trouble, plain for all to see, is that there are Irish Protestants and English Catholics. Being Protestant does not exclude one from Irish culture, but it may qualify one, together with one's German counterpart, as belonging to something called a Protestant culture.

This is not the muddle that it appears to be. What I am pointing to is the fact that not all cultures are demarcated in the same way: different considerations are taken into account in different situations. To belong to one culture, therefore, need not exclude one from membership of another.

But some people balk at so flexible a view of culture. The concept, they contend, is more fixed in its application than my brief comments suggest. According to their view, every state or society manifests a particular culture, so that if one properly belongs to a given society, one belongs to its culture alone. The view is strongly exclusivist and finds considerable political support among the popular political movements of the New and Not-so-new Right. It is a view which seems to depend on an organic conception of culture according to which a culture is not just the vital "driving force" of a society, but is integrally related to that society and its members in much the way that the human mind is related to the human body. And just as one person cannot be located in different minds, so, on this account, a person or a society cannot properly be located in different cultures.

To my knowledge, this view has never seriously been advocated by philosophers of any repute. It does, however, derive a good deal of its impetus from G. F. W. Hegel—although it would be quite wrong to ascribe doctrines of cultural exclusivity to him. It would also be wrong to think that Hegel dwells at any length on the concept "culture." He does not. What he does say, however, is quite specific, and is integrally related to his view of history. In *The Phenomenology of Mind* he tells us:

That which, in reference to the single individual, appears as his culture, is the essential moment of spiritual substance as such . . . or otherwise put, culture is the single soul of this substance, in virtue of which the essentially inherent (*Ansich*) becomes something explicitly acknowledged, and assumes definite objective existence.[4]

Put simply, Hegel believes that culture has to be identified with a particular stage in the development of the "spiritual substance"—that is, in the development or evolution of *Geist*. It is this which is objectively instantiated in the institutions of any society, and which helps distinguish the society in the eyes of its members. This stage in the development of Spirit is what Hegel calls the *Volksgeist*, and he insists on its organic nature by maintaining that

the individual is an individual in this substance. . . . . No individual can step beyond it; he can separate himself certainly from other particular individuals, but not from the *Volksgeist*.[5]

Culture, then, is identified by Hegel as a "moment" of *Geist*, which in its turn is identified as the *Volksgeist*—that is, as the national spirit which is not only responsible for various cultural manifestations, but in some sense guides the growth and development of a society, and furnishes its members with a notion of their own identity. Hegel elaborates on this in his *Lectures on the Philosophy of History*, where he contends that

World history represents . . . the evolution of the awareness of Spirit of its own freedom. . . . Every step being different from every other one, has its own determined and peculiar principle. In history such a principle becomes the determination of Spirit—a peculiar National Spirit [*ein besonderer Volksgeist*]. It is here that it expresses all the aspects of its consciousness and will . . . ; it is this that imparts a common stamp to its religion, its political constitution, its art and its technical skills. These particular individual qualities must be understood as deriving from that common peculiarity—the particular peculiarity which characterises a nation. Conversely, it is from the facts of history that the general character of this peculiarity has to be inferred.[6]

For Hegel there clearly is a sense in which culture as a "peculiar National Spirit" or *Volksgeist* helps determine the growth and development of a society. His is in many ways an attractive account of "culture," since it not only explains the dynamics of social change, but also accounts for social cohesion. For according to this organic view, each individual is only the individual that he or she is, by being located within a particular culture. Just as the human mind imparts a personal identity to a person, so every society, and every individual within that society, derives a sense of his or her cultural identity from the culture (or *Volksgeist*) that infuses the society.

It is true, of course, that there is no way of distinguishing or discerning the *Volksgeist* independently of the cultural manifestations for which it is said to be responsible, for, as we have just seen, it is from the facts of history that the general character of the *Volksgeist* has to be inferred. This, of course, does not constitute an objection to Hegel's account of culture. It simply attests to its metaphysical character. For if I understand Hegel correctly, culture, like *Geist* and *Volksgeist*, is essentially unobservable.

Nor is there any reason why unobservable entities should not be allowed a place in our explanations. On my view they certainly can be allowed a place provided that there is no other way of explaining the behavior of a particular system. To take an example from Daniel Dennett, we readily posit unobservable beliefs, intentions, and desires when explaining the behavior of a chess-playing computer.[7] Our reason for doing so is simple. The design of a computer and its physical state at any given time are simply too complex to be usefully invoked in an explanation or prediction of the computer's play.[8] Here it seems both more plausible and more useful to invoke certain unobservables in an explanation by treating the computer as an "intentional system"—that is, as a system whose behavior can be explained or predicted by assuming that it has certain information (beliefs), and by supposing its behavior to be directed by certain goals (intentions), and then by calculating the most reasonable action for it to take relative to its intentions and beliefs.[9]

Now, it is not without interest that Hegel chooses to do something very similar by attempting to explain the development of society—and especially its cultural manifestations—by attributing to it an unobservable spiritual substance which is the seat of various beliefs and intentions. Hegel, it would seem, chooses to treat society as an intentional system whose cultural manifestations are properly explained only by appeal to the intentions and beliefs (will and consciousness) of an underlying cultural spirit, the *Volksgeist.*

In response to this it is sometimes suggested that society simply is not the type of thing which can have intentions and beliefs. Hegel, it is suggested, is guilty of an elementary type or category confusion, since only individuals, but not societies, are capable of taking these ascriptions. But this sort of objection cannot be sustained. It simply begs the question against Hegel, whose argument, after all, can plausibly be construed as an attempt to offer an alternative to our individualistic conception of human society. Still more, the objection is not even relevant, for if Dennett is correct it always makes sense to explain the behavior of a system by *assuming* (rather than asserting) that it has beliefs and intentions; and it is arguably this that Hegel attempts to do. It would seem, then, that one cannot undermine Hegel's position by appealing to the inappropriateness of his intentional ascriptions. Rather, one has to show that the method of explanation invoked in this case is not adequate to the task of explaining the behavior or cultural manifestations of society.

That it is not adequate to this task becomes apparent when we reflect on Dennett's observation that in order to explain the behavior of any system in terms of beliefs and intentions, one must assume the rationality of that system.[10] One must assume, that is, that the system will pursue its goals, or attempt to fulfill its intentions, in ways appropriate to the information or beliefs which it possesses. Now, if we decide to treat a society as an intentional system, it seems perfectly reasonable to assume that it has as a goal the welfare of its members, and that given certain information (beliefs), it will pursue this goal by the most appropriate means. However, in the light of the information available to us, it is frequently possible to show that societies behave in ways which run counter to this aim: they blunder into wars, destabilize their economies, create mass poverty, and so on. In the face of this sort of evidence, it becomes progressively more difficult to assume the rationality of the system in question; and once one abandons this assumption, one effectively admits that societies are not intentional systems.

It might, of course, be the case that societies *are* intentional systems, but that they habitually function on the basis of false beliefs. This, it is argued, accounts for their failure to achieve their goals while at the same time preserving the assumption of their rationality. On this view, societies pursue their goals in ways appropriate to the beliefs that they happen to have. The contingent fact that most of these beliefs turn out to be false, it is argued, does not make the system any the less rational. But this is a desperate maneuver. For if it were the case, say, that a chess-playing computer were frequently to operate on the basis of false beliefs—the belief that a knight is a king, or that pawns move like bishops—it would be misplaced to attest to its rationality in anything but the weakest sense. We would be much more inclined to say of the computer that it is malfunctioning. The case is somewhat different for persons, for unlike computers we do not ascribe malfunctions to them—although if they regularly pursue their goals in terms of false beliefs we would be forced to doubt their rationality. We do so not because they are acting in ways that are inappropriate to their beliefs, but because they appear unable to assess and interpret evidence. And this is an important, indeed a vital, criterion of a person's rationality, such that anyone who is unable to fulfill it would be deemed irrational in a perfectly straightforward sense of the word. So although a society which standardly seeks its goals in ways appropriate to false beliefs satisfies one criterion of rationality, it fails to satisfy another. And for this reason it becomes impossible to assume its rationality, and hence impossible to treat it as an intentional system.

It is, of course, open to us to try to preserve the rationality of society by contending that we can have no adequate idea of the intentions and beliefs which motivate and guide it. It is because we invariably make false assumptions about the nature of these, the argument goes, that we wrongly consider society irrational. But this move, we should notice, only preserves the rationality of the system at the cost of making it impossible to say anything about the beliefs and intentions which it is presumed to have. And this gives the game away, for it effectively concedes that we cannot explain and predict the behavior of a society by ascribing beliefs and intentions to it; it concedes, in other words, that society is not an intentional system.

Hegel, however, makes no such mistake. On his view, the goals of a society are never hidden or mysterious. On the contrary, they are to be identified with those of Spirit, and can be comprehended by a competent Philosopher. Hegel's mistake, rather, is that he tries to preserve the rationality of society by specifying its goal (the "will") so generally as to make any state of affairs compatible with the achievement of it. On his view, the ultimate aim of Spirit is to achieve full self-awareness by making the world congruent to itself—thereby maximizing human freedom.[11] But if this is the goal, then *any* historical or social event, inasmuch as it enters into the dialectical process whereby Spirit achieves its goal, must be thought of as serving that end. This conclusion is sometimes denied, but here I agree with E. H. Gombrich who contends that "it certainly is part of Hegel's conception of History as an unfolding of divine reasoning that whatever is must also be right, right because meaningful as a step towards the self-realization of the spirit."[12] And Hegel seems to say as much when he writes that "world history exhibits *nothing other* than the plan of providence"—where this plan is to be explained as the goal of Spirit.[13] It follows, I think, that there can no longer be any point in treating society as an intentional system, for we cannot hope to explain or predict the behavior of a society by appealing to intentions which will be served *no matter how* things turn out.

The mistake of those who advance an organic account of "culture" along Hegelian lines, is, so it seems to me, that they think of culture as having a function in society analogous to that of the human mind in a person. On their view, culture is nothing less than Descartes's ghost in a societal machine. But we have now seen that their attempt to treat society as an intentional system must fail, for one can only preserve the assumption of its rationality either by rendering its assumed intentions totally mysterious and opaque, or else by specifying them so generally as to make intentional explanations and predictions impossible. This is not to deny that there are rational intentional systems of a social sort: a tennis club, a peace group, a university, could all qualify. It could even turn out that the behavior of a larger social group—what I have loosely called a society, and what Hegel calls the State—is largely rational. However, in the latter case, the weight of evidence suggests that it is always implausible to assume that societies are rational; and without such an assumption one cannot treat society as an intentional system, and hence offer a mentalistic account of its culture.

Culture and Colligation

There is no reason at all, then, to suppose that culture has to be explained along Hegelian lines: as a mentalistic entity which rigidly determines cultural identities, and which controls and shapes the destiny of a society. This so-called idealist view of culture, I have said, receives much popular, but little philosophical, support. There is another view that, to return to my analogy, takes us away from the Cartesian "ghost" to something like a Humean "bundle." For we appear to use the word "culture" of a vast and complex field of human behavior, which, to the untutored, must appear bewildering in its diversity and apparent randomness. Those who are puzzled by it try to make sense of it. Precisely how they do this is a difficult question which requires attention both to genetic epistemology and to the methodology of the social sciences. What is clear, however, is that those who study and observe human beings soon discover patterns and sequences in human behavior and interaction. Social scientists distinguish rituals, customs, traditions, manners, types of play, and even modes of dress. They discern distinctive linguistic habits, distinctive political and economic systems, and, of course, distinctive religions and art forms. Each, in turn, is seen to reflect certain values, systems of belief, and bodies of knowledge which form the bedrock for action and interaction between human beings.

Such beliefs, values, and practices, and the institutions founded upon them, hang together in important, complex, and varying ways. Political beliefs, values, and behavior usually reinforce, but sometimes undermine, established economic practices. Similarly, religious values, rituals, and pronouncements may strengthen, or may on occasions emasculate, dominant modes of political and economic interaction. And the artist's voice can bolster or sap the prevailing economic, political, and religious order, and can reciprocally be bolstered or sapped by it. It is largely in order to mark these intricate and variable relationships that social scientists use the word "culture."[14] Used in this way, "culture" is a colligatory concept.[15] It is employed in a way which marks off groups of people by collecting together their characteristic and mutually dependent patterns of action and interaction, as well as the values, attitudes, beliefs, and knowledge which guide them.

There is nothing very original about a colligatory account of culture. Edward Tylor, after all, advanced a similar account as early as 1871.[16] Nevertheless, it is an account in need of considerable elaboration and defense. Those who are wedded to an idealist or Hegelian view of culture will no doubt think it incapable of explaining cultural identity, societal change, or the organic nature of a culture. That these fears are groundless will emerge as we proceed. What seems clear enough even now is that not everything correctly regarded as a culture can adequately be construed on the model of an organism. For the idealist, cultures ought always to be organic wholes. And yet, European culture is not very well integrated, but consists of strands of more or less independent beliefs, practices, and institutions. Protestant culture is rather more integrated, while Catholic culture can usefully be construed as an organic whole which consists of mutually interdependent parts. A colligatory account has the virtue of allowing us to distinguish these degrees of integration without implying, as an idealist account must, that weakly integrated cultures are in some sense deviant or ailing.

Then, too, a colligatory account has the obvious advantage of being able to explain exactly what is involved in coming to know a culture. There are, above all, no inferences to a closet *Geist*. Rather, when we speak of Greek, Pueblo, or Jewish culture, we demarcate different patterns of behavior, values, and beliefs, and we help draw attention to the fact that they hang together in different ways. To be acquainted with these cultures, therefore, is to know about these different patterns. And it is in the light of such knowledge that various actions and pronouncements assume a significance which they would otherwise lack. Thus, for instance, we know that (ancient) Greek and Jewish cultures include drinking rituals, and that Pueblo culture does not.[17] Pop culture rejects religion; Jewish, like Pueblo and Greek culture, embraces and elevates it. As a result we can gauge the significance that a Pueblo Indian, a devotee of Pop, an ancient Greek, or a Jew would attach to the consumption of alcohol during a religious ceremony. It seems clear from this that a colligatory account allows the concept "culture" a useful diagnostic role—for it can usefully be employed in explanations and predictions of human behavior and social change.

No doubt for reasons such as these, something like a colligatory account of culture has come to dominate among anthropologists. A. L. Kroeber and Clyde Kluckhohn surveyed several hundred definitions of culture in order to distill an account which they believed would be acceptable to most social scientists. In so doing they arrived at the pattern theory of culture, according to which culture consists in part of patterns of, and for, behavior.[18] Bronislaw Malinowski saw culture as an active, well-organized unity, and this colligatory view is also to be found, in one form or another, in the work of Edward Sapir and Morris Opler.[19] All, however, fail to see the implications of, and problems posed by, their colligatory theories. Thus, for instance, because different social scientists colligate human phenomena differently, it is sometimes held that the word "culture" has many overlapping and contradictory meanings. As James Spradley says, "Social scientists have made it a regular practice to expropriate this term for their special purposes. As each new definition is added to the list, the semantic battle lines are drawn and the verbal warfare continues."[20] But there really is no need for such warfare. The acrimony, it seems, takes root in a failure to understand the colligatory function of the word "culture." Once this is grasped, it becomes plain that the word is standardly used to bring together *different* patterns of behavior, values, belief, and knowledge in *different ways*. And this in no way entails that the meaning of the word is in constant flux. What it is used to refer to may no doubt change, but its sense will remain unchanged.

This becomes clearer, I think, when we attend to collective nouns such as "pile," "collection," "heap," and so on. I may speak both of a pile (collection, heap) of books, and a pile (collection, heap) of stones. And although the word "pile" ("collection," "heap") brings different things together on each occasion, its sense does not alter in each case. Of course, when used referringly, the phrase "the pile" may have different referents from one occasion to the next; but as Frege has long since pointed out, we must beware of confusing sense with reference.[21] The same cautionary tale can be told of all colligatory concepts. When historians speak of the Roman era and the Elizabethan era, they clearly speak of different periods and happenings, but in each case the word "era" retains its sense. And when an art critic speaks of Cézanne's style in one breath, and Rembrandt's style in another, the word "style" has but one sense, although what is referred to on each occasion differs. It is precisely in this way that the word "culture" retains its sense no matter what collection of institutions, behavior patterns, values, ideologies, or bodies of knowledge and belief it is used to colligate and to refer to. When we speak of American culture, we speak, *inter alia*, of a capitalist economic system; when we speak of Jewish culture we refer to no economic system at all. But this, I have been at pains to show, does not entail that we attach different meanings to the word on each occasion.

Even those social scientists who have tried to put an end to the continuing dispute about "culture" have failed in the final analysis to take the colligatory function of the word seriously enough. Ward Goodenough, for instance, thinks it best to allow two meanings of the word: one which distinguishes patterns of behavior, and another which distinguishes patterns of ideas.[22] What he fails to see is that the word functions in the same way in each case. It merely colligates. Consequently, there is no distinction of sense in these cases, and the only distinction that can plausibly be made is a distinction of *what* is colligated—a distinction of reference, not meaning. Not only this, for when we speak of British culture, Maori culture, elitist culture, or even Coca-Cola® culture, we bring together patterns of behavior *and* patterns of ideas. If Goodenough is to be believed, such phrases as "British culture," "Italian culture," "Protestant culture," and "feminine culture" are all ambiguous. But this seems most unlikely.

The lesson to be learned from all of this is not that cultures do not really exist—of course they do, but not as some kind of mentalistic substance. Rather, as we have seen, cultures exist in the way that collections exist. They are nothing but collections of behavior patterns, institutions, values, bodies of knowledge, and systems of belief. And it is the nature of these ingredients, as well as the way in which they hang together, that determines the character of any particular culture. It would be quite mistaken, then, to suppose that I have de-ontologized culture. At best I have re-ontologized it.

Demarcating Cultures

To say that "culture" is a colligatory concept is just to say that we use it to collect and bring together certain phenomena in certain ways. And, of course, what we collect and how we collect it depend importantly on our concerns and interests. Even the most enthusiastic philatelists do not collect all the stamps that they can lay their hands on. Rather, given their particular interests, philatelists collect only certain types of stamps, and then only in very special ways. They may collect according to the "one of each" or "sheet of each" principle, or they may collect according to countries, years of origin, pictorial motifs, or printing errors. The resultant collections will be distinguished not only by the stamps that each contains, but also by the different principles used in selecting and ordering them. The collections, one might say, hang together in different ways.

In my view, collections always reflect the particular concerns and interests of the collector, and this is seldom more obvious than when people gather, organize, and relate human phenomena under the term "culture." Examples are many and familiar. At times political and economic interests dominate. Thus, for instance, a Vatican scholar will think it proper to inquire into the Catholic contribution to British history, theology, moral values, politics—in short, to British culture. However, certain Protestant politicians in Northern Ireland would not only deny the validity of the inquiry, but would also deny that "popery" has any place in British culture.

In a similar, but less obviously extreme way, people often try to demarcate their own culture in a way which places it in a very favorable light. So, for instance, a proud Briton may be reluctant to see prostitution, racism, or occultism as part of British culture, and might indignantly deny that war and its glorification are integral to the British cultural heritage. The same desire to commend one's own culture prevents Americans and Russians alike from regarding economic colonialism as part of their respective cultures.

There are, of course, many other interests and concerns which affect the ways in which we demarcate cultures. The late nineteenth-century aesthetic movement, for example, and the resultant growth of esoteric art, so affected values and interests in the West that it brought successive generations to the view that the term "culture" was coextensive with the production and appreciation of "high" art. On this view, the only activities that could properly be brought under the label "culture" were the activities of the first-night-fur-coat-brigade, and those who pandered to it.[23] An altogether different restriction on the scope of the word can be found among those anthropologists who are concerned to make their subject scientific. In their bid to do so they prefer to confine the term "culture" to public behavior alone, thereby excluding the nonquantifiable ideational or cognitive aspects of culture.[24]

Our allegiances, our preferences, our prejudices clearly can intrude, and will often influence the principles according to which cultures are discerned and demarcated. These principles, we have now seen, help determine which human phenomena we are willing to include under our various cultural banners. However, this does not entail that we are at liberty to include or exclude whatever we wish when speaking of a culture. There are obvious constraints, both of evidence and consistency. If, for example, one chooses to demarcate American culture in terms of its technological achievements, this will no doubt influence one's perception of what is and what is not properly a part of this culture. One is likely to attend only to those institutions, sequences of behavior, values, and frames of reference which we regard as pertinent to American technology. But one could, of course, object to the principle used on this occasion by pointing out that it reflects neither the intricacy nor the diversity of American life. For in concentrating on General Electric, Coca-Cola®, and Boeing, it overlooks the spiritual dimension of America: American religion, art, literature, science, philosophy, and so on.

Of course, if the incentives are right, there will always be some people who are willing to demarcate this (or any other) culture in a way which affords an impoverished view of it. In the end, however, it is the actual patterns of action and interaction, and the beliefs and values that guide them, which attest to the adequacy of any attempt to demarcate a culture.

It seems plain, then, that we can appeal to evidence in order to demonstrate the inadequacies of demarcating (and so defining) a culture in one way rather than another. But this, while correct, is not as uncomplicated as might first appear. The trouble is that what we count as evidence for a particular demarcation might itself be the product of our political, economic, religious, or sentimental interests. And this difficulty is compounded by the fact that in most, perhaps all, societies the dominant classes not only demarcate their culture to suit their interests but attempt, with the help of the media, religion, and education, to bring others to their view of the culture. In so doing, they attempt to achieve what Antonio Gramsci has called "hegemony": a situation in which the dominant classes can pursue their own interests within the community and can do so with the consent of the dominated classes.[25] According to Gramsci, such hegemony is not just necessary for stable government, but involves developing what Marx has called "false consciousness" in the dominated classes. This suggests that it will be difficult to isolate evidence which can disabuse people of a particular way of demarcating or seeing their culture. The task is not impossible, however, for if it were there could be no way of recognizing that our cultural perceptions are either mistaken or correct.[26] There could, as a result, be no way of recognizing the dimensions and degrees of cultural hegemony within one's society and no way at all of ascertaining its effects.

It is the case, then, that we can appeal to evidence in order to demonstrate the inadequacies of demarcating a culture in one way rather than another. But this is not the only constraint on the demarcation of cultures. For once one adopts a specific way of demarcating a culture—a principle of cultural demarcation, so to speak—one is obliged to apply it consistently.

A member of the Ku Klux Klan, for instance, may prefer to demarcate American culture in terms of its technological achievements, but may at the same time insist that Jews have no place in this culture. However, if a survey of those institutions and practices which the Klansman wants most to include under the banner of American culture reveals a continuing Jewish contribution to them, it is simply inconsistent to maintain that Jews have no place in this conception of American culture.

The problem of consistency runs deeper than this, for however we choose to demarcate a particular culture, we are bound to come up against the question of whether some other culture can properly be regarded as a part of it. There clearly is no *a priori* reason why one culture cannot be said to be part of another. Just as my Victorian jug collection can be part of my ceramics collection, so we could find that Jewish culture is properly speaking a part of European culture. Of course, the fact that Jewish individuals contribute to the institutions which characterize European culture cannot of itself establish that the one culture forms part of the other. For one could find a situation, say, in which a Jewish scholar contributes greatly to the corpus of Catholic theology; yet it would be ridiculous to infer from this that Jewish culture is part of Catholic culture. Whatever Jewish scholars may do, one wants to insist that Jewish culture can never form part of Catholic culture.

Why not? Well, consider the elementary task of collecting stamps, or classifying them, according to their shape. Here the same principle is used to collect or classify all stamps, although, of course, various stamps will satisfy the principle differently. As a result, there will be a collection of square stamps, a collection of triangular ones, circular ones, and so on. It is only because each collection of stamps satisfies *the same* classificatory principle, but does so *differently*, that the resultant collections or classes are necessarily exclusive of each other. A collection of rectangular stamps cannot form part of a collection of circular ones.

It is, on my view, precisely this rule of classificatory logic which makes it impossible for Jewish culture to form part of Catholic culture. For in each case we colligate (or collect) human phenomena according to the same principle—that is, according to the way in which sets of human beings conceive of—and worship a godhead. Accordingly, if they do so differently, they must constitute different and exclusive cultures. Of course, it is no part of my argument to suggest that this is the only principle operative in the demarcation of these cultures—although it certainly is the predominant one. Rather, mine is the conceptual remark that when the same colligatory principle is used to demarcate cultures, groups of phenomena which satisfy the principle differently *must* form different and exclusive cultures.

Consequently, it is only when two cultures are demarcated according to different principles that it becomes possible for the one to form part of the other. Thus, for instance, we tend to demarcate Western culture in terms of the shared origins of the political, economic, religious, literary, and artistic traditions of the geographical West. All countries or groups of people who have contributed importantly to the origins of these institutions are said, according to this principle, to belong to Western culture. Jewish culture, we have seen, is demarcated according to a totally different principle, and this is why it is possible for Jewish culture to form part of Western culture; although whether it does or not must depend on the extent to which it can be seen to have contributed to the origins of the institutions and traditions of the geographical West. It is likewise possible for Hindu culture to form part of Western culture—this simply because different principles of cultural demarcation are used to distinguish the two cultures. However, there is considerable historical evidence which suggests that the Hindu religion has had little, if any, direct influence on the religious, political, and economic traditions of the West. Hence, while it remains *possible* that Hindu culture may be a part of Western culture, all the evidence suggests that it is not *in fact* a part of that culture.

The Cry for a Cultural Identity

We are now in a position to return to the question with which we began: what is it that people want when they search for a cultural identity? At root, I think, they are in search of a unified view of their culture: a coherent way of thinking about and understanding it. The people concerned could, of course, form a very large group—a nation—in which case the search for a cultural identity would coincide with the search for a national identity. But the group could be much smaller than this. It could be a group of women or Maori or Jews who live within a broader society and are in search of their respective identities. Whatever its size and constitution, the trouble is that members of a group may have many different views about the nature of their shared culture, none of which need be widely held within the group. And in any such case there remains a perfectly obvious sense in which the group as a whole lacks a cultural identity. The quest, then, is not just for a unified view, but also for a widely held or shared view of the culture: a view which, because it is shared, will help unite and bind the group. The problem is to know how to arrive at this.

The usual strategy is to attempt to discover something distinctive about one's culture, something which can be appealed to in order to develop a collective view of the culture. What this amounts to, however, is by no means clear. Earlier I argued that cultures which satisfy the same principle of cultural demarcation, but which do so differently, are necessarily different and exclusive of each other. But such differences are never sufficient for cultural distinctiveness. One can agree, for instance, that New Zealand and Italian culture are distinct and exclusive of each other, but this does not entail that there is anything distinctive about New Zealand culture, let alone that there is a New Zealand cultural identity. Nor are qualitative differences between cultures sufficient for cultural distinctiveness. The fact of the matter is that there are recognized qualitative differences between, say, New Zealand, Australian, British, and American cultures, but that these seem totally unremarkable to a person in search of something distinctive about New Zealand culture: something on which to found a cultural identity.

The quest for identity and distinctiveness is never just a quest for fixed boundaries and quantifiable properties. It is, in part, a search for the remarkable, the extraordinary, the outstanding, or the importantly different traits of a group. And the belief often is that once these are attended to, we will think differently about our group, we will be able to notice its strengths and weaknesses and the welcome or unwelcome influences operative upon it. What is more, we will be able to appeal to these traits in order to enlist loyalties, to summon a national pride, to articulate grievances, to alter our sense of self, to rethink our role within the group, and to demand the sort of action which will alter or strengthen the fabric of the society.

The search for cultural distinctiveness and identity is plainly intentional. It is, in the broadest sense, a political but not a scientific quest. It is one which sets its own criteria of success. There are no independent, widely accepted, and objectively specifiable conditions for the success of such a search. Rather, the conditions of success are determined by what those who search for a cultural identity regard as desirable.

Even so, such a search can be ill conceived. People frequently look to the "ingredients" of their society—to its languages, institutions, religions, art forms, and technological achievements—in order to discover something distinctive which, they hope, will serve to mark their cultural identity. Conceived of in this way, the search is often doomed to failure, and the reasons for this, while complex, have much to do with an inability to understand the concept "culture."

In order to see the point more clearly, we must remind ourselves that "culture" is a colligatory concept, that it brings together different human phenomena in different ways, that is, under different principles of cultural demarcation. It follows from this, and from our earlier discussion in this chapter, that there are at least two ways in which cultures may be seen to be distinctive. They may be regarded as distinctive in respect of the *phenomena* that they bring together; or they may be thought of as distinctive in respect of *the way* in which they bring them together.

Consider once more our band of philatelists. The stamps that they collect may be quite remarkable, say, for their pictorial design; or they may be run-of-the-mill and very ordinary in this respect. In the latter case we would scarcely describe the collection as distinctive—even if it contained stamps which were numerically and pictorially different from any other collection. What we need to remember, though, is that the same group of stamps can be collected together in different ways. It is possible for a collection based on pictorial motifs to contain exactly the same stamps as one based, say, on printing techniques. The first collection of stamps, moreover, could be regarded as very ordinary and commonplace. "There are many collections of bird stamps," one might say, "and this one is scarcely out of the ordinary. It is not at all distinctive." However, the same stamps collected together in respect of printing techniques might constitute a very unusual collection, *not* because the printing techniques are themselves remarkable, but because it is unusual to collect stamps *in this way*. And here we *would* describe the collection as distinctive.

What emerges, then, is that while a collection may be seen to be distinctive simply in virtue of the things collected, it may also be considered distinctive in virtue of the way in which it collects them. I have maintained that the same is true of cultures. Consider an example which is especially close to my home: the search among New Zealanders for a cultural identity. Many of my countrymen and countrywomen despair of ever finding or creating such an animal—and they despair, I think, because they are blinded by the fact that the various phenomena that are usually collected together under the banner of New Zealand culture are so very like the cultural phenomena found in Australia, Canada, Great Britain, and America.

But there is more than one way of demarcating a culture. The tendency among New Zealanders has been to employ only one principle, a geographical principle of cultural demarcation, according to which all social phenomena between certain lines of longitude and latitude constitute New Zealand culture. And because the culture thus demarcated seems totally nondistinctive, the tendency is to hunt for increasingly idiosyncratic phenomena, and to add these to the collection in order to remedy the deficiency. But this does little to create or uncover a New Zealand cultural identity.

The fault has to do with excessive reliance on a geographical principle of cultural demarcation. And this can be seen as a relic of Hegel, for on his view geographically (and temporally) delimited human phenomena are invariably manifestations of the *Volksgeist*. They are indicative of a special national character, of what could be called the national culture. But if my earlier objections are correct, and if it really is inappropriate in this case to rely too extensively on a geographical principle of cultural demarcation, how else are we to demarcate New Zealand culture?

Well, it is sometimes suggested—most often by politicians and social scientists—that social phenomena in New Zealand cluster around an imperialist principle: that the political and economic systems in New Zealand, its religions, language, art, and philosophy, its sports and forms of recreation, its news media and education system, have all to be seen as linked in a common colonial cause which directs the people of New Zealand to serve the material ends of the imperial master. If we demarcate New Zealand culture according to this principle—that is, if we think of its various institutions, traditions, and values, as bound together in this common cause— not only does the apparently commonplace acquire a new significance, but New Zealand culture itself seems to become more distinctive. Certainly it is not distinctive in the way that some would want it to be, but when looked at in these terms it can nonetheless be seen to be importantly, indeed remarkably, different from American and British culture. For whereas America and Britain are cast in the role of colonizer, New Zealand and its institutions are to be understood as the colonized.

There clearly are alternative ways of demarcating New Zealand culture, ways that may have the effect of making the culture seem altogether more distinctive. In this case, though, what is perceived to be distinctive about New Zealand culture—namely, the way in which its "ingredients" are organized and "hang together" because of colonialism—is the cause of some dissatisfaction, and this could very well produce a sense of common deprivation among those New Zealanders who perceive their culture in this way. Not only this, for such individuals, having once imbibed this view of their culture, will alter their view of themselves, and will therefore, in all likelihood, act as a group in order to offset their perceived disadvantage.

It goes without saying, though, that this particular way of demarcating New Zealand culture can properly be adopted only if there is some evidence to support it. It is, after all, no more than a hypothesis—a product of the fanciful imagination whose formulation is no doubt constrained, but under-determined, by the available evidence. So unless it accurately reflects the ways in which human phenomena hang together in New Zealand, it may well mislead us as to the actual nature of the culture. Earlier I said that the search for distinctiveness is an inherently political search, and so it is. But this is not to say that distinctiveness is simply a political fiction. It is true that what we count as distinctive, as remarkable, or as significantly different is up to us and will depend on our values, attitudes, and political aspirations. Nonetheless, we can properly regard something as a distinctive feature of our culture only if it actually *is* a feature of our culture. Our principles of cultural demarcation may enable us to uncover actual features of our culture, but they may also mislead us—with notoriously unhappy consequences. Aryan superiority, for example, was for a short time regarded by many Germans as the distinctive feature of German culture, but it was not really a feature of that culture.[27] It was a fiction bred of a spurious, racial, principle of cultural demarcation which did not accurately reflect the ways in which human phenomena clustered together in that society.

How we demarcate our culture clearly is important, for, as we have now seen, it can foment a sense of cultural distinctiveness and identity. It is a powerful political and ideological tool which, if uncritically applied, may have exceedingly unwelcome consequences. This presumably is why social scientists characteristically defend their cultural demarcations by amassing evidence, and by testing the explanatory, predictive, and descriptive utility of the colligatory principles that they have employed. Politicians are less scrupulous in this regard, and authors even less so.

Of particular interest, though, is the fact that many writers of the last one hundred years have produced novels and plays which promote new ways of demarcating, and hence new ways of thinking about, their own and other cultures. These novels, one could say, impart both strategic and conceptual skills, for they give us new ways of demarcating and thinking about particular cultures.[28] This is scarcely surprising, for if, as I have already intimated, the principles that we adopt in demarcating our cultures are inventions bred of fancy, we should expect to find some such principles in the fanciful constructions of authors who write about people and the societies in which they live.

In *The Great Gatsby*, for instance, F. Scott Fitzgerald invites us to think of American life as organized around the dream and promise of individual wealth and the happiness supposedly bred of it. As a result, and in ways that I outlined earlier, readers may come to think of American religion, education, art, science, technology, and industry as bound together in an unholy quest for this nebulous, so-called American, dream. And it is this dream, we are led to believe, which brings the elements of American culture together, and which can be appealed to as a principle in terms of which to demarcate the culture.

Nor is Fitzgerald the only author to offer new and insightful ways of demarcating cultures. In *A Portrait of the Artist as a Young Man,* James Joyce brings us to think of Irish culture as organized around the fearful and debilitating power of the priest. Then, too, there are the authors of the so-called new or emerging nations who seemingly strive to demarcate their respective cultures. According to Paul Rich, for instance, John Buchan's novel *Prester John* (written during and after his sojourn in South Africa) furnished the racial idiom in terms of which many white South Africans later came to identify and demarcate their culture.[29] By contrast, the rebel Afrikaner novelist André Brink has, through a succession of novels, brought readers to see Afrikaner patterns of behavior, religion, education, art, and science, as bound together in the promotion of an enormous illusion: a massive exercise in deception designed solely to perpetuate the political advantage of a privileged few. Here the desire to deceive and beguile is seen as the colligatory principle which binds and demarcates Afrikaner culture. In New Zealand, authors such as Jean Devanny and Bruce Mason have encouraged readers to think of the political and economic system, their frames of reference and value, as clustering around a single and very ruthless slaughterhouse principle. On their view, the preparation of flesh for the tables of others is the primary colligatory principle which binds New Zealand culture and renders it distinctive.

Literary works of art clearly can provide new ways of thinking about and demarcating cultures. Whether or not Fitzgerald intended as much, his readers may come, in time, to think of American life as organized around a single pervasive illusion: an infinitely desirable, yet infinitely elusive, goal which affords both structure and significance to human phenomena in the United States of America. And once people begin to think of America in this way, once they attempt to demarcate American culture in these terms, they may come to notice features of the culture which were previously unnoticed. Alternatively, as we have seen, they may simply invent such features. Either way, people may be brought with the passing of time to regard these features as important enough to mark what is distinctive about their culture. And they may use this to develop a communal view of their culture—to develop a cultural identity. This, in its turn, may help to cement loyalties, to stimulate pride, to articulate grievances, and to invite group action.

It would be wrong, of course, to think that Fitzgerald's novel actually achieved all of this. For even if a substantial number of Americans were led by the work to embrace the principle of cultural demarcation which it suggests, it does not follow that American culture thus demarcated will come to be regarded as distinctive, or that it will promote a shared or widely held view of the culture. Whether or not it does do all of this, I have stressed, must depend on the beliefs, the values, the attitudes and aspirations that readers bring to the work. In matters of cultural distinctiveness and identity, the beholders' share is vital.

Despite this, there may be copious evidence to suggest that the principle of cultural demarcation conveyed in *The Great Gatsby* accurately reveals the ways in which human phenomena hang together in America. In such a case, one clearly has reason to maintain that this principle marks certain features of American culture, and that it should be allowed to mold and inform the American sense of identity. The trouble, of course, is that evidence does not always have its due effect on the search for an identity. For, as we have seen, the preferences and interests of people in a particular society can encourage them to ignore the evidence, and, with it, important aspects of their culture. They adopt an impoverished view of their culture which, at times, totally misconstrues its nature.

It seems plain, then, that even though literary works of art can furnish principles of cultural demarcation, they cannot ensure the development of a cultural identity. This must depend on the preferences, values, and interests that people bring to literature.

From Cultural to Individual Identity

One could say that, insofar as literature helps people to discover their cultural identity, it does so by telling a story. For the fact of the matter is that any story must embody certain organizational principles in accordance with which the objects and events in the narrative are made to hang together. To compose and tell a story is just to apply such a principle to certain imaginary or nonimaginary things and events. On my view, then, whenever literature enables people to discover (or invent) a cultural identity, it does so by telling a story which suggests to its audience a particular way of organizing and relating human phenomena. It imparts a principle of cultural demarcation—a colligatory principle which enables us to see human phenomena in our society as a more or less coherent and organized whole.

Such colligatory principles need not be derived from literature. We can invent and tell our own stories about our society; we can imagine ways in which apparently discrete human phenomena hang together and coalesce, and having done so, we are left with a hypothesis—a historical or sociological hypothesis—which needs to be tested. If our interests and concerns are strong enough, we may, as we have seen, assent to the hypothesis without ever testing it, and we may continue to assent to it even in the light of obvious counterevidence.

Much the same is true of what I shall call "individual identity." Most people carry around in their heads some or other image of themselves: what we call a self-image. In calling it an image, however, I do not mean to suggest that it is a piece of visual imagery. While it may involve visual imagery, it is usually much more discursive than this. It is more like a story, a life-narrative, in terms of which people are disposed to see themselves and make sense of their lives. Some people think of themselves (or are disposed to think of themselves) as pious, devout, humble, chaste, and all that this implies; and they would prefer to see the events of their lives in these terms. Others prefer to construe their lives in terms of their own bravery, boldness, and manliness, while there are those who regard themselves as gentle, caring, and just, and acquire a sense of worthiness from construing their lives in these terms. Then, too, there are people who would prefer to think that they are important, wordly, and of consequence, while others are disposed to see themselves as sensible, reliable, unruffled, and rational. It would be difficult, I think, to exaggerate the variety of life-narratives that people embrace, or the lengths to which they will go to protect them.

It would be wrong, of course, to think of a life-narrative as a story constantly buzzing in one's head, commenting on and directing one's life. Rather, a life-narrative (individual identity, self-image) must be thought of as a disposition of individuals to organize, relate, and see the events in their lives in specific ways. Bearing this in mind, we may say that each life-narrative or self-image furnishes an individual with a way of making sense of his or her life. Each provides us with a way of ordering or colligating our various actions, activities, and enterprises. Such narratives are not god-given or natural to the individual. Infants are not born secure in their view of themselves. They acquire a view of themselves. Individual identities, it seems to me, are invented and learned. They may, of course, be based on past experience, but past experience is often too complicated, amorphous, and anomalous to admit of a coherent self-image. Most often, individual identities are bred of fancy—they are fanciful constructs that people adopt and impose on the various events which crowd their lives. It is this construct, this invention, this story, which often lends order and purpose to a life, and which is frequently of profound value to an individual.

The view that individuals are disposed to take of themselves I have called an individual identity. That people actually have such an identity or life-narrative emerges most clearly when we reflect on the phenomenon sometimes referred to as agent regret.[30] As a young teenager at a school debating society meeting, Mary C. was guilty of a minor howler, a malapropism, which her teacher drew to her attention after the event. Mary blushed furiously at the time, and now, some twenty years later, continues to blush when she thinks of the mistake. She regrets the error even now, and the oddity is that she knows that no one else remembers it. No one was hurt by her mistake, and there were no long-term or untoward consequences. In fact, her team won the debate. Why, then, does she continue to regret the mistake? On my view, she regrets it because the error is not part of the story she would like to be able to tell of herself; it sits uneasily with her self-image, her individual identity. Mary is disposed to think of herself as an articulate, intelligent, and fluent debater, a stimulating and informed speaker whom people like to hear. Malapropisms have no place in this picture. Her regret, it seems, is an aesthetic response to what she now regards as a blemished narrative.

Of course, we could just say that Mary's pride was hurt, and hope to explain her regret in this way. But appeals to pride explain too little, for it is never clear what we are to say about the source of human pride. On my view, pride itself needs to be accounted for, and can best be accounted for in terms of individual identity; although not just in terms of this, for it is also the desire to preserve and retain this identity or life-narrative which helps account for the regrets, stubbornness, and arrogance of some people.

In order to see this more clearly, we need to remind ourselves that individual identity is the source of one's self-esteem. Those who have reasonably high levels of self-esteem, perhaps because they are disposed to think of themselves as efficient, intelligent, likable, generous, and kind, will tend to be guided in what they do by this sense of self. Any construal of their actions that challenges their self-image, that suggests, say, that they are less than generous, or that they are inefficient or unkind, will be the cause of some consternation. People whose positive self-image is threatened in this way will generally defend themselves against such accusations—either by regarding, say, their lack of generosity as momentary and untypical, or else by denying the charge altogether. People are generally obliged, for reasons of their own psychological well-being, to defend themselves in this way. For any successful attack on an individual's positive self-image will induce a lack of confidence, a measure of trauma, depression, and even neurosis. In short, it will produce a damaging crisis of confidence within the individual. It is in order to avoid this sort of crisis that we sometimes protect ourselves by clinging stubbornly to our identity, our self-image, even at the cost of denying the obvious. Sometimes, moreover, rather than risk this sort of upset, we embrace a life-narrative which seriously underestimates our own worth, and provides us with little to live up to.

These last observations have more, I suspect, to do with empirical psychology than they have to do with philosophy. And although I cannot pretend to any expertise as an experimental psychologist, it is nonetheless important for us to see how large a role these narratives play in our lives. On my view, as we have seen, one's life-narrative tends to guide and regulate one's behavior. Take, for instance, those individuals who have an impoverished life-narrative, and who think of themselves as generally inefficient and unintelligent, as unlucky and as losers. This must affect their expectations of what they can hope to achieve. As a result, they are likely to underachieve since they simply will not strive in situations where others, with a better sense of self, will both try and on occasions succeed.

The notion of a life-narrative also helps to explain why people are often immune to reason and rational argument. Individuals are sometimes confronted by sound arguments which tend to undermine important aspects of their self-image, and so pose the threat of personal confusion, upheaval, and crisis. Thus, for instance, people who think of themselves as devout, pious, and obedient, and who think favorably of themselves on this account, will not generally be persuaded by an argument—no matter how strong it is—which demonstrates the incoherence of the traditional concept of God. For whatever else our individual identities do, they help determine what we consider to be important. Hence a few contradictions and *non sequiturs* may be considered utterly inconsequential by those who see themselves as primarily devout and obedient theists. On my view, only those people who think of themselves as fundamentally rational will take seriously the accusation of irrationality. If my earlier analysis is correct, to accuse such people, as theists are wont to do, of intellectual pride is to attack their individual identity or self-image. It is an attempt to replace it with a self-image more conducive to the interests of those who are embarrassed by rational argument, and who regard it as a threat to their identity.

It should be clear enough by now that all reflective human beings enjoy an individual identity: a way of seeing themselves and construing their lives. Such an identity, I have tried to show, is vitally important to each and every individual. It is crucial as well to the societies in which they live, for how we see ourselves, I have argued, affects not only what we regard as important and unimportant, but also how we act with regard to our fellow human beings. This is why many societies often assume a proprietorial interest in our individual identities. They are concerned to see them develop in certain ways but not in others. Schools, the media, censorship, and religion are only some of the vehicles used to affect our self-image and self-esteem, and this, of course, suggests that initially the individual identities that we adopt bear little or no relation to the sorts of people we actually are. Our individual identities, like our cultural ones, seem to be a product of the fanciful imagination, although, as we shall see, what we do not invent for ourselves, others invent for us.

People often dream about the sort of person they would like to be. Looking to the future, they see themselves as rich, bold, ruthless, powerful, fearless, glamorous; as intelligent, perceptive, sensitive, caring. There is a sense in which they imagine a certain life for themselves, and they may, after a while, begin to see and think of themselves in the light of their imaginings. For the most part, though, we do not pluck these visions out of the air. They are usually suggested to us in many different ways. Our parents, our teachers, priests, and friends all play a role in our socialization, and in so doing they impart values and instill ideals. In the light of these, we may prefer to imagine ourselves as ruthless rather than sensitive, powerful rather than caring, fearless rather than intelligent.

This process of suggestion, we learned in Chapter Six, is greatly facilitated by the novels people read, the films and plays that they see, and even (I can now add) the advertising to which they are exposed and the games that they play. In the light of all or any of these, we may derivatively imagine ourselves in certain ways: as a latter-day Robin Hood, as a sagacious Mr. Knightley, as a soulful and unhappy Maggie Tulliver. Most often, however, because we already have certain socially instilled ideals and values, we creatively combine selected aspects of real and fictional people, and we tend to think of ourselves in terms of the models that these provide. The process, at this point, is inherently fanciful and fraught with risk, for it is plain that by thinking of ourselves in terms of these models, we not only discern some sort of sense in our lives, but we begin to organize priorities and to act accordingly.

The element of risk in all of this is most apparent in the case of people who suffer low self-esteem, who have impoverished individual identities, and who tend to think of themselves, say, as unintelligent, unlucky, disadvantaged, and generally powerless. This self-image may, of course, be shaped to some extent by past experience; and partly because they find the reality hard to live with, and partly, too, because they have imbibed a range of values, not all of which find general favor, they may select surrogate identities which are threatening to the society at large. We are all acquainted with the underachiever who, looking to television, chooses to act out the role of gangster, Casanova, Nazi, thug, torturer, Klansman, rapist, and so on. After thinking of themselves in this way for some time, the role play is frequently forgotten and fancy becomes fact.

We plainly cannot allow people to adopt just any identity. The cost to society is too great. It is the general, although tacit, recognition of this fact—a recognition, I should add, which reveals considerable deference to the powers and scope of the fanciful imagination—which leads to a tendency in our society to create institutions that invent and proscribe identities for others. It is not too much of an exaggeration to see the education system, our boards of censors, and a good deal of religious instruction as bent on this task. Usually individuals accept only some aspects of these identities, reject others, and do a good deal of inventing for themselves. It is possible, though, for other people to do all the inventing and imagining, and to project ready-made individual identities on to others. J. M. Synge's *The Playboy of the Western World* provides a fictional example of this phenomenon, but it occurs as well among actual people in the world we inhabit. People do have greatness thrust upon them: in being treated as folk-heroes, they think of themselves as folk-heroes, and begin to act accordingly. They internalize the role of judge, bishop, rabbi, doctor, or pope, and begin to think of themselves in the sometimes sterile ways suggested by the institutions to which they belong.

Conclusion

It seems plain from all of this that fictional literature can facilitate the process of demarcating one's culture. It seems plain, too, that it can contribute in important ways to the development both of a cultural and an individual identity. My aim in this concluding chapter has been to explain how all of this is possible, and in so doing to bring together the several themes of this book in a way which demonstrates their importance, not just for the individual, but for society generally.

In my introduction to this book, I suggested that there were three distinct but related ways of looking at its arguments. We can see them, I said, as a study in romantic theory, as a study in the imagination and its powers, and as a study in the philosophy of literature. The theories of literature advocated by the New Critics and their successors, I argued, have effectively silenced literature, leaving it with nothing to say and nothing to do. It was my aim to show that fictional literature, relying as it does on the fanciful imagination, can and does impart knowledge not just of a propositional variety, but also knowledge of skills, values, and feelings. In so doing, I sought to show how a romantic epistemology could rise above the limitations placed on epistemology by the rise of science and its emphasis on propositional knowledge as the only knowledge worthy of philosophical attention.

The task has been a lengthy one, and has involved developing a romantic epistemology which is not prone to the usual romantic excesses. I argued at some length that this epistemology, even though it elevates the fanciful imagination and regards it as crucial to the acquisition and growth of empirical knowledge, need not commit us to the romantic idealism of Schelling and Coleridge, still less to a variety of Derridean textualism or Kuhnian relativism. Indeed, I take myself to have established that romantic realism is a tenable position which, if properly understood, will entail neither a conceptual nor a cultural relativism. All of this was to be found in my first three chapters, and prepared the way for a better understanding in later chapters of the comprehension and interpretation of fictional literature. In addition, we were able, in the light of the early chapters, to explain how we learn both from fiction and from the metaphors of fiction. At every turn I have felt obliged to show that my position in this book is not liable to the usual romantic blunders—and my account of metaphor was no exception, for I there defended myself against the romantic extremes of Nietzsche and Derrida, and tried to steer a course between their positions and the neopositivist position of Davidson.

In many ways this final chapter is an attempt to use some of these earlier observations in order to develop an adequate account of culture and cultural identity. Such an account was called for, not just because of our interest in the question of whether fictional literature can ever contribute to a culture and cultural identity, but also in order to complement my arguments against relativism. For in Chapter Five, I argued that it is possible to verify an interpretation of a literary work, but that we can do so only if we have knowledge of the appropriate culture or period of the culture within which the work was produced. Margolis's notion of cultural emergence was uncritically embraced and used to support this view; and it is to be hoped that my account of culture helps inform his concept of cultural emergence.

In developing this account, I was forced (yet again) to guard against certain romantic excesses. My concern, of course, was with a Hegelian theory of culture and identity, and after criticizing and disposing of this view, I offered a colligatory account of culture. Whatever its faults, the account offered has the undeniable virtue of demystifying the notions of culture and cultural identity. How we demarcate a culture, I argued, will depend on the colligatory principles we adopt, and these, we saw, are often the offspring of the fanciful imagination, suggested to us in works of literature.

In this way, fictional literature is seen to acquire the social function which contemporary literary theory witholds from it. For it is now apparent that the fanciful imagination in general (and fictional literature in particular) does suggest ways of construing human and social phenomena. In so doing, it sometimes excites criticism and protest, enlists loyalties, and even encourages group action. Most often, of course, it performs a less strident role, and merely gives people particular ways of seeing and thinking about their society and their culture. In addition, we found, both in this chapter and in Chapter Six, that fiction, like the fanciful imagination, may affect our sense of self. It can and does provide new ways of construing and making sense of the various happenings and events in our lives, and in doing so often furnishes us with new ways of thinking about ourselves. These self-images or individual identities, we found, are profoundly important not just for the individuals who bear them, but also for the societies in which we live.

According to my argument in this book, it is the fanciful imagination and its progeny which enable us to make sense of, and to come to know, the physical and social world in which we live. Science, on this view, is just one of the products of fancy, for we cannot invent theories and formulate hypotheses without fancifully construing the phenomena of our world in one way or another. Fiction, we have seen, is another of the products of the fanciful, creative, or originative imagination, although the knowledge which it affords is richer and more varied than that afforded by empirical science.

Borrowing Hume's words, we may say that it is the fanciful imagination rather than the principle of the association of ideas which is the cement of our universe. By emphasizing and explaining its role in the acquisition and growth of knowledge, I have challenged the positivist tendencies of contemporary epistemology: tendencies, I have suggested, which are bred of the hegemony of empirical science. In so doing, I have preserved and defended a few of the basic insights of romantic theory without tumbling, together with Coleridge, Schelling, Hegel, and others, into the abyss below.

NOTES

Chapter One

1. Not all were equally thorough in this regard. Wordsworth appeared to believe that one could subvert idealism, and regain some knowledge of an external reality, through the sense of touch. See Mary Warnock, *Imagination* (Faber, London, 1976), p. 103.

2. F. W. J. Schelling, *Schellings Sämtliche Werke*, K. F. A. Schelling, ed. (14 vols., Cotta, Stuttgart, 1856–61), part I, vol. 3, p. 626.

3. Samuel Taylor Coleridge, *Biographia Literaria*, George Watson, ed. (Dent, London, 1975), ch. 13.

4. For the most part, these ideas are developed in G. F. W. Hegel, *Hegel's Philosophy of Right*, T. M. Knox, trans. (Clarendon Press, Oxford, 1967), part 1. It is true, of course, that for Hegel freedom consists in doing one's rationally apprehended duty.

5. Friedrich Nietzsche, "On Truth and Falsity in their Ultramoral Sense," in Oscar Levy, ed., Maximilian A. Mügge, trans., *The Complete Works of Friedrich Nietzsche* (18 vols., Allen & Unwin, London, 1911), vol. 2, pp. 171–92.

6. *Schelling's Sämliche Werke*, part I, vol. 1, p. 383.

7. Ibid., vol. 4, p. 289.

8. Ibid., vol. 1, pp. 390–91.

9. Romantic idealists differ about the extent to which this is possible. Fichte believed that we could have absolutely certain knowledge only of those things of which we could be conscious—things in time and space. Our knowledge of the absolute ego was a theoretical construction, and hence less certain. In this respect he differed from Schelling, who not only allowed knowledge of the absolute ego, but also insisted that it was more certain than our knowledge of objects in space and time. See J. G. Fichte, *Ausgewählte Werke in Sechs Bänden*, Fritz Medicus, ed. (6 vols., Fritz Eckardt Verlag, Leipzig, 1911–12), vol. 1, pp. 10, 22, 80.

10. *Schellings Sämtliche Werke*, vol. 7, p. 201.

11. Richard Rorty, "Nineteenth Century Idealism and Twentieth Century Textualism," in *Consequences of Pragmatism* (University of Minnesota Press, Minneapolis, 1982), pp. 142–43, 148–49. Although Rorty is here explaining the rise of textualism with reference to romanticism, he gives every appearance of

agreeing with this view, and actually maintains that the textualists have won the day.

12. The seminal work is, of course, T. S. Kuhn, *The Structure of Scientific Revolutions*, 2d ed. (University of Chicago Press, Chicago, 1970).

13. Jacques Derrida, *Of Grammatology*, Gayatri Chakravorty Spivak, trans. (Johns Hopkins University Press, Baltimore, 1974), pp. 49–50.

14. Gilbert Ryle, *The Concept of Mind* (Penguin, Harmondsworth, England, 1963), pp. 242–43.

15. Ibid., p. 243.

16. Gerald Graff, *Literature Against Itself: Literary Ideas in Modern Society* (University of Chicago Press, Chicago, 1979), p. 5.

17. Monroe C. Beardsley, "Intentions and Interpretations: A Fallacy Revived," in Michael J. Wreen and Donald M. Callen, eds., *The Aesthetic Point of View* (Cornell University Press, Ithaca, N.Y., 1982), p. 188.

18. I. A. Richards, *Science and Poetry* (Kegan Paul, Trench, Trubner & Co., London, 1935), chs. 1, 5, 6.

19. Ibid., p. 58.

20. Ibid.

21. I. A. Richards, *Principles of Literary Criticism* (Kegan Paul, Trench, Trubner & Co., London, 1945, pp. 226–27), where he defines a poem as "a class of experiences."

22. W. K. Wimsatt, Jr., and Monroe C. Beardsley, "The Intentional Fallacy," in Joseph Margolis, ed., *Philosophy Looks at the Arts: Contemporary Readings in Aesthetics*, rev. ed. (Temple University Press, Philadelphia, 1978), p. 294.

23. Richards, *Science and Poetry*, p. 65.

24. Ibid., p. 73.

25. I. A. Richards, *Coleridge on Imagination*, 2d ed. (Routledge & Kegan Paul, London, 1950), pp. 226–28.

26. John Crowe Ransom, *The World's Body* (Scribners, New York, 1938), pp. 115–16. See, as well, his *The New Criticism* (Folcroft Library Editions, Norfolk, Conn., 1971), pp. 333–34.

27. T. S. Eliot, *Christianity and Culture* (Harvest Books, New York, 1949), p. 99.

28. Cleanth Brooks, *Modern Poetry and the Tradition* (Oxford University Press, Oxford, 1965), pp. 147–48.

29. The exception, perhaps, is Northrop Frye, although there is a clear sense in which he adapts the procedures of science to suit his romantic allegiances. See his *The Educated Imagination* (Indiana University Press, Bloomington, 1964).

30. Cleanth Brooks, *The Well Wrought Urn* (Harvest Books, New York, 1947), p. 18.

31. Allen Tate, *The Man of Letters in the Modern World* (Meridian Books, New York, 1955), p. 335.

32. Brooks, *The Well Wrought Urn*, pp. 190–91.

33. Ibid., pp. 255–56.

34. Graff, *Literature Against Itself*, p. 142.

35. T. S. Eliot, *The Use of Poetry and the Use of Criticism* (Faber, London,

1964), p. 18. In endorsing these words, Eliot attributes them to Richards. Brooks does the same in *The Well Wrought Urn*, p. 265.

36. Wimsatt and Beardsley, "The Intentional Fallacy," p. 294.

37. Graff, *Literature Against Itself*, p. 139.

38. Richards, *Principles of Literary Criticism*, pp. 251, 252.

39. See, for example, Geoffrey Hartman, "Literary Criticism and its Discontents," *Critical Inquiry* 3 (1976), 203–20, esp. p. 217.

40. Richard Palmer, *Hermeneutics: Interpretation Theory in Schleiermacher, Dilthey, Heidegger and Gadamer* (Northwestern University Press, Evanston, Ill., 1969), pp. 4–5.

41. See Graff, *Literature Against Itself*, pp. 140–46, for an illuminating discussion of these tensions.

42. Ibid., p. 143.

43. Ibid., p. 144.

44. Susan Sontag, *Against Interpretation* (Delta, New York, 1967).

45. See, for example, Brooks, *The Well Wrought Urn*, p. 266, where, writing of Urban and Richards, he says: "Both point the literary critic to a reading of the poem itself—to the fullest realization of the symbolic structure that *is* the poem. The task is not easy; it is important; it is basic to any valid literary criticism."

46. See J. Hillis Miller, "Steven's Rock and Criticism as Cure" in Morris Philipson and Paul J. Gudel, eds., *Aesthetics Today* (New American Library, New York, 1980), pp. 524–25. See, as well, Jonathan Culler, *On Deconstruction: Theory and Criticism after Structuralism* (Cornell University Press, Ithaca, N.Y. 1982), pp. 22–28.

47. Many of Derrida's remarks and doctrines are taken over by Paul de Man and applied to the New Criticism in his *Blindness and Insight: Essays in the Rhetoric of Contemporary Criticism* (Oxford University Press, Oxford, 1971).

48. Frye, *The Educated Imagination*, p. 80.

Chapter Two

1. Plato, *Phaedrus*, R. Hackworth, trans. (Cambridge University Press, Cambridge, 1952), 245a. See, as well, *Ion* in *The Dialogues of Plato*, B. Jowett, trans. (5 vols., Clarendon Press, Oxford, 1892), vol. 1, pp. 501–2.

2. Saint Augustine, *Letters*, in *A Select Library of the Nicene and Post-Nicene Fathers*, J. Cunningham, trans. (14 vols., Wm. B. Eerdmans, Grand Rapids, Mich., 1956), vol. 1, letter VII, iii, 6 to Nebredius, A.D. 389, pp. 255–56.

3. R. Descartes, *The Philosophical Works of Descartes*, E. S. Haldane and G. R. T. Ross, trans. (Cambridge University Press, Cambridge, 1931), p. 7.

4. Ibid., p. 186.

5.. Nicholas Malebranche, *The Search after Truth*, T. M. Lemmon and P. J. Olscamp, trans. (Ohio State University Press, Columbus, 1980).

6. Francis Bacon, *Works*, J. Spedding, R. L. Ellis, and D. D. Heath, eds. (14 vols., Longmans, London, 1864–74), vol. 3, p. 343.

7. Ibid., vol. 4, p. 406.

8. Thomas Hobbes, *Leviathan* (Dent, London, 1962), p. 3.

9. Ibid., p. 5.

10. Ibid., p. 6.

11. Ibid., p. 8.

12. Ibid., p. 9.

13. Ibid., p. 33.

14. Ibid.

15. John Locke, *An Essay Concerning Human Understanding*, John W. Yolton, ed. (2 vols., Dent, London, 1961), vol. 1, II, xii, 2, p. 130.

16. Ibid., vol. 1, II, xxxiii, 5–8, pp. 336–37.

17. Ibid., vol. 1, II, xxxiii, 10, p. 338.

18. Ibid., vol. 1, II, xi, 2, p. 123.

19. John Locke, *Of the Conduct of the Understanding*, 3d ed. (Clarendon Press, Oxford, 1890), section 33, p. 75.

20. Locke, *Essay Concerning Human Understanding*, vol. 2, III, 8, 34, pp. 105–6. For more on Locke's attitude to metaphor, see Chapter Seven.

21. David Hume, *A Treatise of Human Nature*, L. A. Selby-Bigge, ed. (Clarendon Press, Oxford, 1941), I.1.iii, p. 9. Further references to this work will be given in the text.

22. Immanuel Kant, *Critique of Pure Reason*, Norman Kemp Smith, trans. (Macmillan, London, 1964), B152.

23. H. J. Paton, *Kant's Metaphysic of Experience* (2 vols., Allen & Unwin, London, 1961), vol. 2, p. 227.

24. N. R. Hanson, *Patterns of Discovery* (Cambridge University Press, Cambridge, 1958), ch. 1.

25. Michael Frayn, *Constructions* (Wildwood House, London, 1974), para. 6.

26. See R. L. Gregory, *The Intelligent Eye* (Weidenfeld & Nicolson, London, 1970). See, as well, the case studies cited by Jean Piaget, *The Origins of Intelligence in the Child*, Margaret Cook, trans. (Penguin, Harmondsworth, England, 1977), pp. 37–42. It is doubtful whether the earlier Piaget (1936) would have agreed with my account at this point since he attempts to explain the infant's initial accommodation to the breast entirely in terms of physiological reflexes—despite the fact that his case studies give clear indication of trial and error (searching) activities on the part of the infant (pp. 38–39). However, the later Piaget (1970), in his article "Piaget's Theory" in *Carmichael's Manual of Child Psychology*, P. Mussen, ed. (Wiley & Sons, New York, 1970) insists that in order to know an object, an organism must in some sense act upon it, thereby transforming not only the object but also its own psychological structures. Although my thesis in this chapter is compatible with, and can be seen as an extension of, Piaget's later theory, to my knowledge he nowhere explores the possibility of the imagination actively contributing to the initial cognitive process.

27. There is no need to suppose on this account that scientific discoveries require the total rejection of established bodies of knowledge or belief. It seems much more likely that scientists sometimes suspend aspects of these bodies, and that this facilitates discoveries and insights bred of fancy. But even so, it would be wrong to suppose in such a case that the scientist's fanciful construals are totally

unconstrained by beliefs bred of past experience. *Cf.* Paul Feyerabend, *Against Method* (New Left Books, London, 1974).

Chapter Three

1. F. W. J. Schelling, *Schellings Werke*, Manfred Schröter, ed. (6 vols., Beck, Munich, 1927–28), vol. 3, p. 626.

2. Samuel Taylor Coleridge, *Biographia Literaria*, George Watson, ed. (Dent, London, 1967), ch. 13, p. 167.

3. Friedrich Nietzsche, "On Truth and Falsity in their Ultramoral Sense," in Oscar Levy, ed., Maximilian A. Mügge, trans., *The Complete Works of Friedrich Nietzsche* (18 vols., Allen & Unwin, London, 1911), vol. 2, p. 180. All further references to this article in this chapter will be given in the text.

4. Richard Rorty, "Introduction: Pragmatism and Philosophy" in *Consequences of Pragmatism* (University of Minnesota Press, Minneapolis, 1982), p. xvii.

5. This claim is discussed in detail in Chapter Seven.

6. Jacques Derrida, *Of Grammatology*, Gayatri Chakravorty Spivak, trans. (Johns Hopkins University Press, Baltimore, 1974), p. 49.

7. Ibid. See, as well, p. 139, where Derrida insists that cultures have to repress the true nature of language.

8. Jacques Derrida, *Positions* (University of Chicago Press, Chicago, 1981), p. 41.

9. Jacques Derrida, *Limited Inc.*, Samuel Weber, trans., supplement to *Glyph* 2 (1977), 162–254, esp. p. 236.

10. Derrida, *Positions*, p. 41.

11. Jonathan Culler, *On Deconstruction: Theory and Criticism after Structuralism* (Cornell University Press, Ithaca, N.Y., 1982), p. 86.

12. Derrida, *Grammatology*, p. 50.

13. Culler, *On Deconstruction*, pp. 121–25.

14. See Ferdinand de Saussure, *Course in General Linguistics*, Wade Baskin, trans. (Routledge & Kegan Paul, London, 1974), esp. pp. 3, 13–14, 68, 80. See, as well, Jonathan Culler, *Saussure* (Fontana, London, 1976), ch. 2.

15. Derrida, *Grammatology*, pp. 34–43.

16. Ibid., p. 166. See, as well, Jacques Derrida, "Différance" in *Speech and Phenomena and Other Essays in Husserl's Theory of Signs*, David B. Allison, trans. (Northwestern University Press, Evanston, Ill., 1973), p. 147.

17. Culler, *On Deconstruction*, p. 95.

18. Derrida, *Grammatology*, p. 157, where he writes: "Immediacy is derived. Everything begins with the intermediary."

19. Derrida, *Positions*, p. 26.

20. See, for example, Jean Piaget, *The Origin of Intelligence in the Child*, Margaret Cook, trans. (Penguin, Harmondsworth, England, 1977), pp. 46–47.

21. H. P. Grice, "Meaning," *The Philosophical Review* 66 (1957), 377–88.

22. Karl Popper, "Truth, Rationality and the Growth of Scientific Knowl-

edge" in *Conjectures and Refutations: The Growth of Scientific Knowledge*, 5th ed. (Routledge & Kegan Paul, London, 1974), pp. 215–50; Gilbert Ryle, *The Concept of Mind* (Penguin, Harmondsworth, England, 1963), ch. 7; N. R. Hanson, *Patterns of Discovery* (Cambridge University Press, Cambridge, 1965), ch. 1.

23. Derrida, "Différance," p. 141.

24. Richard Rorty, "Nineteenth-Century Idealism and Twentieth-Century Textualism" in *Consequences of Pragmatism*, p. 154.

25. Richard Rorty, "Philosophy as a Kind of Writing: An Essay on Derrida" in *Consequences of Pragmatism*, p. 104.

26. On this, see Culler, *On Deconstruction*, pp. 149–51.

27. Steven Fuller, "A French Science (With English Subtitles)," *Philosophy and Literature* 7 (1983), 3.

28. For an account of this procedure, see Spivak's preface to Derrida, *Grammatology*, pp. xiii–xx.

29. Ibid., p. xviii. See, as well, Derrida, *Speech and Phenomena*, p. 147.

30. Derrida, *Grammatology*, p. 61.

31. Cited and translated by Spivak in her preface to Derrida, *Grammatology*, p. xviii. Emphasis added.

32. Rorty, *Consequences of Pragmatism*, pp. 93, 98, 142, where he suggests that Derrida, following Hegel, does not think that there is any need for argumentation in philosophy. Philosophy does not proceed by logic, but by rhetoric. If the latter is true, it also explains the need to create the illusion of argument. On this, see Newton Garver's preface to Derrida, *Speech and Phenomena*, pp. ix–xi.

33. Jacques Derrida, *Writing and Difference*, Alan Bass, trans. (Routledge & Kegan Paul, London, 1978), p. 3.

34. It is true that Derrida's ontology commits him to the existence only of signs. Strictly speaking, therefore, he countenances neither persons nor the imagination. However, his ontology is clearly reductionist, and provided that we remember that this is his preferred analysis of all entities, including persons and the imagination, there is no harm in his (or our) continuing to speak of these entities. It seems clear that "the play of signs" has the same role in Derrida's epistemology and metaphysics as the imagination does in traditional romantic theory.

35. See Richard Macksey and Eugenio Donato, eds., *The Structuralist Controversy: The Languages of Criticism and the Sciences of Aran* (Johns Hopkins University Press, Baltimore, 1970), p. 272, where Derrida says: "I don't believe there is any perception."

36. Michael Dummett argues that reductionist theses such as phenomenalism are not, properly speaking, antirealist. I shall consider this view presently. See Michael Dummett, "Realism," in *Truth and Other Enigmas* (Harvard University Press, Cambridge, 1978), pp. 145–65.

37. David Hume, *A Treatise of Human Nature*, L. A. Selby-Bigge, ed. (Clarendon Press, Oxford, 1941), book I, part IV, section II.

38. Ibid.

39. Bertrand Russell, *The Problems of Philosophy* (Oxford University Press, Oxford, 1912), chs. 2 and 3.

40. Bertrand Russell, *The Analysis of Mind* (George Allen & Unwin, London, 1921), lectures 4 and 7.

41. On this, see Chapter One, "An Excursion into Romantic Theory."

42. Rorty, "Introduction," in *Consequences of Pragmatism*, p. xxxix.

43. Richard Rorty, "Pragmatism, Davidson and Truth," unpublished, 1983.

44. Dummett, "Realism," p. 146.

45. Ibid. For further support of this interpretation, see Michael Devitt, *Realism & Truth* (Basil Blackwell, Oxford, 1984), pp. 196–223.

46. See, for example, Richard J. Bernstein, *Beyond Relativism and Objectivism* (University of Pennsylvania Press, Philadelphia, 1983).

47. Hume, *A Treatise of Human Nature*, book I, part IV, section II, p. 187.

48. Hilary Putnam, *Reason, Truth and History* (Cambridge University Press, Cambridge, 1981), pp. 55–56.

49. This will have important consequences for any theory of morality, although I cannot pursue this here.

50. As people become vulnerable in different sorts of ways, perhaps (as a Marxist would say) because of the changes in the "material conditions" of their existence, they will tend to adopt different construals, and embrace different beliefs. However, as we shall see in Chapter Five, the romantic realist argues that it is possible to adjudicate between these beliefs.

Chapter Four

1. It is, of course, true that a play or a novel need not be entirely fictional. For the purpose of this chapter, however, I shall make the simplifying assumption that the plays and novels mentioned are purely fictional.

2. Cf. Kendall Walton, "Fearing Fictions," *The Journal of Philosophy* 75 (1978), 5–27, esp. p. 6. Walton appears to support a version of this argument, and in consequence maintains that anyone who properly understands fiction is never actually moved by fictional events. Rather, it is only make-believe true that the reader is so moved.

3. To this extent my argument coincides with Walton's in "Fearing Fictions." Unlike Walton, however, I attempt to preserve our basic intuitions about being moved by fiction, and defend the view that we really are amused, saddened, or aroused by fictional characters and events without thereby misunderstanding the fiction.

4. Kendall Walton appears to support such a view at one point in his article "How Remote are Fictional Worlds from the Real World," *The Journal of Aesthetics and Art Criticism* 37 (1978), 18. He writes that we should regard "fictional statements as occurring, implicitly if not explicitly, within the scope of an intensional operator, 'It is fictional that,' and hence as analogous to statements of the form "It is believed that,' "It is wished that,' etc."

5. My talk of worlds at this point need not commit me to the existence of imaginary, fictional, or possible worlds. Any group of interconnected imaginings,

whether or not they delineate a possible state of affairs, I shall call an imaginary world.

6. Gilbert Ryle, "Symposium on Imaginary Objects," *Proceedings of the Aristotelian Society* suppl. vol. 13 (1933), 32.

7. Michael Weston, "How Can We Be Moved by the Fate of Anna Karenina?" *Proceedings of the Aristotelian Society*, suppl. vol. 49 (1975), 81–93; and Eva Schaper, "Fiction and the Suspension of Disbelief," *The British Journal of Aesthetics* 18 (1978), 31–44. Page references to these articles will be given in the text.

8. See, for example, Colin Radford, "How Can We Be Moved by the Fate of Anna Karenina?," *Proceedings of the Aristotelian Society* suppl. vol. 49 (1975), 67–80, who defends the view that it is irrational to be moved by creatures of fiction. A similar position is taken by H. H. Price, *Belief* (Allen & Unwin, London, 1969), pp. 307ff.

9. See Walton, "Fearing Fictions," p. 14, where he maintains that the fact that a person has certain physiological sensations of fear "as a result of realizing that make-believedly the slime threatens him generates the truth that make-believedly he is afraid of the slime."

10. Walton's account of make-believe, if we are to go by the examples that he uses, is clearly intended to capture our ordinary use of this term. See Walton, "Fearing Fictions," pp. 11–12. See, as well, his "Pictures and Make-Believe," *The Philosophical Review* 82 (1973), 283–319, esp. pp. 287–92.

11. Walton, "Fearing Fictions," p. 16.

12. Ibid., pp. 13–14.

13. Ibid., p. 6.

14. Walton, "How Remote are Fictional Worlds," p. 12.

15. Walton, "Fearing Fictions," p. 9.

Chapter Five

1. See, for example, Lionel Trilling, "The Sense of the Past" in *The Liberal Imagination* (Viking Press, New York, 1950); Joseph Margolis, "Describing and Interpreting Works of Art" in F. J. Coleman, ed., *Contemporary Studies in Aesthetics* (McGraw-Hill, New York, 1968).

2. Chapter Three, "The Rage for Deconstruction," "In Defense of Deconstruction," and "Presence Regained."

3. Among the more prominent opponents of interpretative relativism are Monroe C. Beardsley, *The Possibility of Criticism* (Wayne State University Press, Detroit, 1970); and Anthony Savile, *The Test of Time: An Essay in Philosophical Aesthetics* (Oxford University Press, Oxford, 1982).

4. Joseph Margolis, "Robust Relativism," *The Journal of Aesthetics and Art Criticism* 35 (1976), 37–46. See, as well, Joseph Margolis, *Art and Philosophy: Conceptual Issues in Aesthetics* (Humanities Press, Atlantic Highlands, N.J., 1980), chs. 3 and 6. More recently a similar view has been expounded in Joseph Margolis, "The Nature and Strategies of Relativism," *Mind* 92 (1983), 548–67;

"Historicism, Universalism and the Threat of Relativism," *The Monist* 67 (1984), 308–26; and "Relativism, History and Objectivity in the Human Sciences," *Journal for the Theory of Social Behaviour* 14 (1984), 1–23. In the latter papers, Margolis maintains that there are some domains in which a number of interpretations may be forthcoming which are formally incompatible and yet equiplausible. I do not want to dispute that there may be such domains. My dispute is with the claim that fictional literature invariably constitutes one such domain.

5. See Chapter Two.

6. Cf. C. L. Stevenson, "On the Reasons That Can Be Given for the Interpretation of a Poem," in Joseph Margolis, ed., *Philosophy Looks at the Arts*, 1st ed. (Scribners, New York, 1962), pp. 121–39.

7. Thomas Leddy, "Robust Realism Rejected," *The Journal of Aesthetics and Art Criticism* 52 (1984), 317–19.

8. Ibid., p. 318. Leddy is responding to an earlier version of the present chapter which appeared under the title "Towards a Robust Realism," *The Journal of Aesthetics and Art Criticism* 41 (1982), 171–85.

9. Attempts to understand the theme of a work or the motives of a fictional character cannot plausibly be construed as a search for linguistic meaning. This point is clearly made by Stuart Hampshire, "Types of Interpretation" in S. Hook, ed., *Art and Philosophy* (New York University Press, New York, 1966), pp. 101–8. Despite this, we often speak of attempts to grasp the theme of a work as attempts to understand *the meaning* of the work. I shall adopt this convention in this chapter.

10. Robert J. Matthews, "Describing and Interpreting a Work of Art," *The Journal of Aesthetics and Art Criticism* 36 (1977), 5–14.

11. Monroe C. Beardsley, "The Limits of Critical Interpretation," in S. Hook, ed., *Art and Philosophy*, pp. 61–62. The point is taken up by Matthews, "Describing and Interpreting a Work of Art," p. 9.

12. Margolis, *Art and Philosophy*, p. 111.

13. C. L. Stevenson, "Interpretation and Evaluation in Aesthetics," in Max Black, ed., *Philosophical Analysis* (Prentice-Hall, Englewood Cliffs, N.J., 1950).

14. An insincere description will contain the very strong suggestion or "conversational implicature" that the speaker knows or believes whatever is conveyed by the description. See H. P. Grice, "Logic and Conversation" in Donald Davidson and Gilbert Harman, eds., *The Logic of Grammar* (Dickenson, Encino, Calif., 1975), pp. 64–75. I am indebted to Matthews, "Describing and Interpreting a Work of Art," for this point.

15. See, for example, Roger Trigg, *Reason and Commitment* (Cambridge University Press, Cambridge, 1973); as well as Savile, *The Test of Time*, chs. 3 and 4.

16. Margolis, "Robust Relativism." Wherever possible, page references to this article will be given in the text.

17. Joseph Margolis, *The Language of Art and Art Criticism* (Wayne State University Press, Detroit, 1965), p. 88. The same view is advanced by Margolis, *Art and Philosophy*, pp. 148–49.

18. This view is shared by Margaret MacDonald, "Some Distinctive Features

of Arguments Used in Criticism of the Arts," in William Elton, ed., *Aesthetics and Language* (Basil Blackwell, Oxford, 1959); and Richard Wollheim, *Art and Its Objects* (Penguin, Harmondsworth, England, 1970), p. 103.

19. Margolis, *The Language of Art and Art Criticism*, p. 71; *Art and Philosophy*, p. 111.

20. Margolis, *The Language of Art and Art Criticism*, p. 88; *Art and Philosophy*, pp. 120–21.

21. Beardsley, *The Possibility of Criticism*, pp. 43–44.

22. E. D. Hirsch, Jr., *Validity in Interpretation* (Yale University Press, New Haven and London, 1967), pp. 140ff; E. D. Hirsch, Jr., *The Aims of Interpretation* (University of Chicago Press, Chicago, 1976), pp. 1–13.

23. Joseph Margolis, "Works of Art as Physically Embodied and Culturally Emergent Entities," *The British Journal of Aesthetics* 14 (1974), pp. 187–96. All further page references to this article will be given in the text.

24. Margolis, *Art and Philosophy*, p. 167.

25. In this respect I differ not only from relativists, but also from much less skeptical theorists such as Hirsch, *Validity in Interpretation*, p. 173, where he writes: "Correctness is precisely the goal of interpretation and may in fact be achieved, even though it can never be known to be achieved."

26. I shall not offer a more comprehensive defense of this claim here. For more on this topic, see Savile, *The Test of Time*, chs. 1–6.

27. H. P. Grice, "Meaning," *The Philosophical Review* 66 (1957), 377–88; and H. P. Grice, "Utterer's Meaning and Intentions," *The Philosophical Review* 78 (1969), 147–77.

28. Hirsch, *Validity in Interpretation*, p. 23.

29. Ibid., ch. 1.

30. Beardsley, *The Possibility of Criticism*, pp. 18–19. See, as well, Laurent Stern, "On Interpreting," *The Journal of Aesthetics and Art Criticism* 39 (1980), 119–29, esp. p. 123 where he offers two interesting arguments designed to undermine Hirsch's view.

31. See Grice, "Utterer's Meaning and Intentions," pp. 147–48.

32. It is true, of course, that the context in which such a device is used may reveal a tension between its standard meaning and the authorial intention made apparent in the rest of the text. However, this is always contingent on the structure of the text, and it remains possible that such a tension may be undetectable.

33. I develop a theory of culture in Chapter Ten.

34. Cf. Anthony Savile, "The Place of Intention in the Concept of Art," in Harold Osborne, ed., *Aesthetics* (Oxford University Press, Oxford, 1972), p. 169. For my account of standard or literal meaning, see Chapter Seven.

35. Jack W. Meiland, "Interpretation as a Cognitive Discipline," *Philosophy and Literature* 2 (1978), 22–45, esp. p. 38.

36. Svante Nordin, *Interpretation and Method: Studies in the Explication of Literature* (Lunds Universitet, Lund, Sweden, 1978).

37. Kendall Walton, "Categories of Art," *The Philosophical Review* 39 (1970), 334–67, esp. pp. 340–41.

38. Joseph Margolis, "Critics and Literature," *The British Journal of Aesthetics* 11 (1971), 369–84, esp. p. 378.

39. Margolis, "Works of Art as Physically Embodied and Culturally Emergent Entities," pp. 187–96.

40. Leddy, "Robust Realism Rejected," p. 318.

41. Trilling, "The Sense of the Past," p. 186.

42. This radical view finds considerable philosophical support in the works of, for example, W. V. Quine, *Word and Object* (M.I.T. Press, Cambridge, Mass., 1960) and "Ontological Relativity," and "Speaking of Objects," in *Ontological Relativity and Other Essays* (Columbia University Press, New York, 1969); T. S. Kuhn, *The Structure of Scientific Revolutions*, 2d ed. (University of Chicago Press, Chicago, 1970); Paul K. Feyerabend, *Against Method* (New Left Books, London, 1975); Ludwig Wittgenstein, *On Certainty*, G. E. M. Anscombe and G.H. von Wright, eds., Denis Paul and G. E. M. Anscombe, trans. (Basil Blackwell, Oxford, 1974).

43. See, for example, Quine, *Word and Object*, ch. 2, sections 7–8.

44. This, of course, is the problem of the indeterminacy of translation as delineated by Quine, *Word and Object*, pp. 27ff.

45. See, for example, Trigg, *Reason and Commitment*; Savile, *The Test of Time*; Margolis, "Robust Relativism," pp. 37–38; Donald Davidson, "On the Very Idea of a Conceptual Scheme," *Proceedings and Addresses of the American Philosophical Association* 47 (1973–74), 5–20; W. Newton-Smith, "Relativism and the Possibility of Interpretation," in Martin Hollis and Steven Lukes, eds., *Rationality and Relativism* (Basil Blackwell, Oxford, 1982), pp. 106–22.

46. A similar point is made by Trigg, *Reason and Commitment*, pp. 101–2.

47. Cf. Quine, "Ontological Relativity," pp. 48–49.

48. I am, of course, thinking of doctrines such as incommensurability, translational indeterminacy, and ontological relativity.

49. See, for example, W. V. Quine and J. S. Ullian, *The Web of Belief* (Random House, New York, 1970), ch. 1.

50. Quine, *Word and Object*, pp. 28ff.

51. See Chapters Seven and Eight, where I explore Davidson's interpretation program. See, as well, Donald Davidson, "Radical Interpretation," *Dialectica* 27 (1973), 313–27; and Hans-Georg Gadamer, *Truth and Method*, Garrett Barden and John Cumming, trans. (Seabury Press, New York, 1975).

52. Margolis, *Art and Philosophy*, p. 111.

53. Margolis, "Describing and Interpreting Works of Art," p. 186.

54. Margolis, "Critics and Literature," p. 381.

Chapter Six

1. See Chapter Two for an account of Hume on the fanciful imagination.

2. See, for example, W. V. Quine, "Epistemology Naturalized," in *Ontological Relativity and Other Essays* (Columbia University Press, New York, 1969), pp. 69–90; Karl Popper, "Epistemology Without a Knowing Subject," in *Objective Knowledge: An Evolutionary Approach* (Oxford University Press, Oxford, 1972), pp. 106–52. See, as well, Ian Hacking, *Why Does Language Matter to Philosophy?* (Cambridge University Press, Cambridge, 1975), pp. 160ff.

3. The coherence in question need not be logical, for it is well known that not all fictional worlds are logically possible. The world of Dr. Who, for instance, is clearly not a logically coherent world since it involves time travel and so breaches the law of contradiction. In such a case, the requirement of coherence amounts to no more than that the sentences of the fiction should "hang together" in a way which presents a unified narrative. There is, of course, a good deal more to be said about fictional worlds, but I shall not address this topic here.

4. See Chapter Four.

5. See, for example, John Hospers, "Implied Truths in Literature," in Francis J. Coleman, ed., *Contemporary Studies in Aesthetics* (McGraw-Hill, New York, 1968), pp. 233–46; John Hospers, *Meaning and Truth in the Arts* (University of North Carolina Press, Chapel Hill, 1946), p. 206; Dorothy Walsh, "The Cognitive Content of Art," in Coleman, ed., *Contemporary Studies in Aesthetics*, pp. 285, 296–97; Dorothy Walsh, *Literature and Knowledge* (Wesleyan University Press, Middletown, Conn., 1969), chs. 6–8; Jacob Bronowski, *The Visionary Eye* (MIT Press, Cambridge, 1978), pp. 117–20; Julian Mitchell, "Truth and Fiction," in *Philosophy and the Arts*, Royal Institute of Philosophy Lectures, vol. 6, 1971–72 (Macmillan, London, 1973), pp. 1–22.

6. See Chapter Four.

7. There is a sense in which such beliefs are self-fulfilling, for they can condition our emotional responses to future situations. For this reason it is arguable, although I will not argue the case here, that in some instances first-person empathic beliefs constitute empathic knowledge.

8. See, for example, Nelson Goodman, *Languages of Art* (Oxford University Press, London, 1969), ch. 1; Max Black, "How Do Pictures Represent?" in E. H. Gombrich, Julian Hochberg, and Max Black, *Art Perception and Reality* (Johns Hopkins University Press, Baltimore, 1972), pp. 117–22; Roger Squires, "Depicting," *Philosophy* 44 (1969), 193–204, esp. pp. 193–94; Søren Kjørup, "Film as a Meeting-place of Multiple Codes," in David Perkins and Barbara Leanders, eds., *The Arts and Cognition* (Johns Hopkins University Press, Baltimore, 1977), pp. 26ff. I have responded to some of these criticisms in my *Pictures and Their Use in Communication: A Philosophical Essay* (Martinus Nijhoff, The Hague, 1977), ch. 1.

9. Black, "How Do Pictures Represent?," p. 122.

10. Joseph Margolis, *Art and Philosophy* (Humanities Press, Atlantic Highlands, N.J., 1980), p. 100–101.

11. Kendal Walton, "Pictures and Make-Believe," *The Philosophical Review* 82 (1973), 283–319, esp. p. 316.

12. Margolis, *Art and Philosophy*, p. 101.

13. Ibid., p. 100.

14. Kjørup, "Film as a Meetingplace," p. 27.

15. J. L. Austin, *Sense and Sensibilia* (Oxford University Press, Oxford, 1962), ch. 7.

16. Cf. Kjørup, "Film as a Meetingplace," p. 27.

17. My argument in this and the next section may be regarded as an argument in support of this view.

18. Kjørup, "Film as a Meetingplace," p. 27.

19. John Searle, *Expression and Meaning* (Cambridge University Press, Cambridge, 1979), p. 95. The same view is expressed by Squires, "Depicting," p. 193.

20. James W. Manns, "Representation, Relativism and Resemblance," *The British Journal of Aesthetics* 11 (1971), 281–87. Manns is critical of this view.

21. Goodman, *Languages of Art*, p. 5.

22. See my "Picturing," *The Journal of Aesthetics and Art Criticism* 34 (1975), 145–55, for an extended defense of this view. See, as well, Manns, "Representation, Relativism and Resemblance." I shall discuss this claim in more detail later on.

23. Popper, "Epistemology Without a Knowing Subject," pp. 121–22.

24. See my *Pictures and Their Use in Communication*, pp. 13–18, where similar arguments are developed.

25. Margolis, *Art and Philosophy*, p. 100.

26. Hospers, *Meaning and Truth in the Arts*, p. 206.

27. This view was defended in my "Learning from Fiction," *Philosophical Papers* 9 (1980), 60–73, esp. pp. 67–69. For reasons soon to be apparent, I no longer consider this an adequate theory.

28. See Chapter Two.

29. Here I am indebted to Philip Catton.

30. See, for example, Walsh, "The Cognitive Content of Art," p. 287.

31. See Chapter Two.

32. This is an adaptation of an example employed by Hilary Putnam, "Literature, Science and Reflection," in *Meaning and the Moral Sciences* (Routledge & Kegan Paul, London, 1978), pp. 83–94.

33. See Chapter Four.

34. Putnam, "Literature, Science and Reflection," p. 87.

Chapter Seven

1. Friedrich Nietzsche, "On Truth and Falsity in Their Ultramoral Sense" in Oscar Levy, ed., Maximilian A. Mügge, trans., *The Complete Works of Friedrich Nietzsche* (18 vols., Allen & Unwin, London, 1911), vol. 2, p. 178. A similar view can be found more rigorously argued in George Lakoff and Mark Johnson, "Conceptual Metaphor in Everyday Language," *The Journal of Philosophy* 77 (1980), 453–86. See, as well, Paul de Man, "The Epistemology of Metaphor," *Critical Inquiry* 5 (1978), 13–20.

2. Nietzsche, "On Truth and Falsity," p. 178.

3. Ibid., p. 180.

4. Friedrich Nietzsche, *The Birth of Tradegy and the Case of Wagner*, Walter Kaufmann, ed. (Vintage, New York, 1966), pp. 17–27.

5. Thomas Hobbes, *Leviathan* (Dent, London, 1962), pp. 13 and 22.

6. John Locke, *An Essay Concerning Human Understanding*, J. W. Yolton, ed. (2 vols., Dent, London, 1961), vol. 2, pp. 105–6.

7. A. J. Ayer, *Language, Truth and Logic* (Penguin, Harmondsworth, England, 1975), p. 59.

8. Ibid., p. 60.

9. See Chapter Three.

10. I am indebted to Donald Callen for drawing this point to my attention.

11. I. A. Richards, *The Philosophy of Rhetoric* (Oxford University Press, Oxford, 1936), p. 92.

12. See Chapter Three, "The Rage for Deconstruction."

13. On this, see Newton Garver's preface to Jacques Derrida, *Speech and Phenomena and Other Essays in Husserl's Theory of Signs*, David B. Allison, trans. (Northwestern University Press, Evanston, Ill., 1973), pp. ix–xlii, esp. pp. xx ff., where Garver explores similarities between the later Wittgenstein's and Derrida's views of meaning.

14. Derrida, *Speech and Phenomena*, p. 85. See, as well, Nietzsche, "On Truth and Falsity," p. 180.

15. Jacques Derrida, *Of Grammatology*, Gayatri Chakravorty Spivak, trans. (Johns Hopkins University Press, Baltimore, 1974), p. 15.

16. Cf. Christopher Norris, *Deconstruction: Theory and Practice* (Methuen, London, 1982), p. 66. Norris appears mistakenly to locate the metaphoricity of language in *différance*. It is, rather, the artificial constraints placed on *différance* (the endless deferring and displacement of meaning), in order to generate the illusion of a fixed and settled meaning, which gives rise to what Derrida regards as the intrinsically metaphorical nature of intelligible discourse.

17. A view similar to Derrida's is to be found in Nietzsche, "On Truth and Falsity"; Richard Rorty, "Philosophy as a Kind of Writing: An Essay on Derrida," *Consequences of Pragmatism* (University of Minnesota Press, Minneapolis, 1982), pp. 90–109; Christopher Norris, *The Deconstructive Turn: Essays in the Rhetoric of Philosophy* (Methuen, London and New York, 1983), pp. 1–12.

18. Jacques Derrida, "White Mythology: Metaphor in the Text of Philosophy," *New Literary History* 6 (1974–75), 60.

19. Norris, *Deconstruction*, pp. 18–19.

20. Rorty, "Philosophy as a Kind of Writing," pp. 98–99. Rorty points to the fact that this is the serious element in Derrida's otherwise playful writings.

21. Chapter Three, "The Rage for Deconstruction," "In Defense of Deconstruction," and "Presence Regained."

22. Jacques Derrida, *Writing and Difference*, Alan Bass, trans. (Routledge & Kegan Paul, London, 1978), p. 3.

23. Nietzsche, "On Truth and Falsity," p. 178.

24. Ibid., p. 184.

25. My arguments for all of this are to be found in Chapter Three, "Presence Regained," "Realisim, Idealism, and the Occlusive Fallacy," and "A Romantic Realism."

26. Donald Davidson, "What Metaphors Mean," in Sheldon Sacks, ed., *On Metaphor* (University of Chicago Press, Chicago, 1979), pp. 29–45. Further references to this article are given in the text.

27. He also offers a number of rather less well-developed objections to a semantic interpretation of metaphor. These have been canvassed and, in my view, decisively refuted, by Max Black, "How Metaphors Work: A Reply to Donald Davidson," in Sheldon Sacks, ed., *On Metaphor*, pp. 190–92. In part, I am indebted to Jan Crosthwaite for my rendering of Davidson's arguments. Her views

on metaphorical meaning, however, differ diametrically from my own. See her "The Meaning of Metaphors," *Australasian Journal of Philosophy* 63 (1985), 230–335.

28. My argument does not commit me to the view that metaphors occur only in illocutionary acts. Unlike Max Black, however, it seems plain to me that in thinking we can perform illocutionary acts which are parasitic on public illocutions. Still more, when these are performed with the help of metaphors, they can frighten or cheer us, and in this sense do have a perlocutionary dimension. Cf. Black, "How Metaphors Work," pp. 188–89.

29. Cf. Stephen Davies, "Truth-Values and Metaphors," *The Journal of Aesthetics and Art Criticism* 42 (1984), 291–302, esp. p. 298.

30. I deal with this point in some detail in Chapters Eight and Nine.

31. Janet Martin Soskice, *Metaphor and Religious Language* (Clarendon Press, Oxford, 1985), p. 29.

32. Ibid., p. 30.

33. Ibid.

34. Donald Davidson, "Semantics for Natural Languages," in *Inquiries into Truth & Interpretation* (Clarendon Press, Oxford, 1984), p. 55.

35. Ibid.

36. Ibid., p. 56.

37. Donald Davidson, "Belief and the Basis of Meaning," *Synthese* 27 (1974), 309–23, esp. p. 318.

38. A. Tarski, "The Concept of Truth in Formalized Languages," in *Logic, Semantics, Mathematics* (Clarendon Press, Oxford, 1956).

39. Davidson, "Semantics for Natural Languages," p. 60.

40. Ibid., p. 61.

41. Ibid.

42. Ibid., p. 58.

43. Ibid.

44. Ibid. pp. 57, 61.

45. For a full account of the relation between T-sentences and meaning, see Donald Davidson, "Truth and Meaning," *Synthèse* 17 (1967), 304–23, esp. p. 322. See, as well, his "Semantics for Natural Languages."

46. Davidson, "Belief and the Basis of Meaning," pp. 310–11. See, as well, his "Radical Interpretation," *Dialectica* 27 (1973), 313–27, esp. p. 315.

47. Davidson, "Radical Interpretation," p. 324.

48. Davidson, "Belief and the Basis of Meaning," p. 316.

49. Davidson, "Radical Interpretation," p. 323.

50. Davidson, "Truth and Meaning," esp. pp. 310, 312.

51. It is sometimes held that Davidson is wholly skeptical about meanings, and that this is why a T-sentence cannot be thought to give the meaning of a metaphor. It is true that Davidson does not countenance the existence of meanings as Platonic entities. In "Truth and Meaning" he tells us that "they have no demonstrated use" (p. 307). However, in "What Metaphors Mean" we are told that "the point of the concept of linguistic meaning is to explain what can be done with words" (p. 38), while in "Belief and the Basis of Meaning" it becomes clear that on Davidson's view T-sentences can "give the meaning" of linguistic utterance,

relative always to certain constraints. He writes: "A theory of truth will yield interpretations only if its T-sentences state truth conditions in terms that may be treated as 'giving the meaning' of object language sentences. Our problem is to find constraints on a theory strong enough to guarantee that it can be used for interpretation." And in his "Semantics for Natural Languages" (pp. 60–61), Davidson sets out explicitly to "support . . . the claim that a theory of truth does 'give the meaning' of sentences."

52. The example, but not the objection, comes from Josef Stern, "Metaphor as Demonstrative," *The Journal of Philosophy* 82 (1985), 677–710, esp. pp. 663–64; and A. C. Danto, *The Transfiguration of the Commonplace* (Harvard University Press, Cambridge, 1981), pp. 179ff. The objection was suggested in the comments of an anonymous reader to whom I am indebted.

53. Davidson, "Radical Interpretation," p. 322.

54. Davidson, "Belief and the Basis of Meaning," pp. 318–21.

55. Davidson, "Semantics for Natural Languages," pp. 60–61.

56. Davidson, "Belief and the Basis of Meaning," pp. 320–21.

57. Davidson, "Semantics for Natural Languages," p. 56.

58. Max Black, "More About Metaphor," in Andrew Ortony, ed., *Metaphor and Thought* (Cambridge University Press, Cambridge, 1979), p. 26. It might be objected that the connotations, like the implications, of an utterance are not properly a part of its meaning. But such an objection, in my view, applies only to the literal (what Grice has called the "timeless") meaning of the utterance. If it is clear that the connotations and implications are being exploited on this occasion, then I can see no reason why they should not be regarded as part of the "occasion meaning" (Grice) of the utterance—even where the occasion meaning is not entirely determinate. And it is *this* meaning which Davidson's program seeks initially to uncover.

59. Ibid. A metaphor may also be emphatic for purely semantic reasons, but I have already discussed this possibility, and have shown that it does not deter us from applying Davidson's program to metaphors.

60. John McDowell, "Truth Conditions, Bivalence and Verificationism," in Gareth Evans and John McDowell, eds., *Truth and Meaning: Essays in Semantics* (Clarendon Press, Oxford, 1976), pp. 42–66. Davidson has argued for this in his "Moods and Performances," in Avishai Margalit, ed., *Meaning and Use* (Reidel, Dordrecht, Netherlands, 1979), pp. 9–20, esp. pp. 17–18.

61. See Donald Davidson, "Reality Without Reference," in Mark Platts, ed., *Reference, Truth and Reality* (Routledge & Kegan Paul, London, 1980), pp. 131–40, esp. pp. 134–37.

62. Donald Davidson, "On the Very Idea of a Conceptual Scheme," *Proceedings and Addresses of the American Philosophical Association* 17 (1973–74), 5–20.

Chapter Eight

1. See Donald Davidson, "What Metaphors Mean," in Sheldon Sacks, ed., *On Metaphor* (University of Chicago Press, Chicago, 1979), pp. 29–45. His view

has found wide acceptance. See, for example, F. T. C. Moore, "On Taking Metaphor Literally," in David S. Miall, ed., *Metaphor: Problems and Perspectives* (Harvester Press, Sussex, 1982), pp. 1–13; Stein Haugom Olsen, "Understanding Literary Metaphors," in Miall, ed., *Metaphor: Problems and Perspectives*, pp. 36–54; Stephen Davies, "Truth-Values and Metaphors," *The Journal of Aesthetics and Art Criticism* 42 (1984), 291–302.

2. See Donald Davidson, "Moods and Performances," in Avishai Margalit, ed., *Meaning and Use* (Reidel, Dordrecht, Netherlands, 1979), pp. 9–20, esp. pp. 17–18.

3. Donald Davidson, "Radical Interpretation," *Dialectica* 27 (1973), 313–27, esp. p. 315.

4. See Chapter Seven.

5. I am indebted to Julian Novitz for this metaphor.

6. Davidson, "Radical Interpretation," p. 324.

7. Donald Davidson, "Truth and Meaning," *Synthèse* 17 (1967), 304–23, esp. pp. 310, 312; "Radical Interpretation," p. 313.

8. Max Black, "More About Metaphor," in Andrew Ortony, ed., *Metaphor and Thought* (Cambridge University Press, Cambridge, 1979), pp. 21–41.

9. Ibid., pp. 26–27.

10. Max Black, "How Metaphors Work: A Reply to Donald Davidson," in Sacks, ed., *On Metaphor*, p. 191.

11. Ibid., pp. 183, 187, 188.

12. Black, "More About Metaphor," p. 30. As will become apparent from my analysis, I doubt whether the suggestiveness of a metaphor necessarily leads to ambiguity; not all of the associations which are properly a part of the metaphor's suggestiveness need be part of its meaning.

13. Davidson, "What Metaphors Mean," p. 36.

14. Max Black, "Metaphor," in Mark Johnson, ed., *Philosophical Perspectives on Metaphor* (University of Minnesota Press, Minneapolis, 1981), pp. 63–82, esp. p. 74. Black contends that our knowledge of this system does not amount to knowledge of the literal meaning of the word in question. He gives no reasons for this view, and if my contentions above are correct, he must be mistaken.

15. Black, "More About Metaphor," p. 28.

16. The image of "filtering" is, of course, Max Black's. See his "Metaphor," p. 74.

17. Both Black, "More About Metaphor," p. 30, and John Searle, "Metaphor" in Johnson, ed., *Philosophical Perspectives on Metaphor*, pp. 273–81, produce principles according to which metaphors may be understood. On my view, the principles that they produce *describe* various ways of coming to understand. They are not rules for understanding.

18. Davidson endorses this view when he emphasizes the "assumptions" that we have to make, and the "hunches" on which we rely, in interpretation. See, for example, Donald Davidson, "On the Very Idea of a Conceptual Scheme," *Proceedings and Addresses of the American Philosophical Association* 47 (1973), 5–20, esp. pp. 18–19. See, as well, Davidson, "Truth and Meaning," pp. 312–13, where he writes that "the theory-builder must not be assumed to have direct insight into likely equivalences between his own tongue and the alien. What he

must do is find out, *however he can*, what sentences the alien holds true in his own tongue." (Emphasis added.) On my view this will often involve fanciful conjectures of one sort or another.

19. Donald Davidson, "Belief and the Basis of Meaning," *Synthèse* 27 (1974), 309–23, esp. p. 317.

20. I am grateful to Anthony Savile and Flint Schier for raising this objection.

21. Cf. Davidson, "On the Very Idea of a Conceptual Scheme," pp. 5–20.

22. I have explained how imaginative constructions can affect us emotionally in Chapter Four.

23. Cf. Davidson, "What Metaphors Mean," p. 44.

24. Ibid.

25. Ibid.

Chapter Nine

1. See Chapter Six, "Fictional Worlds and Resemblance."

2. Donald Davidson, "What Metaphors Mean," in Sheldon Sacks, ed., *On Metaphor* (University of Chicago Press, Chicago, 1979), pp. 29–45. See, as well, Stein Haugom Olsen, "Understanding Literary Metaphors," in David S. Miall, ed., *Metaphor: Problems and Perspectives* (Harvester Press, Sussex, 1982), pp. 36–54. So far as I know, Olsen is the only philosopher to have applied Davidson's theory of metaphor to the metaphors of fiction.

3. Cf. Nelson Goodman, *Ways of Worldmaking* (Harvester Press, Sussex, 1978), pp. 57–58.

4. James Joyce, *A Portrait of the Artist as a Young Man* (Penguin, Harmondsworth, England, 1965), p. 59. Further references to this work are given in the text.

5. See Max Black, "More About Metaphor," in Andrew Ortony, ed., *Metaphor and Thought* (Cambridge University Press, Cambridge, 1979), pp. 29–31; and John Searle, "Metaphor," in Mark Johnson, ed., *Philosophical Perspectives on Metaphor* (University of Minnesota Press, Minneapolis, 1981), pp. 273–85.

6. The fact that Davidson maintains that "there is no limit to what a metaphor draws to our attention" ("What Metaphors Mean," p. 44), should not be taken to suggest that everything drawn to our attention is appropriate to the metaphor; still less that all emotional responses to a metaphor are appropriate. This would leave no room for the notion of misconstruing a metaphor.

7. Olsen, "Understanding Literary Metaphors." Where possible, further references to this article are given in the text.

8. Cf. Olsen, "Understanding Literary Metaphors," pp. 39–48.

9. Virginia Woolf, *Orlando* (Harcourt, Brace, New York, 1928), p. 188.

10. Sandra M. Gilbert, "Costumes of the Mind: Transvestism as Metaphor in Modern Literature," *Critical Inquiry* 7 (1980), 391–417.

11. I am indebted to Peter McCormick, "Moral Knowledge and Fiction," *The Journal of Aesthetics and Art Criticism* 41 (1983), 399–410, for this example.

12. McCormick, "Moral Knowledge," p. 399.

13. Ibid.

14. John Irving, *The World According to Garp* (Corgi Books, London, 1982), p. 89.

15. See Chapter Five.

16. See, for example, Nelson Goodman, *Languages of Art* (Oxford University Press, Oxford, 1969), whose study of symbol systems never touches on this sense of the word "symbol." See, as well, Humphrey House, "The Ancient Mariner," in M. H. Abrams, ed., *English Romantic Poets: Modern Essays in Criticism* (Oxford University Press, New York, 1960), p. 189.

17. Goodman, *Ways of Worldmaking*, p. 58.

18. Many of these confusions are to be found in Monroe Beardsley, *Aesthetics*, 2d ed. (Hackett, Indianapolis, 1981), pp. 288–93.

19. Ibid., p. 288; and John Hospers, *Understanding the Arts* (Prentice-Hall, Englewood Cliffs, N.J., 1982), p. 177. So far as I can see, this claim is false. In ordinary, nontechnical discourse, there appear to be only two central ways of using the word.

20. Cited by Goodman, *Ways of Worldmaking*, pp. 57–58.

21. See Beardsley, *Aesthetics*, p. 291. Beardsley is sensitive to the problem, and although sympathetic to the New Criticism, is not willing to abandon the notion of a literary symbol.

22. House, "The Ancient Mariner," p. 189.

23. See Beardsley, *Aesthetics*, pp. 291–92.

24. Hospers, *Understanding the Arts*, p. 179.

25. Isabel Hungerland, *Poetic Discourse* (University of California Press, Berkeley, 1958), p. 137.

26. Melvin Rader and Bertrum Jessup, *Art and Human Values* (Prentice-Hall, Englewood Cliffs, N.J., 1976), p. 276.

27. Robert Penn Warren, "A Poem of Pure Imagination," in *Selected Essays* (Vintage Books, New York, 1958).

28. See House, "The Ancient Mariner," pp. 184–85.

29. Beardsley, *Aesthetics*, pp. 288–93. (Further references to this volume will be given in the text.) Hospers also tends to assimilate the two, but I shall not discuss his account here. See Hospers, *Understanding the Arts*, p. 178, where he writes: "[W]e . . . cover most of the cases in which symbolism has been imputed to objects in works of art, if we explore the cases in which there is a convention by which A *stands for* B." Emphasis added.

30. I say "usually" because it seems plain that demagogues can construct contexts within which to introduce such metaphors. A skillful orator can also exploit a pre-existing context to this end.

Chapter Ten

1. See, for example, Leo Lowenthal, *Literature, Popular Culture and Society* (Pacific Books, Palo Alto, Calif., 1968), pp. xii–xvi; Howard Lee Nostrand,

"Literature in the Describing of a Literature Culture," in Milton Albrecht, James H. Barnett, and Mason Griff, eds., *The Sociology of Art and Literature* (Praeger, New York, 1970), p. 562; Belinda Bezzoli, "History, Experience and Culture," in Belinda Bezzoli, ed., *Town and Countryside in the Transvaal* (Ravan Press, Johannesburg, 1983), pp. 19–21.

2. See, for example, W. K. Wimsatt, *The Verbal Icon: Studies in the Meaning of Poetry* (University of Kentucky Press, Lexington, 1954); Paul de Man, *Blindness and Insight: Essays in the Rhetoric of Contemporary Criticism* (Oxford University Press, Oxford, 1971).

3. Albert Guerard, *Literature and Society* (Cooper Square, New York, 1970), p. 120.

4. G. F. W. Hegel, *The Phenomenology of Mind*, J. D. Baillie, trans. (Allen & Unwin, London, 1949), p. 516.

5. Cited by Charles Taylor, *Hegel and Modern Society* (Cambridge University Press, Cambridge, 1969), p. 86.

6. G. F. W. Hegel, "Vorlesungen über die Philosophie der Geschichte," in Hermann Glockner, ed., *Sämtliche Werke* (26 vols., Friedrich Fromann Verlag, Stuttgart, 1971), vol. 11, p. 101.

7. Daniel C. Dennett, *Brainstorms: Philosophical Essays on Mind and Psychology* (Harvester Press, Sussex, 1981), ch. 1.

8. Ibid., pp. 3–5.

9. Ibid., p. 6.

10. Ibid., pp. 6, 9–12.

11. G. F. W. Hegel, *Die Vernunft in der Geschichte*, Johannes Hoffmeister, ed. (F. Meiner, Hamburg, 1955), p. 74.

12. E. H. Gombrich, *In Search of a Cultural History* (Oxford University Press, Oxford, 1969), p. 7.

13. Hegel, *Die Vernunft in der Geschichte*, p. 77. (Emphasis added.)

14. They also use the term "social structure"—partly, I think, to avoid treating society as an intentional system. Unlike A. R. Radcliffe-Brown, however, I am not persuaded that a study of social structure is any more scientific than a study of culture.

15. See W. H. Walsh, "Colligatory Concepts in History," in Patrick Gardiner, ed., *The Philosophy of History* (Oxford University Press, Oxford, 1974), pp. 127–44.

16. Edward B. Tylor, *Primitive Culture* (2 vols., John Murray, London, 1871), vol. 1, pp. 1–7. Tylor defined "culture" (or "civilization") as "that complex whole which includes knowledge, belief, art, morals, law, customs, and any other capabilities and habits acquired by man as a member of society" (p. 7).

17. Ruth Benedict, *Patterns of Culture* (Routledge, London, 1935), p. 82.

18. A. L. Kroeber and Clyde Kluckhohn, *Culture: A Critical Review of Concepts and Definitions* (Harvard University, Peabody Museum of American Archaeology and Ethnology Papers, Cambridge, 1952), vol. 47, no. 1, p. 181.

19. Bronislaw Malinowski, "Culture," in *The Encyclopedia of the Social Sciences* (Macmillan, New York, 1931), vol. 4, pp. 621–45; Edward Sapir, "The Unconscious Patterning of Behaviour in Society," in David G. Mandelbaum, ed.,

Selected Writings of Edward Sapir in Language, Culture and Personality (University of California Press, Berkeley, 1958), pp. 544–59; Morris E. Opler, "Component Assemblage and Theme in Cultural Integration and Differentiation," *American Anthropologist* 61 (1959), 955–64.

20. James P. Spradley, ed., *Culture and Cognition: Rules, Maps and Plans* (Chandler, San Francisco, 1972), p. 6.

21. G. Frege, "On Sense and Reference," in Peter Geach and Max Black, eds., *Translations from the Philosophical Writings of Gottlob Frege* (Basil Blackwell, Oxford, 1966).

22. Ward Goodenough, ed., *Explorations in Cultural Anthropology* (McGraw-Hill, New York, 1964), pp. 1–24, esp. p. 11.

23. Here I disagree with Raymond Williams, *Culture* (Fontana, Glasgow, 1981), p. 11, who treats this as a distinct sense of the word "culture."

24. Goodenough, *Explorations in Cultural Anthropology*, p. 11.

25. Antonio Gramsci, *Selections from the Prison Notebooks of Antonio Gramsci*, Quintin Hoare and Geoffery Nowell Smith, eds., trans. (Lawrence & Wishart, London, 1971), pp. 210–78, esp. pp. 245ff.

26. I have defended this claim in Chapter Five.

27. That is to say, Aryan people were not actually superior to non-Aryan people. Of course, the *belief* in Aryan superiority was, for about fifteen years, an actual feature of German culture, and the presence of that belief helps explain certain aspects of that culture during the Nazi era. The belief itself, however, was false.

28. See Chapter Six for an account of how such skills are acquired from fiction.

29. Paul Rich, " 'Milnerism and a Ripping Yarn': Transvaal Land Settlement and John Buchan's Novel 'Prester John,' 1901–1910," in Bezzoli, ed., *Town and Countryside in the Transvaal*, pp. 421–33.

30. I am indebted to Flint Schier for this example, and for drawing my attention to this phenomenon.

INDEX

Anna Karenina (in *Anna Karenina*), 80, 83, 86, 91, 126, 134, 136, 141, 196, 197
Antirealism, 56, 57, 60–61, 68. *See also* Idealism; Romantic idealism
Aristotle, 151
Austen, Jane, 137; *Emma*, 137; *Sense and Sensibility*, 98, 99, 115
Austin, J. L., 123
Ayer, A. J., 144–45

Bacon, Francis, 23
Beardsley, Monroe C., 16, 94, 99; on interpretation, 99–100, 101, 106; on literary symbols, 199, 203–4
Black, Max, 121, 151, 166, 167, 169, 173–74, 183, 186, 187, 193
Bloom, Harold, 20
Brink, André, 225
Brooks, Cleanth, 13, 14–15, 17, 237n.45
Broyard, Anatole, 194, 196, 202
Buchan, John, 225; *Prester John*, 225

Chekov, Anton, 103
Classification, 219–20
Coleridge, Samuel Taylor, 2; on imagination, 4; and occlusive fallacy, 58; and reality, 4; "The Rime of the Ancient Mariner," 199, 202; and romantic idealism, 37–38, 58, 232
Colligatory concepts, 213
Constructive imagination: and growth of knowledge, 35–36; Hume on 22, 25–26, 34, 35; Kant on, 22, 36; in traditional epistemology, 22, 34. *See also* Fanciful imagination
Culler, Jonathan, 44–46

Cultural identity, 206, 220–26; and cultural demarcation, 222–24; and fiction, 224–26
Culture: colligatory account of, 213–16, 233; and cultural emergence, 100, 101, 104, 105, 107, 115, 196, 197; and cultural stabilities, 102, 115; demarcation of, 216–20, 222–24; Hegel on, 208–13; and identity, 205; and interpretation, 97–98, 196, 197; and knowledge of other cultures, 112–13, 114, 115–16, 197; and literature, 205; and perception, 115. *See also* Cultural identity

Dada, 119
Davidson, Donald: and Derrida, 169–70; on knowledge of other cultures, 113; on metaphor, 145, 151, 153–70, 183, 184, 187, 205, 232, 252n.6; against metaphorical meaning, 154–55, 157, 171, 183, 249n.51; on radical interpretation, 159–67, 171, 173
Deconstruction: and "aporia," 48; and determinate meaning, 44–46, 47–50, 89; and *différance*, 47, 52; exposition of, 42–48, 51–55; of "hierarchical oppositions," 43, 46, 51, 151; and historicism, 51–53; and interpretation, 89–90; and logocentrism, 42–43, 45, 53–54, 151–52; and metaphysics of presence, 43–48, 51, 52–55, 58, 147, 151–52; and Nietzsche, 40–41, 44; and phonocentrism, 45–46; and romantic idealism, 38, 40–41, 44, 45, 51; and systems of signs, 48–50, 58; and traces, 46, 55; and Wittgenstein, 48; and "writing" or *archi-écriture*, 47, 48, 50, 58. *See also* Derrida, Jacques
Defoe, Daniel, 140; *Robinson Crusoe*, 140

de Man, Paul, 18, 20
Dennett, Daniel, 210–13
Derrida, Jacques: and antirealism, 45–48, 51,
  55; and *archi-écriture*, 47, 48, 58, 150; and
  Davidson, 169–70; on deconstruction,
  42–55; and *différance*, 47, 52; and historicism, 51; as an idealist, 45, 55, 72, 232;
  on logocentrism, 6, 40, 48, 53–54, 147; on
  metaphor, 54, 145, 147, 149, 150–52, 205;
  and Nietzsche, 40–41, 45, 54, 152; and
  occlusive fallacy, 58; and perception, 56,
  240n.35; on philosophy, 151, 240n.32; on
  presence and absence, 47–48, 51, 52, 58; as
  a romantic, 3, 5, 6, 45, 55–56, 240n.34;
  and Schelling, 45. *See also* Deconstruction
Descartes, R., 23
Description: compared with interpretation,
  93–97, 102, 103–4, 114; epistemic structure of, 93–97
Devanny, Jean, 225
Dewey, John, 68
Dickens, Charles, 77, 78, 79, 122, 123;
  Pickwick Papers, 75, 76, 77, 78, 79
Dostoyevsky, F., 137; *Crime and Punishment*,
  137, 141
Dummett, Michael: on realism and anti-
  realism, 60–61, 69, 70

Elinor Dashwood (in *Sense and Sensibility*),
  98, 115
Eliot, George, 193, 202; *The Mill on the
  Floss*, 193, 201
Eliot, T. S., 13, 14, 16, 17, 194
Emma Woodhouse (in *Emma*), 99
Emotional responses to fiction, 73–87, 120,
  133; and identification with characters, 86,
  120, 133, 140; and meta-emotions, 86;
  rationality of, 74, 75, 80, 87; Walton on,
  84–86
Enlightenment, the, 1, 112, 142, 143, 144;
  and metaphor, 143, 144; and positivism, 1
Enobarbus (in *Antony and Cleopatra*), 154,
  161, 165
Epistemology: Derrida's, 46–47; and fiction,
  11, 117–20, 130–42; and perception, 53,
  56, 58–59; as realist, 60, 62; social dimension of, 65–66; traditional, xi, 21–27, 117;
  and verification, 60–61. *See also* Romantic
  epistemology
Experience: mediated by linguistic concepts,

53, 58, 59; socially determined, 66–67;
  unmediated by concepts, 66

Fanciful imagination: and conjecture, 32–33,
  34; constraints on, 34–35, 65, 67, 93;
  defined, 27; and fiction, 118, 121, 122–23;
  Hume on, 26–27, 33–34; and hypotheses,
  34–35, 227; and individuation of objects,
  31–32; and interpretation, 90–97; Kant
  on, 26–27; and knowledge, 3, 11, 19,
  31–36, 55, 57, 60, 67, 71, 118, 133, 232;
  and metaphor, 143, 184, 205; Nietzsche
  on, 39, 152–53; and reality, 55, 67; relation
  to fact, 27–33; and romantic idealism, 37;
  and romantic theory, 4–5, 15, 37; verification of, 59–60. *See also* Imagination;
  Romantic epistemology
Feyerabend, Paul, 40
Fichte, J. G., 4, 235n.9
Fiction: and cultural identity, 224–26,
  231–32; emotional responses to, 73–87;
  and fanciful imagination, 118, 122–23; as
  a functional object, xi–xii, 11, 117–42,
  224–26, 230–31, 233; imaginative
  response to, 81–84, 90–97, 133–37, 186;
  and intentional objects, 122; and knowledge, 11, 19, 117–20, 130–42; language of,
  19, 78, 118, 124–25, 184; and metaphor,
  184–98; and New Criticism, 11; and real
  entities, 123–24; understanding of, 73, 74,
  81, 87–88, 89–116; and values, 139–42.
  See also Fictional entities
Fictional entities: creation of, 122–23; as
  intentional objects, 122; properties of,
  122–23, 124, 127; vs. real entities,
  123–24; and resemblance, 121–30; as
  worlds, 118–21, 241n.5, 246n.3. *See also*
  Fiction
Fitzgerald, F. Scott, 224–26; *The Great
  Gatsby*, 224–26
Foucault, M., 3
Frayn, Michael, 29
Frege, Gottlob, 215
Frye, Northrop, 15, 19
Fugard, Athol, 139
Fuller, Steven, 54

Gadamer, Hans-Georg, 63, 113
Geist, 208–9, 214
Genre, 108–9

Gilbert, Sandra M., 194
Gombrich, E. H., 212
Goodenough, Ward, 216
Goodman, Nelson, 3, 123, 198, 203
Graff, Gerald, 12, 15, 16, 17, 20
Gramsci, Antonio, 218
Grice, H. P., 50, 106, 243n.14

Hanson, N. R., 29, 51
Hardy, Thomas, 194; *Far from the Madding Crowd*, 124, 194
Hartley, David, 24
Hartman, Geoffrey, 18, 20
Hegel, G. F. W.: on culture, 208–13, 214; and *Geist*, 208–9; and reality, 4; and *Volksgeist*, 209
Hegemony, cultural, 218
Heidegger, Martin, 3, 54
Herbert, Frank, 125; *Dune*, 125
Hirsch, E. D., 99, 106, 244n.25
Historicism, 51–53, 66
Hobbes, Thomas, 23–24, 144
Hospers, John, 130, 200, 203, 253n.29
House, Humphrey, 199
Hume, David, 4, 22, 34, 57, 117; on constructive imagination, 22, 25–26, 34; and external world, 57, 64; on fanciful imagination, 26–27, 117; on individuation of objects, 31; and induction, 30–31; and knowledge, 33–36, 117; naturalism of, 57, 64; and occlusive fallacy, 58
Hungerland, Isabel, 200
Hypotheses, 34–36, 131–32, 135, 227

Idealism, 61–63, 67. *See also* Antirealism; Romantic idealism
Imagination: as autonomous, 11, 13; Bacon on, 23; Coleridge on, 4; defined, 10–11; and derivative imagining, 10, 79, 118, 121; Descartes on, 23; Hobbes on, 23–24; Hume on, 25–27; and interpretation, 90–97; Kant on, 26–27; and learning from fiction, 133–37; Locke on, 24–25; Malebranche on, 23; as a mental entity, 8–9; and New Criticism, 11, 13, 15; as romantic, 15; Ryle on, 8–11; Saint Augustine on, 22–23; study of, 7–11; and understanding fiction, 75–79, 81–84. *See also* Constructive imagination; Fanciful imagination
Individual identity, 226–31; and fiction, 230–31; and life-narrative, 227–29

Induction, 30, 131, 133
Intentional systems, 210–13
Interpretation, 19, 89–116, 195–98; aims of, 98, 105; ambiguity of, 116; Beardsley on, 99; and biography, 109; compared with description, 93–97, 102, 103–4, 114; and cultural myths, 97–99; elaborative vs. elucidatory, 91–93, 98, 99, 102, 103, 114; epistemic structure of, 93–97; and genres, 108–9; Hirsch on, 99; and juxtapository metaphors, 195–98; rational disputation about, 111; and relativism, 89–90, 97–104; and superimpositions, 99–100; vagueness of, 116; verification of, 97, 100, 104–9, 113
Irving, John, 194–95; *The World According to Garp*, 194–95, 202

Joyce, James, 185–86, 188, 191, 192, 193, 202; *A Portrait of the Artist as a Young Man*, 185–86, 192, 201

Kant, Immanuel, 3, 55, 70; on constructive imagination, 22, 26; on fanciful imagination, 26–27; reaction to Hume, 4; on reproductive imagination, 26
Kluckhohn, Clyde, 214
Knowledge: of culture, 112–13, 114, 115–16; explicit vs. tacit, 83; and fanciful imagination, 21–36, 55, 60, 67, 71, 133; and fiction, 11, 12–13, 19, 74, 81–84, 117–20, 127, 130–42; and justification, 132; propositional, 117, 119; and a romantic epistemology, 19, 21–36; and science, 74, 114, 132–33; of skills, 119–20, 132–37, 137–39; of values, 139–42. *See also* Learning from fiction
Kroeber, A. L., 214
Kuhn, T. S., 6, 40, 110

Language: Derrida on, 42–55; and literal meaning, 146–47; Saussure on, 45–48; as a system of differences, 48–49
La langue, 46, 47–48
Lawrence, D. H., 194
Learning from fiction, 117–20, 130–42; about human beings, 136, 141; attitudes, 119; empathic beliefs and knowledge, 120, 133, 135–37; and hypotheses, 131–32, 135; through imaginative involvement in, 133–37; by induction, 131, 133; proposi-

Learning from fiction *(continued)*
  tional and factual beliefs, 119, 130–32;
  propositional knowledge, 119, 132, 133;
  and resemblance, 130–31; values, 118,
  139–42
Leddy, Thomas, 92, 110, 113, 115
Literary symbols, 185, 198–204; context of,
  201; and images, 201; and incongruity,
  202; and interaction theory of metaphor,
  200; as juxtapository metaphors, 200–204;
  and purely referential symbols, 199, 202–4
Literary works: cultural emergence of, 101,
  105; individuation of, 100, 101–2, 104
Literature. *See* Fiction; Poetry
Locke, John: on imagination, 24–25; on
  metaphor, 144

McCarthy, Mary, 199
McDowell, John, 167
Maggie Tulliver (in *The Mill on the Floss*),
  193, 195
Make-believe, 79, 84–86
Malebranch, Nicholas, 23
Malinowski, Bronislaw, 215
Margolis, Joseph: and cultural emergence,
  100, 101, 105, 107; on interpretation, 95,
  97–104, 105, 108; on resemblance, 121;
  and robust relativism, 97–104, 110, 114,
  242–43n.4
Marianne Dashwood (in *Sense and Sensibility*), 91, 94, 115
Mark Antony (in *Antony and Cleopatra*),
  146, 154, 161, 165
Mason, Bruce, 225
Matthews, Robert J., 94, 243n.14
Meaning: and *archi-écriture,* 47, 48; and
  context, 188; as a culturally emergent
  property, 107; and Davidson, 159–67; and
  deconstruction, 44–47, 150; and *différance,*
  47–52; H. P. Grice on, 50; and historicism,
  51–52; and intention, 106; and interpretation, 99–100, 106, 243n.9; and linguistic
  convention, 107; as literal, 145–46, 151; of
  metaphors, 154–55, 157, 161–67, 171,
  172–75, 175–80, 183, 184, 187, 188, 189;
  and relativism, 112; stimulus theory of,
  112; and systems of signs, 48–50; text as a
  source of, 107–8
Meiland, Jack, 107
Metaphorical meaning: arguments against,

154–55, 157, 167–68, 171; arguments for,
  155–56, 158, 161–67, 187; and construction of T-sentences, 171–72; and context,
  187, 188, 189, 190, 192, 205; and
  emotional effects, 180–82, 187, 188;
  interaction theory of, 175–80, 184, 187,
  195, 200; and radical interpretation,
  159–67, 172–80; utterance as bearer of,
  172. *See also* Metaphors; Metaphors of
  fiction
Metaphors: and acquisition of conceptual
  skills, 139, 182; Ayer on, 144–45; Black
  on, 166, 167, 169, 173–74, 183, 186;
  Davidson on, 145, 153–70, 181, 187;
  demarcation of, 147–49; Derrida on, 54,
  145, 150–52; effects of, 155, 175, 180–83;
  and Enlightenment, 144–45; of fiction,
  184–98; Hobbes on, 144; interaction
  theory of, 175–80, 184, 187, 191, 200;
  Locke on, 144; metaphorical vs. literal
  discourse, 19, 145–49, 153, 187–89;
  Nietzsche on, 4, 38, 41, 143–44; Olsen on,
  187; and logical positivism, 144–45; as
  "resonant" and "emphatic," 174; and
  speech acts, 155, 171–72. *See also* Metaphorical meaning; Metaphors of fiction
Metaphors of fiction, 184–98; in context,
  185, 186, 187, 188, 189, 190, 192, 205;
  emotional responses to, 186, 187, 188; and
  incongruity, 195–97, 202; as juxtapository
  metaphors, 192–98; as literary symbols,
  200–204; Olsen on, 187; as ornamental,
  189–90; as sentential metaphors, 185–92,·
  205; as thematic, 190–92. *See also*
  Metaphorical meaning; Metaphors

New Criticism, the, 11–19, 205; attacks on,
  17–18; and experience, 14–15; Graff on,
  12; and literary symbols, 199, 200; and
  meaning, 16; problems posed by, 17–18,
  232; and I. A. Richards, 12, 14, 16; and
  romanticism, 12–19; and science, 12–14,
  16–17
Nietzsche, Friedrich: and cognitive relativism,
  40; and deconstruction, 44; and Derrida,
  41, 44, 45, 152; and fancy, 39, 152–53; on
  metaphor, 4, 38–39, 41, 143–44, 150,
  152–53, 205, 232; and the real world, 4,
  38, 55, 147; and romantic idealism, 38–42,
  55, 72, 153; on truth, 38–40, 41, 153

Nordin, Svante, 107
Norris, Christopher, 18, 248n.16

Objectivism, 63, 90
Occlusive fallacy, 55, 56–60
Olsen, Stein Haugom, 187, 189
Opler, Morris, 215

Parole, 46, 47–48
Perception: conceptual mediation of, 53,
    58–59; conditions for observation, 68–69;
    and culture, 115; and identity, 220; of
    resemblances, 127–30; and society, 65–66
Phonocentrism, 45–47
Piaget, Jean, 49, 238n.26
Pictures of fictions, 121–30
Pickwick (in *Pickwick Papers*), 75, 77,
    78–79, 122, 123, 124, 129
Plato, 46
Poetry, 12–13, 14, 15
Popper, Karl, 51, 117, 127
Post-modernism, 16, 17, 18
Pragmatism: and occlusive fallacy, 58, 67;
    and realism, 41; and romantic idealism, 38
Putnam, Hilary, 68, 69, 142

Quine, W. V., 117

Rader, Melvyn, 200
Radical interpretation, 159–67, 172
Ransom, John Crowe, 13, 14, 17
Raskolnikov (in *Crime and Punishment*),
    129, 141
Realism: and deconstruction, 41, 53, 55; and
    Dummett, 60–61; and epistemology, 60,
    63; explained, 60–63; and fanciful
    imagination, 3, 55, 60; and Hume, 57; and
    pragmatism, 41; and romantic idealism, 41;
    and romantic theory, 4–7; three senses of,
    62–63. *See also* Romantic idealism;
    Romantic realism
Relativism: and possibility of communication,
    112; and fanciful imagination, 3; as
    incoherent, 109–13; and interpretation,
    89–90, 97–104; and meaning, 112; and
    radical relativism, 110–11; and realism, 62,
    64; of reference, 111; and robust relativism,
    90, 97–104, 110, 114; and romantic
    idealism, 38
Resemblance: assertion of, 126, 127–29; and
    description, 125, 127–29; between fictional

and nonfictional entities, 121–30; Good-
    man on, 126; independent discernment of,
    122, 127–29; recognition of, 127–30;
    Searle on, 126
Richards, I. A., 12, 14, 16, 17, 149
Romantic epistemology: and fanciful imagina-
    tion, 19, 64, 67; and idealism, 37, 55–56,
    59, 60; and knowledge, 3, 11, 19, 31–36,
    55, 57, 60, 67, 206, 232; and Nietzsche,
    38, 55; and occlusive fallacy, 59–60; and
    perception, 56, 58–59, 64; and realism, 42,
    59–60, 63–71; and romantic imagination,
    15; social dimension of, 65; and verifica-
    tion, 59–60, 61
Romantic idealism, 5–6, 19, 37, 56, 57, 59;
    and absolute ego, 6; Coleridge on, 37–38;
    and fanciful imagination, 37; and the New
    Criticism, 16; Nietzsche on, 38–42; and
    occlusive fallacy, 57–58, 59, 67;
    vs. realism, 41; Schelling on, 37
Romantic realism, 7, 63–71, 232; and
    Dummett, 60–61; dependence on fanciful
    construals, 67; and Hume, 64; and percep-
    tion, 64–65; and Putnam, 68
Romanticism, xi–xii, 2, 3–7, 38–42, 55, 72,
    117, 153; against the Enlightenment, 1–2,
    12, 117; and idealism, 5, 55; influence of,
    3; and the New Criticism, 12–19; and
    Nietzsche, 38–42, 55, 72, 153; and the real
    world, 4–7; and romantic theory, 2, 232.
    See also Romantic epistemology; Romantic
    idealism; Romantic realism
Rorty, Richard: on an extralinguistic world, 6,
    58; and occlusive fallacy, 58; and percep-
    tion, 53, 58–59, 65–66; pragmatism of,
    58–59; as a romantic, 3, 6, 72, 235n.11
Rousseau, Jean-Jacques, 46
Russell, Bertrand, 58
Ryle, Gilbert, 3, 8–11, 51

Saint Augustine, 22–23
Sapir, Edward, 215
Saussure, Ferdinand de, 45–48
Schaper, Eva, 80, 81–84, 86, 88
Schelling, F. W. J., 4, 5–6, 37–38, 45, 58, 72
Schopenhauer, A., 4
Science: as an authority, 1–2, 42–43, 74, 117;
    and deconstruction, 42–43; and imagina-
    tion, 73; and knowledge, 1, 74, 132–33,
    232; and metaphor, 144

Searle, John, 126, 186
Shakespeare, William, 74, 94, 110, 113, 190;
  Hamlet, 74, 100, 105, 110, 111, 112;
  A Midsummer Night's Dream, 189
Simile, 155, 196, 201
Skills: conceptual or cognitive, 119–20,
  137–39; and factual beliefs, 137–38;
  acquired from fiction, 132–39, 232; and
  imagination, 133–37, 232; acquired
  through metaphor, 138, 182; of strategy,
  119, 132–37
Socrates, 22, 130
Sontag, Susan, 17
Soskice, Janet, 158
Spradley, James, 215
Stanislavsky, Konstantin, 103
Stephen Dedalus (in *A Portrait of the Artist as
  a Young Man*), 185–86, 187, 191, 193, 201
Stevenson, C. L., 95
Synge, J. M., 231; *The Playboy of the Western
  World*, 231

Textualism, 52, 57, 58, 232
Tolkien, J. R. R., 130; *The Hobbit*, 130
Tolstoy, Leo N., 83, 91, 134, 141, 198, 202;
  Anna Karenina, 93, 135, 193, 194
Trilling, Lionel, 110
Truth: correspondence theory of, 69–70;
  Dewey on, 68; and fiction, 78, 83; and
  fundamental wants, 65, 70, 71; of interpre-
  tation, 97, 100, 104–9, 114, 115–16; and
  metaphor, 150; Nietzsche's theory of,
  38–40, 153; objectivity of truth conditions,
  60–62; and romantic realism, 64, 65
Tylor, Edward, 214

Understanding fiction, 73–88, 89–116; and
  belief or disbelief, 76–78, 78–79, 80, 83,
  88; and culture, 97–98, 100, 101, 104; and
  imagination, 75–79, 80, 81; impediments
  to, 76–78, 78–79, 80, 83, 88; through
  interpretation, 89–116; and make-believe,
  79, 84–86; proper ways of understanding,
  75, 76–77, 87–88; and role of emotion,
  75, 79; and Schaper on knowledge, 74

Verification: and authorial intention, 106; and
  context, 109; with help genres, 108–9; of
  interpretation, 104–9, 113, 115; in terms
  of linguistic conventions, 107
Volksgeist, 209
Vonnegut, Kurt, 124

Walton, Kendall: on categories of art, 108; on
  emotional responses to fiction, 84–86,
  241n.2, 241n.3, 241n.4, 242n.9; on resem-
  blance, 121
Warren, Robert Penn, 13, 202
Weston, Michael, 80–81, 88
Willoughby (in *Sense and Sensibility*), 91, 94,
  98, 115
Wimsatt, W. K., 16
Wittgenstein, Ludwig, 3, 48
Woolf, Virginia, 194
Wordsworth, William, 2, 4, 235n.1